Children ask questions. Teenager: apologist and musician, provide: find those answers. Whether it is esoteric 'are there vampires?', D

I know at least one teenager who will be enjoying this. My daughter!

DAVID ROBERTSON,

SOLAS CPC, ST PETERS FREE CHURCH , DUNDEE

Professor Bill Edgar is the ideal person to help teenagers think through the Christian faith. Harvard educated, and once school master extraordinaire, then Professor of Apologetics in Aix-en-Provence, for two decades now he has taught hundreds of appreciative students at Westminster Seminary in Philadelphia. And this is just the beginning! Widely read in, and sensitive to, contemporary culture (as his other books make clear), he is also a jazz pianist who has toured throughout Europe. And there is much more! But perhaps best of all, Bill Edgar is a listening and deeply respectful Christian whose presence brings others (and especially young people) immediately into the circle of his life-long friends. I suspect that *You Asked* will add to that circle every teenager who reads it!

SINCLAIR B FERGUSON,

SENIOR MINISTER, FIRST PRESBYTERIAN CHURCH, COLUMBIA, SOUTH CAROLINA

Teens struggle with doubts, anxiety, and peer pressure regularly. *You Asked* provides a thought-provoking launching point from which teens can wrestle with these unique dilemmas. Each chapter provides insight and guidance into specific questions and concerns, which can be explored discretely or as part of the larger narrative. Combined with follow-up discussion, this book can go a long way to helping mitigate the philosophical and ethical minefield known as adolescence.

MICHAEL KELLER,

REFORMED UNIVERSITY FELLOWSHIP CAMPUS MINISTER, NEW YORK CITY

Dr. Edgar offers a brilliant, thorough, and, yet, accessible apologetic for teens regarding the Christian faith. So many students know bits and pieces of Christianity; *You Asked* provides a cohesive systematic theology in a personal manner that a teen can understand. Intelligent but personal., *You Asked* has great value for non-believing, new-believing, and long-believing teens. Every Christian teen should read You Asked before they attend college to equip them for the challenges to their worldview. Every non-Christian teen should read *You Asked* in order to hear a fair and accurate presentation of Christianity and The Gospel.

CAMERON COLE,

DIRECTOR OF YOUTH MINISTRIES, CATHEDRAL CHURCH OF THE ADVENT;BIRMINGHAM, ALABAMA

Perhaps the highest praise I can give this volume is that I feel confident in giving it to my students. Many books for youth water things down and don't really deal with their tough questions. But not this one. I know that here they'll find clear and compelling answers to the questions they are asking in language they understand. I am delighted it's available and will be directing students to it for years to come.

BIJAN MIRTOLOOI,
YOUTH MINISTRY STAFF, REDEEMER PRESBYTERIAN CHURCH, NEW YORK CITY

Apologetics for Dummies? Absolutely not: apologetics for thoughtful, inquiring young teens! I wish I had known someone like Bill Edgar when I was 13 or 14. I wouldn't have had to start with other people's questions, including the Church's—but with my own. The modern pastor will find endless hints here on great ways to connect with youth of all ages. Bill talks to young people without a hint of talking down to them.

PETER C. MOORE,
MINISTER OF DISCIPLESHIP, ST. MICHAEL'S CHURCH, CHARLESTON, SOUTH CAROLINA

YOU ASKED

Your Questions.
God's Answers.

William Edgar

CF4·K

Dr William Edgar is Professor of Apologetics at Westminster Theological Seminary, Philadelphia. He is ordained in the Presbyterian Church in America and directs the gospel-jazz band *Renewal*. His wife, Barbara, and he, have two children and three grandchildren.

© Copyright 2013 William Edgar

paperback ISBN 978-1-78191-143-3
epub ISBN 978-1-78191-189-1
mobi ISBN 978-1-78191-191-4

First published in 2013
by
Christian Focus Publications,
Geanies House, Fearn,
Ross-shire, IV20 1TW, U.K.
www.christianfocus.com

Cover design by Paul Lewis
Printed by Bell and Bain, Glasgow

Contents

Dedication

To our grandchildren, William Morgan, John Gordon and Ava Boatwright, who are now in their most formative years.

"I write to you, children, because you know the Father" (I John 2:13).

With love from your Papi.

Foreword

The present volume is the fruit of years of reflection as well as personal involvement with young people. It has become ever more clear that the ability to defend and commend the Christian faith is urgently needed, not only for believers in general, but for young people in particular. My first employment after graduate school was in a marvelous American independent school, called Brunswick. I was privileged there not only to teach subjects pertaining to the faith, but also to befriend and mentor adolescent young people during a period in life that presents unique challenges. My family and I have also been deeply involved in a youth ministry called FOCUS (Fellowship of Christians in Universities and Schools) which sponsors local fellowship groups, summer camps and the like.

In preparation for this book we interviewed many young people, church groups, youth leaders and the like. I would like to express my warm gratitude to all of them. The youth of Lansdale Presbyterian Church was especially helpful in giving feedback for the questions and answers explored in the text. Particularly inspired advice came from a Westminster Seminary student, currently Coordinator of the Junior and Senior High groups at Redeemer Presbyterian Church, New York City. Bijan Mirtolooi painstakingly read the entire manuscript and made invaluable suggestions, both in the content and the structure, most of which were incorporated.

Thanks go to Christian Focus Publications who first suggested I write this book, and have encouraged me all along. Special thanks to Catherine Mackenzie, Children's Editor of CF4K (Christian Focus for Kids) for her careful editorial work, allowing for many improvements to the text. Throughout she helped me keep the balance between accessibility to young people and not "talking down" to them.

I would like to thank Westminster Theological Seminary, where I currently teach Apologetics. By special arrangement I have been able to take time off from teaching in the Spring semester, and hence produce the present text. And as ever, I want to thank my dear wife, Barbara, who has patiently worked with me in this project, as she has in every ministry in which we have engaged.

It is my wish, and my prayer, that this book encourage young people, in whose hands will be the future of the church and the public square. May it assist them to face the issues not only with the correct answers, but "with gentleness and respect," and the godliness that should distinguish us from simply being good debaters in a generation increasingly ignorant, if not hostile to the Gospel.

William Edgar

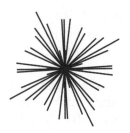

So You Are
a Teenager

So you are a teenager! Or maybe on the way?[1] Well, first of all, congratulations! It is a wonderful, rich, fun, crazy, confusing, deepening time of life. Adolescence, to use the technical term, gets a bad wrap. Sometimes fairly so. After all, as you move toward adulthood, you are developing into your own person. You are moving from dependence to independence. This can be hazardous. You may put adult authority to the test. You may fight with parents or teachers. You may try things you shouldn't. But mostly, it's great. God wants you to grow and more fully become the person you are meant to be. Adults who have never quite left childhood, while perhaps amusing, have a problem. Peter Pan is a fun character, but not a good model. God wants his people to be properly nurtured so that they may become mature and balanced adults. (Eph. 6:4) Just as staying physically undeveloped isn't good, so stunted growth in the Christian life isn't normal.

Adolescence is the time when many young people start to drive a car. They become more free to hang out with friends, without parental supervision. They learn about money, and how to use it for themselves. Eventually, it is the time when they will leave home for university or for the work place. All of this is normal and good.

The transition from childhood to adulthood is bound to come with bumps along the road. There will be special strains and temptations. You may be in for major disappointments. Some young people contract nasty health problems, or just embarrassing ones, such as acne.

---

1. Technically, specialists tell us, adolescence can begin as early as 10 years old in developed countries.

Much worse, a good friend might betray you. This can happen at any age, but it is particularly painful when you are an emerging adult. It just seems to hurt more.

Perhaps things won't always go so well between you and your parents, your teachers, or other authorities. Now that you are beginning to see life less as a totally reliant child and more as an emerging grown-up, you may become critical of the way your elders handle things. And you may be right, at least some of the time! You will have different ways of doing things, you will develop different tastes and nurture different career goals than what your elders might recommend. That's not a bad thing, unless it leads to conflicts.

Disagreements with adults are to be expected. But much popular culture simply assumes the youth are right. It sides with the rebel, although, ironically, in films or music it often is paid for by an adult business! You know those teen movies about kids having a good time, and nerdy adults who can't understand? Teens listen to music today of many styles, rap, heavy metal, folk, rock and roll, and much more. Often there is no "deep" meaning to the songs, just music. Some of it, however, carries strong messages about doing what you want, whatever the authorities might say. When I was a young man rock and roll music was being born (that's how old I am!). Some of it was wonderful, creative, rooted in the African-American tradition. In the best of it there was a healthy kind of protest against injustice in society. For example, Woody Guthrie's *This Land Is Your Land* or Elvis Presley's *Mystery Train* reminded us of everyone's responsibility to take care of their country. But some of it was destructive. Although playful and fun, Chuck Berry's *Roll Over Beethoven* encouraged us to part company with our parents and their values. We embodied the "generation gap." We protested against "the establishment" as if we knew better than our leaders what life was all about. In a word, we were rebellious. This was no fun at all, really.

Today the issues and the music are somewhat different, yet there is still the good and the bad. A good deal, though not all, of rap music is anti-authority, sometimes violently

against the police or even anti-women. Yet some of
it cries out in an authentic way against injustice.
I find generally that young people have much more
social concern than my generation did, and they
care more about abuses, such as trafficking, sustainable
farming, cruelty to animals, and the like. This is partly
because they have many advantages we did not, including
far more opportunities to travel the world and experience
other cultures and thus see their strengths, but also their
great need.

Still, there are many temptations toward self-centeredness, much that teaches, "just do it," from the old Nike
advert. And of course they have access to an enormous
number of ways to attain various pleasures. Because they
are computer savvy and know how to navigate the internet, they can get information and be entertained instantly.

The internet is a mixed bag. You can download favorite
tunes, get on Facebook, Twitter, and the rest, seeming to
improve communication a hundred fold. Texting is now
a major form of communication for young people. If you
are typical, you spend hours texting friends, whereas older
people use email, the telephone, even personal visits. So
what? Such modern forms of communication are not all
bad. However, texting can mean you do not necessarily have
to meet someone face-to-face. While you may gain from
efficiency, you may lose true and personal communication.
Also, texting may give you a false sense of freedom. You
allow yourself to write things you might never say in
person. You can't see your friend's face or gestures, so you
are deprived of the body language that usually goes with
a personal conversation. At the extreme another person is
simply a text, not a real, live human being.[2]

Here's another thing. As an emerging adult today,
you live with a contradiction. On the one hand, you are
more compassionate than previous generations. At least
that is the direction you are moving in. You care more
about justice, and issues such as sex trafficking and
embezzlement, and the like. Tragically, too, there is more

---

2. One characteristic of people, not just teens, who use these means
of communication, is known as FOMO, or "fear of missing out."

brokenness today, and families are more dysfunctional than in previous generations. You are more likely to have been affected by such brokenness than in previous times. Your experience may lead you to have special concern for others who are suffering. On the other hand, you are more self-oriented, and have real difficulty caring about an objective world beyond yourself. Much of your morality is based upon the live-and-let-live philosophy of relativism. Less true of Christian young people than of unbelievers, but still, seeing the world from the perspective of your own head, not God's standards, is characteristic of people within the church as well as those outside.

Becoming an Adult

Your growth into adulthood brings several major challenges. As if you had not noticed, your body is changing. Puberty is a transformation that moves you away from childhood and into physical maturity. Among other things, puberty enables you to have children. Hormones may insistently pressure you into discovering the opposite sex, in a way that was never so earlier. This is as it should be. Indeed, it is wonderful! Marriage and having children was God's plan from the very beginning (Gen. 1:26-28). Yet, sexuality is an area where serious problems can develop. There is a great deal of confusion out there. Relationships may get perverted. Premarital or extramarital sex never quite deliver what they promise. The atmosphere is polluted with pornography and lewd images. The ideal of "beauty" which is preached at us by advertisers is usually about very superficial attraction, not real beauty at all. Many young people put themselves under enormous pressure to conform to a hopelessly unrealistic image of beauty. Then come the eating disorders, the macho posturing, and feelings of inadequacy.

Another challenge is the need to become serious about the next step. It might be attending university. It might be finding a job. When things are going well a young person begins to learn how to make decisions, have goals, learn how to handle money, and other processes that ought to lead to financial independence. In almost every culture there is a training time which enables one to learn certain skills. School is meant to provide such preparation. Of course, schooling is more than learning a subject. When it goes well, one also may learn to relate to others, the value of friendship, and athletic training. This too can go wrong, of course. Many young people today have no idea what to do next. They become apathetic. In our advanced technological societies study or work may seem boring. We now can do so much by pushing a button or clicking a mouse, we give up caring at all. Or, the opposite, we may be told that work will save you. Get a job, and all will be well? Nonsense! Some adolescents are under so much pressure to succeed that they break down psychologically. Or perhaps they become apathetic, which is on the surface less of a concern, but in reality a serious problem as well. They cease to care.

Third, and most important for our purposes, this time in your life is often when the deepest questions about religion are raised. Children ask such questions, but when they grow a bit the issues become much more significant, and much more personal. In ancient societies, asking the right questions about religion was even institutionalized. In Israel of old various provisions were made for young people to embrace the true religion as they grew into adulthood. They were expected to understand the faith of their fathers and make it their own. One way this was done was just story-telling. Israelite literature often contained stories about how God's people got to where they were. Psalm 44 begins with, "Our fathers have told us what deeds you [O God] performed in their days." Psalm 78 is one long account of Israel's history from the older to the younger generation. In addition to telling stories there was in the Old Testament a special ritual, just after the Passover celebration.

After the meal, the first son of the family was meant to ask "What does this mean?" which was followed by a recital of the way God redeemed his people out of bondage. (Exod. 13:14; Deut. 6:20) Practicing Jews today still hold the *Bar Mitzvah* for boys and the *Bat Mitzvah* for girls. Have you ever been to one?

Many churches today, reflecting this practice, celebrate "confirmation." This is usually done after a period of instruction, or catechism, where the young person learns how to embrace the faith for himself or herself. While they may have been baptized as infants, they were too young to understand, and so their parents took the vows in their place. Then the time comes when they must make their own commitment. Coming to faith can and does occur at any age, of course. But often the teen years are when a mature decision can be made about the faith.

This book is for you, my friend, if you are thinking about the reasons for faith. I suppose we should let grown-ups listen-in if they'd like. It could even serve as a discussion point in the home or at the church with both generations involved. The book is not a general guide through all things adolescent. Such books exist, although their quality is often mixed. Check out the bibliography in the back. Rather, this book is about apologetics. This field is dedicated to answering questions of many kinds challenging the Christian faith. Such questions are bound to present themselves throughout your growing up years. This book is meant to help you as an emerging adult, to face the inevitable period of questioning, and to grow into a greater confidence in your convictions.

Qualifications

Before you read this book however, you may want to know if you can trust me! Well, I am a professor of apologetics at a theological college. That in itself will not tell you I can connect with young people. But I believe I can. Of course, like you, as I mentioned, I was once a teenager. My memory is pretty good and I remember my own struggles to answer the basic questions which led to my becoming a believer at the age of nineteen. My wife and I had the privilege of raising two children, and we saw them grow from childhood into adulthood. We remember the successes, and we especially remember our mistakes. Also, I taught in an American high school (ages thirteen to eighteen) for close to a decade. I loved my students and felt I could help them with their aspirations and their questions. Furthermore, for several decades, my wife and I have worked for a ministry called FOCUS, which reaches out to high school young people in order to present the gospel to them.

Finally, I am a pretty good listener. So I have engaged in a fair amount of research in preparation for this volume. Part of that was background study in the appropriate articles and books. A most important part of it was some interviews I conducted with a number of church groups, youth leaders and individuals. This was the most enjoyable part of my preparation. Scores of young people told me what was on their minds. And when it might have proved too embarrassing, they scribbled questions on a piece of paper. I have gone through each one of them with care. This book has been examined by a number of young people and youth leaders. It is far from perfect, and no doubt missing some of the concerns that some readers will have, yet it is the result of loving efforts and it comes with a prayer that it may be helpful to my readers. What are the most frequently asked questions? Here they are, in the chapters that follow.

Discussion

1. What is unique to the teenage years?
2. Is it a good time or not so much, for you? Why?
3. How have your family, your church, handled your coming of age?
4. Make a list of questions you've always had about the faith. Are any of them addressed in the pages that follow?

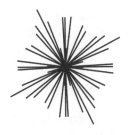

Who Am I?

For my own high school years I went to a boarding school. It was in New England, which is in the northeastern United States, but the place was modeled after the old fashioned British public schools. There were plenty of rules, some trivial, such as tying your necktie correctly, others serious, such as staying on the campus with only a few exceptions. If we were particularly disobedient, say, wandering off campus, for punishment we were sent to the dreaded "rock pile." This consisted of moving rocks in a large pile from one place to another. If we had been extra bad, then we had to return the pile to its original place. And so on. Why was this such a hardship? For one thing, it was demeaning. All your friends could see you out there struggling with these rather large rocks. For another, it was an utterly meaningless exercise. It served no purpose whatsoever. It was hard work for no particular reason.

Human beings are not meant to work for no reason. Work may be hard, or it may be easy. But there has to be a reason to work in the first place. It may sound trite, but it is profoundly true: before engaging in work, or anything else, really, we have to figure out who we are. We have an identity issue. When we interviewed young people in view of writing these pages, that was a constant question we received: what's my true identity? The only sufficient reason to go on living, let alone work or play or perform a thousand tasks as human beings, is to know who I am.

Why exactly are we special? There are lots of answers out there; two main ones are claiming our attention. One of the loudest says we are basically good, and when in doubt, we simply need to feel good about ourselves.

You may have heard this sort of talk. "You are awesome." Or, "She has a great self-image, feels good about herself." In sports commentary we regularly hear, "He has confidence," or, "He looked deep into himself and found the resources he needed," or something of the sort.

The other voice is the opposite. "You're such a loser." Or, more tactfully, "she struggles with a low self-image," or, "right now, she's not a happy camper." When a young person is confused or angry we are told they have "anger issues," and they need some tips in anger management, or the like. In our therapeutic culture, a culture based on feeling good or bad, we tell someone that they have been "insensitive" or "inappropriate," rather than simply wrong.

The darkly cynical "Beavis and Butthead," recently revived, or the tasteless "Unsupervised" on American television appear to address some of the hard questions young people must face, but they do so with such nihilism (death-like meaninglessness) that they leave no real alternative between "you are awesome" or "you're a loser."

Now, we don't want to throw out the baby with the bath water. We certainly do not have to choose between feelings and morals, or between self-image and truth. Both are important. As God's creatures, we are meant to enjoy both. But just trying to feel good about yourself without any reason is not very healthy. Indeed, self-confidence, while a good result sometimes of doing things right, is not usually a good cause. This is particularly true when you are trying to find the meaning of your life. For one thing there is lots not to be proud about. I ought really not to be self-confident about the darker side of my personality. I certainly ought not to feel good about it. Rather, a true diagnosis should indeed lead to a low self-image. My bad habits, my temper, my self-centeredness: these are not subjects for pride. But there is a better way.

Am I Special?

So, then, what is special about me or you? Here is another voice, told to us in the Bible. And it is one of the most revolutionary ideas that has ever made its way into the world. Mankind is created in God's image, after his likeness (Gen. 1:26-27). That is an incredible statement. It is radical. You and I are like God. Just as children are "like" their parents, we resemble God in important ways. We can think his thoughts after him. We are capable of friendships, even of having families, all of which reflect something about God himself, who is a Father, and a Son, and who is the Spirit (more on the Trinity in a subsequent chapter). Even though we are creatures, made by someone else, we are like our Creator. Both our bodies and our souls are made after God's image. We have eyes, because God sees, ears because he hears. We think because God is rational. We are persons, because God is a Person, with a capital P.

Why did God decide to make us with such a noble nature? He could have made robots. They would have been easier to handle! But he did not make us just for his own entertainment. He made us in order to love us. Here is another, related, incredibly revolutionary idea. God had so much love to give that he decided to make creatures fully capable of receiving that love and giving it back. He gave us an extraordinary purpose. We were made first and foremost to be loved by him and to love him back.

If you ever wonder what is the meaning of life, the simple answer is, to be loved by God, and to love him back. God loves us in thousands of ways. He provides for us. He gives us friends and interests. He sets us in the world he made, and directs us to rule over it. But the best of all is that he loves us simply because he loves us! Our friendship with him and his with us are unmovable absolutes, with no deeper explanation. Can this possibly be true? Think about it. Do you love your parents? They are a gift of God. Do you love your friends? A gift from God. Do you love science and technology? A gift. Music? The arts? Gifts, all of them gifts. Well, all of those reflect the more fundamental love of God. To be sure, something has gone terribly wrong, so that God's love is not always evident. We'll get to that shortly. But the love of God is the very heart of the meaning of life.

God loves us, and we are meant to love him back. How do we do that? Well, there are many ways to love God: worshiping him, talking to him (in prayer), ordering our life to honor and please him. Have you ever seen the film, *Chariots of Fire*? It's the story of Eric Liddell, one of the greatest runners the world has ever seen. He won the 400 meter event in the 1924 Paris Summer Olympics, and set a record that took years to overcome. The Liddell family were Christians, committed to missions. But it happens that Eric's sister Jenny once questioned his priorities, wondering why he spent so much time on the track, and not in missions. He remarked to her, "Jenny, I believe God made me for a purpose, but he also made me fast. And when I run I feel His pleasure."[1] Whatever our gifts, be they large or small, they come from God. We should not rank our importance to God in terms of performance, or giftedness. We can be sure God loves us, not because of our gifts, but because he loves sinners like us. That he loves me personally I can know because, first, his Word says so (1 John 3:1), and second he has proved it to us by sending his only son to die and be raised up for me (Rom. 5:6-8). If we are so loved, then we ought certainly to use our gifts for his glory, but they are not the condition for his love. He loves us unconditionally.

The old hit song from the Beatles says it well, "Love Is All You Need." It is not certain that John Lennon fully understood what he was singing, especially since there was no mention of loving God in the song. He did recognize, though, that such a song was radical, and declared that his art was dedicated to changing the world, making it a better place. Taken at face value the statement is true. We can only approach loving God because he first loved us, to be sure. But in this way, love is all we need. Unfortunately in our world today the reverse is often true: all you love is need.[2] We cultivate our needs and we think we deserve everything good just because we are who we are. There is nothing wrong with need in itself. We need food, we need

---

1. Note that this is taken from the film and not the official biography.

2. This is the marvelous title by Tony Walter, *All You Love Is Need*, London: SPCK, 1985.

air, we need security, and indeed, we need God. But need is not an end in itself. God is! So who am I? A creature loved by God.

Things did go very wrong early in human history, and threatened this love, but we're not there quite yet. Before we can address what went wrong, we really have to know that love was the plan. There is a profound statement in the document known as the Westminster Shorter Catechism which many Christians know without necessarily being able to identify the source. In answer to the question, "What is the chief end of man," the answer is, "Man's chief end is to glorify God and enjoy him forever." The word "end" here, means "purpose." What an extraordinary statement! Our purpose in life is to honor God in all things, but also enjoy him. That does not mean simply to feel good in our relation to him. This particular word means to have our entire fulfillment in our relationship with God. The more we honor and obey him, the more joy we experience. Joy becomes a major reason for living. How different from "feeling good about myself."

Beginning Down the Right Path

The Christian religion actually reorients and corrects our deepest aspirations. We are meant for fellowship with God himself. We don't function properly when we don't have that. Of course, many people are not in touch with their deepest longings. Or they confuse them for something else and try to satisfy them with inadequate "gods." These include sex, or music, or money, or just about anything else. All of these objects are good in themselves, but hopelessly inadequate as substitutes for God. The great Saint Augustine once said this prayer to God: "We are restless until we find our rest in thee." We're longing for rest, that is, for true peace, whether we know it or not. One of my favorite thoughts from C.S. Lewis, the marvelous apologist of the previous century, is from a sermon, titled *The Weight of Glory*. He says,

> ...it would seem that Our Lord finds our desires, not too strong, but too weak. We are half-hearted creatures,

fooling about with drink and sex and ambition when infinite joy is offered to us... We are far too easily pleased.[3]

The best kind of apologetics commends this glorious offer. Going deeper, our identity leads to action. Who I am and what I do are deeply connected. More specifically, this loving God gave his human image-bearers, you and me, a task. So his love is purposeful. God made us for several purposes besides pure, Sunday morning worship. Here is what he told the human race at the very dawn of its existence:

> Be fruitful and multiply and fill the earth and subdue it and have dominion over the fish of the sea and over the birds of the heavens and over every living thing that moves on the earth. (Gen. 1:28)

Subduing the earth may sound odd to us today, especially because many people subdue the earth violently, without caring for our planet's welfare. But rightly understood, it is a key concept. God made the world and all its inhabitants very beautiful, but there was still work to be done. Everything was not yet fully tamed. The world and its inhabitants were not fully developed, nor all of its potential fully realized. Forests were still wild, minerals undiscovered, buildings not yet built, melodies not yet written. So that is our task. We are to bring more and more beauty into this world. We've been at it for a long time, but still today things are nowhere near finished. It will take an eternity to finish the job, first here and then in the world to come! How wonderful and rich is this calling. It's the very opposite of the boarding school "rock pile."

Do you worry about the implications of this order to subdue the earth and ecology? Rightly so. A close look at both expressions, "subdue" and "have dominion" shows nothing about the violation of the world that entails pollution. Rather, they are meant to imply a gentle, caring authority over the earth, not a violent one. There have been critics of biblical religion who think that this

---

3. C. S. Lewis, *The Weight of Glory*, MacMillan, 1949, p. 2.

commandment given to our first ancestors somehow justifies achieving progress at any cost, even the pollution of the earth and selfishly robbing our planet of all its resources.[4] Nothing of the kind is implied in the Genesis directive. We learn here, and throughout the Bible that God cares very much for the world he has made, and condemns any kind of disrespect for it. Psalm 104 tells us how he cares for the animals. And Jesus told his disciples that even the flowers of the field have a beauty that is greater than human beauty (Matt. 6:26-30). Although we may enjoy good meat, which obviously comes from slaughtered animals, that is never an excuse for animal abuse. If a donkey stumbles because his load is too heavy, we are not allowed just to stand by and look (Exod. 23:5). Even the trees were protected in ancient Israel (Deut. 20:19). Many young people today are rightly concerned for the environment, and are looking to make ecology their profession.

So then, who are we? We are humans, made after the image of God, and loved by our Creator. God truly loves us! So what are we to do in response?

- First, love God back; thank, worship and adore him. John Calvin tells us in the beginning of his marvelous *Institutes of the Christian Religion* that to know yourself you need to know God, but to know God you need to know yourself.[5] It's both-and!

- Second, we are meant to go out into every continent by ground, sea or air, and explore the world, using our gifts and skills in meaningful work. It is the very opposite of the "rock pile." We are meant to respect creation, while yet lovingly to subdue it. Every legitimate job is meant to be engaged in, and our life should be dedicated to loving God and to making this world a better place for all of his creatures. What a grand purpose! My identity is high and noble indeed.

4. For example, Lynn White, Jr., "The historical Roots of Our Ecological Crisis," *Science* 155: 1203-1207.

5. John Calvin, *Institutes*, 1.1.1-1.1.2.

Discussion

1. Why is tedious work so demeaning?
2. What does it mean to be loved by God?
3. In what way are human tasks meaningful?
4. Is the Christian faith really unique, or do all faiths deal with these questions?

1- rock pile - meaningless work

2. He provides, gives us friends, family, etc.

3. serves greater purpose.

4-

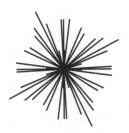

What Went Wrong?

Now we come to the down side. What is clear to every young person I have ever interviewed, is that something is terribly, terribly wrong. Things are not the way they are supposed to be. Children die of leukemia. Husbands abuse their wives. Bank officers cheat their investors. Animals suffer needlessly. Nations go to war. Terrorists hold hostages. The list is long and depressing.

No doubt the issue that most often comes up with young people, or, for that matter, with people of any age, is whether we can believe in a God who is good and powerful, in the face of such horrors. We know this as "the problem of evil."

Because just about everyone recognizes this problem in one way or another, it is important to look at some of the typical answers they give. From the family of Asian philosophies, including Hinduism and Buddhism, comes the response, evil is an illusion. Suffering, pain, death, are basically not real. One of the emphases in Buddhism is detachment. If only we can become free from the illusion of feelings and personality, we can get free from evil, which is a figment of our imagination anyway. But such an answer is hopeless. Ask any mother who has lost her child whether death is an illusion. Ask anyone who has fled for life before a conqueror whether oppression is unreal. It just won't do.

Another answer we often hear is the brave-sounding "get on with it." The Stoic philosophers had a sophisticated form of this answer. Just rise above it, and endure the pain, trying to help our fellow human sufferers along the way. We need to be self-sufficient, calm, never perturbed by poverty or pain. The more popular form of this view is the teacher who says, "stop whining, pull your-self together." Of course, there are times when a stiff upper lip is appropriate. But most of the time, such an attitude makes us insensitive to the plight of destitute people. Furthermore, it does not have the power needed to endure pain and suffering.

Still another answer is called the "silver lining." God has allowed evil because only when we see how bad things are can we see the good in them. Examples of this view abound. When I visit people on their sickbeds, I often ask them something like this: I know how greatly you are suffering; but do you see any good in it at all? Most people will say they do. One will say it gives her a new appreciation for things that really matter, such as the family. Another will say it helps him see how self-reliance will not work, and how he must begin to trust other people more. The Bible actually supports this view. Paul tells his readers that our suffering produces endurance, and endurance character, and character produces a hope that will not fade (Rom. 5:3-5).

One of the most enduring stories in the Bible is the account of Joseph, sold into slavery by his jealous brothers. By a series of divinely ordained circumstances he became Prime Minister of Egypt during the years of feast and famine. When the harvest was good he ordered all the extra grain to be stored up. Then, when a dreadful famine came, Egypt had all it needed. Among the beneficiaries were the Jews, who came for help to Joseph, not knowing at first who he was. When Joseph finally confronted his brothers with his true identity he made this famous declaration: "As for you, you meant evil against me, but God meant it for good" (Gen. 50:20). Jesus himself suffered in order that we may be saved.

The "silver lining" view is undeniable in cases such as these. Still, it is not a good overall answer for why evil? Where was the silver lining in the holocaust? Most serious of all, does God need to stoop to evil in order to bring about good? Put this way, the idea is repugnant.

A Very Different Answer

There are many other answers to the problem of why things are not as they are meant to be, and how a good and powerful God could allow evil. The biblical answer is quite astonishing. It is even shocking. Simply stated, it is that human beings, not God, are at fault. Yet God is fully able to bring us out of our abnormal state. Are we really so guilty?

The concept of sin is not an easy one to explain. Sin? This old-fashioned word is so prone to misunderstanding that even Christians hesitate to use it. Comedians talk of sin as though it were an embarrassing mistake which everyone commits, and which the church takes too seriously. One popular song denounces the false testimony of a man who tells a woman he loves her when he really doesn't. "It's a sin to tell a lie," the song declares with a wink of the eye. In America we call Las Vegas "Sin City," because there are salacious stage shows and alluring gambling devices. But the biblical notion of sin is altogether deeper and far more serious. Sin is one of the main biblical words for human-approved wrongdoing.

This old-fashioned word means opposing God, refusing to submit to him, leaving undone things we ought to have done. Human beings live in a sinful condition. Even more difficult to explain is what we sometimes call original sin. That is, the fact that our first parents brought sin into the world and it infected all of their posterity. In his excellent book, *Orthodoxy*, G. K. Chesterton asserts:

> Certain new theologians dispute original sin, which is the only part of Christian theology which can really be proved.[1]

What he meant is that modern people do not like to speak of original sin. And yet, while many doctrines are a bit removed, or abstract, the doctrine of sin, the presence of evil in each human being, while it may not be very palatable, can be verified empirically. Parents do not have to teach their children to sin. They somehow just know! Sin is everywhere, and we do not have to look very far to find it.

---

1. G. K. Chesterton, *Orthodoxy*, Ignatius Press, 1995, ch. 2.

The great English poet W. H. Auden was an easy-going humanist. He was pretty sure every person was good, deep down. He thought, just give him space, and a man's natural goodness will shine through. He moved to the United States in 1939 and took up residence in New York. To be precise he moved to Yorkville, which was, and still is, a thoroughly German neighborhood of Manhattan. One evening, with a friend, he went to the cinema. They watched a rather gruesome report on Hitler's invasion of Warsaw, entitled *Sieg im Poland* ("War in Poland"). What startled Auden most was the cries, "kill them," "kill the Poles," coming from the mostly German audience. As he reflected later, this was the denial of every humanistic value. These were human beings crying out for blood. He could no longer believe everyone was basically good. But then another question arose. By what right could he call these outbursts evil? How could he call Hitler's invasion of Poland wrong? As he put it, "There had to be some reason why Hitler was wrong." And he found it, in God. Human beings are evil, because God says so.[2] That is, the heart of evil is to be against God, who is good. Otherwise, the line between good and evil would just be arbitrary. And we know that is not so.

The fact that we are evil may lead to great discouragement. In one way, it should. Why are some kids bullies? Why do we seek vengeance upon our offenders? Why do I find a thousand ways to put myself first? This common experience is profoundly discouraging. But, still, there is hope. When you have a clear, honest diagnosis, you are ready to face the facts and maybe do something about it.

According to the Bible, we were not always in this condition. The world into which our first ancestors entered was a paradise. They were to lead their descendents into a life of happiness and maturity. God had only asked one thing of them, a test they had to pass, not to eat of the fruit of a tree, called the "tree of the knowledge of good and evil." Not that God wanted them to be naïve about

---

2. From "The Fatal Flaw of Liberalism," in *The Journey: Our Quest for Faith and Meaning*, Os Guinness, editor, NavPress, 2001, pp. 75-77.

things that mattered, least of all things like good and evil. He wanted them to know the difference between good and evil by a process we might call maturation, not by disobedience. Not, in other words, by actually engaging in evil.

How would we have become full-grown? Very much the way we do in ordinary life today: by being confronted with real choices and making the right decision. When we are told to come home at a certain time, or to be kind to a younger brother or sister, we have a choice. When we make the right choice, we learn things like patience, courage, and we develop character. Unfortunately Adam and Eve, our first parents, did not make the right decision. Rather than listening to God they decided, at the suggestion of a talking serpent, of all things, to take from the forbidden fruit. The serpent argued that God was keeping the fruit from them because he was worried that humans might end up knowing good and evil the way God did. Well, they fell for it, and instead of making them wise, it made them foolish. Not that they acquired no knowledge of good and evil. They did. But the wrong way; by succumbing to it rather than resisting it.

It Gets Worse Before it Gets Better

That is how everything went wrong. Each successive generation continued in this pattern, and even made things worse. Murders, hatred, abuse, corruption, and every other kind of evil permeated humanity. Should we blame Adam for all this? That would make sense if only we were ourselves quite innocent. However, that is the opposite of the truth. Should we blame God? No. The Christian view affirms with great conviction that God hates evil more than anyone. "You who are of purer eyes than to see evil, and cannot look at wrong," the prophet Habakkuk tells us (1:13). Indeed, God is angry at evildoers and will one day bring terrible judgment upon them. "I will punish the world for its evil, and the wicked for their iniquity" (Isa. 13:11). Far from authoring evil, God cannot tempt anyone as he is above evil (James 1:13). Is God powerful? Yes. Is the presence of evil a surprise to him? No. Does his power have anything at all to do with the presence of evil? It must, but we don't know quite how, since he is not responsible for it. So, we are left with three great certainties: God is good, God is all-powerful, human beings are responsible for sin in the world. Until we are convinced of all three, we cannot make much headway in resolving the problem of evil.

So, are we as bad as we could possibly be? No, of course not. That is, we are not demons. There is an old Reformed doctrine known as "total depravity," which does not mean we are utterly and absolutely depraved. We are still made after God's image. We are still capable of good thoughts, words and deeds. So how do these two operate together?

Alexandr Solzhenitsyn, the great Russian historian who played a key role in defeating communism, explains that every human being has two characteristics operating in them at the same time. He was interned in a prison camp for having criticized Joseph Stalin. He found himself in the infamous Gulag, an oppressive series of hard-labor sites. There he saw, first hand, both great acts of bravery, and also enormous crimes perpetrated on the prisoners. He found that prison afforded him the time to reflect for prolonged hours on his condition. Solzhenitsyn came slowly to recognize that without his severe trials he could not have taken the journey that led him to become such an effective prophet for his times.

One incident that occurred marked him for life. His friend Dr. Boris Kornfeld, a Jewish convert to Christianity, tried to teach him that we do not deserve to be spared, since we are all capable of transgression. One night Solzhenitsyn's dear friend had been brutally murdered by the guards, for no good reason. As he reflected on this senseless act, it began to dawn on him that while there was no connection between this murder and a particular evil deed done by the doctor, yet his words rang true: no one deserves to be spared. And then, rather movingly, he describes how it began to be clear to him that he, Solzhenitsyn, was capable of great cruelty. At the same time he began to feel the first real stirrings of good in him.

He concluded: "Gradually it was disclosed to me that the line separating good and evil passes not through states, nor between classes, nor between political parties either, but right through every human heart, and through all human hearts."[3]

So then, in answer to the question we raised in the previous chapter, who am I?, the reply is that there is a twofold reality to each of us. I am God's beloved image-bearer, as we saw, but at the same time I am also inclined toward evil. How can both be true? The book of Genesis tells us how it all began. But the rest of the Bible also tells us to look carefully and honestly at ourselves. This double identity is a verifiable fact. We know deep down that we have high moral standards, we love our friends, we enjoy certain tasks. We also know deep down that we want things we should not have and if we could get away with it we would try many forbidden things. Ask yourself this: if I could be sure no one was watching, would I ... fill in the blank? If we are honest, we might admit we would do more than we ought. Maybe a lot more. We are capable of the worst. The Bible calls this sin.

So, then, we are more noble and more wonderfully made than we can imagine. And we are more sinful and prone to evil than we can imagine. And that is a tremendous beginning to the answer for the problem of evil, because in the diagnosis is a hope for the cure.

Discussion

1. Give your own examples of things "not as they are meant to be."
2. What are the strengths and weaknesses of the view that evil is an illusion?
3. Or, of the "get on with it" view?
4. Or the "silver lining" view?
5. Is the biblical answer really believable? Do you agree with its diagnosis?

---

3. From Alexandr Solzhenitsyn, *The Gulag Archipelago*, New York: HarperCollins Publishers, 1978, IV/1.

— terrible current news?

— evil is an illusion?
  suffering/pain/death are real. It is due to
  sin —

— "stop whining" or "be strong & endure"
  can a human be strong & endure
  by him or herself?

— "silver lining"
  Does God need to ~~be~~ stoop to evil
  in order to bring about good?

I'm God's beloved image bearer/
at the same time I am also
inclined toward evil.

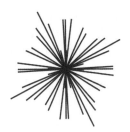

Does God Love Us Anyway?

I s it totally depressing to say we human beings are to blame for evil? Sure, it's awful. And yet, unless we are given an honest diagnosis, we cannot hope for any kind of remedy. Even while he tells us the brutal truth, God does not leave us dangling in despair. The great 17th century apologist Blaise Pascal once said:

> Knowing God without knowing our own wretchedness makes for pride. Knowing our own wretchedness without knowing God makes for despair. Knowing Jesus Christ strikes the balance because he shows us both God and our own wretchedness.[1]

So Jesus Christ helps us find out the best and the worst. Only when we are realistic about the problem, can we have any hope for a solution. If I have a serious tumor, I may not like hearing the bad news from the doctor, but it's my only hope for a cure. If the physician merely tells me not to worry how can that help? I need to know the truth, even if it is profoundly distressing. I have evil running through me, as Solzhenitsyn reminds me. Indeed, the greatest doctor, not Kornfeld, but Jesus Christ, tells it like it is. Of the very nicest persons Jesus says, "If you then, who are evil, know how to give good gifts to your children..." (Matt. 7:11). Not very flattering. But then he brings us to the answer.

An evil person (like me–like you) is exactly the sort of person that God loves. This is what Jesus Christ came to tell us. He loves us not because of our good qualities, or our potential for his service. He doesn't deny these.

---

1. Blaise Pascal, *Pensées*, #192, A. J. Krailsheimer, translator, Penguin Books, 1995, 57.

Yet, he loves us in spite of our bad ones. He has compassion on me and you, stuck as we are in our evil condition. And the astonishing truth is that Jesus Christ not only tells us the answer, he is the answer. The most well-known verse in the Bible reads this way:

> For God so loved the world that he gave his only Son, that whoever believes in him should not perish but have eternal life. (John 3:16)

There are several things to notice here, all of which are relevant to apologetics. First, God so loved the world. He created the world and us in order to show his love. Well, now, despite our fallenness, he has so much more love to give. It seems humanly absurd to think that God would love the world. A first century Jew listening to that statement would have been somewhat shocked. God loves Israel, not the world, they would think. But no, he loves the world, all kinds of people, all of them sinful, in all kinds of places and from every possible background.

Next, this verse makes it clear that the measure of his love is enormous. How great is his love? So great that he was willing to subject his only Son, his cherished Son, to unspeakable torture. And, by the way, the worst part of the torture was not the physical agony of hanging on a gibbet, which was considerable. It was that the eternal Son, Jesus Christ, was being separated from his Father. That is why he cried out, "My God, my God, why have you forsaken me?" (Matt. 27:46). You might ask, why such a terrible price to pay? Why can't God just forgive and forget? No, God cannot lower his standards for justice. We would not want that anyway. Many young people today, as we mentioned in the Introduction, are keenly aware of the issue of justice, much more so, I think, than in the days of my own youth.[2] Once the human race has transgressed, with that evil that cuts into every heart, then even God cannot pretend that evil is not true and just wish it away. Justice must be done. And it was. He sent his only Son to an unthinkable death, the death of crucifixion. Unthinkable, maybe to us.

---

2. More true of those over twenty, but I have found it also in teenagers.

But true! It was the only way that justice could be accomplished, so that we would not have to perish. Jesus was condemned in our place. What an amazing thought!

The Son did this willingly, of course. There are people who see the whole affair as a case of divine child abuse. Nonsense! The Father, the Son, and the Holy Spirit, what we call the divine Trinity, are one, all three agreeing to love the world at the cost of this great sacrifice. This shows the extent of God's love for you and for me: there was never any doubt, never a conflict between the members of the divine Trinity (John 10:17-18). To rescue you or me it would take this incredible solution for the problem of sin.

You Will Need to Believe

So how do we respond? The next part of our great verse says it quite plainly: "Whoever believes in him [Jesus] will not perish, but have eternal life" (John 3:16). Believing is in one way quite simple. It means entrusting yourself to God through Christ. Once you lift the empty hands of faith and ask God for his mercy, then you have become a Christian. And now your new life can begin!

Eternal life refers not only to the duration of this new life, or to living forever, which it does, but to the quality of this life. Eternal life is the unique kind of energy we have when we are in fellowship with God himself. It has little to do with biological existence. It is the way of being of someone who has become a new creation (2 Cor. 5:17). This is our new identity. We do not cease being ourselves, but somehow we become more the self we were meant to be. The power of sin is gone. Even when we die physically, that is not the end. We will be with the Lord forever. And then, when human history ends, we will all be raised again from the dead, and given new bodies with which to live in the final version of God's Kingdom, which we call heaven. That is worth waiting for!

Even now, each person in Christ can find new purpose, and new power. Not that they will be fully freed in the present life from the darker side that plagues them.

Solzhenitsyn, again, added that the line running through us shifts:

> Even within hearts overwhelmed by evil, one small bridgehead of good is retained; and even in the best of all hearts, there remains a small corner of evil.[3]

Full release from evil only happens at death. But today we can still know substantial progress.

We could illustrate it this way. The crucial turning point of World War II was an invasion known as D-Day, or Operation Neptune. It was an extraordinary undertaking. Full of risks, yet a masterpiece of strategy. First, thousands of air strikes were made just after midnight. Then, at 6:30 a.m., close to 200,000 personnel took hundreds of boats and landed on the coast of Normandy, in France. Once they had secured the beach, they were able to move inland and gradually defeat the occupying Germans.

D-Day was June 6, 1944. The war was not officially over until Victory in Europe Day, May 8, 1945, nearly a year later. But the point is, D-Day was the beginning of the end. After its success victory was assured. The same holds for the work of Christ. Once his death and resurrection had occurred, then victory was and is in hand. There remain lots of battles and clean-up exercises, but the war is won. And once we become Christians we are on the right side, with the winning army. Although we will struggle with our old nature and only gradually make some progress in this life, yet the victory is assured.

The Bible puts it this way: "There is therefore now no condemnation for those who are in Christ Jesus" (Rom. 8:1). Think of that. Whatever you may feel, all guilt is gone. You and I are like accused people who have been acquitted by the judge! So, then, who am I? Now a third element needs to be added.

- First, I am a person made after God's image. I am made for God's love.

---

3. *The Gulag Archipelago 1918-1956*, New York: Harper & Row, 1978, p. 615.

- Second, I am frightfully fallen and have lost the privilege of such love.

- Third, if I have come to Christ by faith, I may know his love again.

Today, though I am deeply flawed, yet if I am a believer in Christ, I am being made to be more and more like Jesus Christ. At death I shall enter into his glory and be with him forever. How do you respond? By lifting up the empty hands of faith, and asking God to be merciful to you, a sinner. He'll do it for the asking. Try him out!

Discussion

1. Does God's love have any conditions?
2. If God is all-powerful, why can't he simply say, "I'll forget this evil and let you go?"
3. Describe the agony of the cross. Why did it have to be that way?
4. If all I have to do is believe, how is that not a cop-out?
5. What does "eternal life" mean?

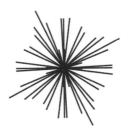

What is a Worldview?

We need to step back for a bit here. The basic issues of identity, good and evil, and the related issues we have been examining are among the most pressing questions we may face as we look into apologetics. They are not bits and pieces of a mysterious puzzle, however. They fit together into a larger picture, sometimes known as a worldview.

What we have been describing, then, is the Christian worldview. Everyone has a worldview, whether they acknowledge it or not. Simply put, a worldview is an understanding of the way things are. Of course, you may have a mistaken worldview. But you have one nevertheless. At a deeper level, a worldview is a heart-commitment. All worldviews begin with some kind of faith.

Usually worldviews include something about an ultimate power: Is there a creator God, or must we face a more atheist principle such as materialism?

They need to explain identity, the way we have tried to do thus far: Who am I? What is my calling?

They also try to answer the question of what is wrong: Was there a fall, the way Christians describe it, or is there some other reason for evil, such as very bad luck, or survival of the fittest? Is death ultimate, worldviews tend to ask, or do we not know, or even care about what is beyond?

Finally, worldviews also try to set forth a way to live in our world: dealing with its blessings and its obstacles. Usually worldviews try to find the path to happiness.

Worldviews are never simply intellectual. They are matters of the heart. They reflect what we worship. Some worldviews are unselfish, seeking the betterment of mankind. Others are more self-centered, looking out only for number one. Some worldviews appear deeply religious, that is, they practice prayer or various rituals. Others appear not to be religious at all. But the reality is, all worldviews are religious in the broadest sense, because they all involve answering the big questions in a way that joins the parts together. The word for religion, *religare*, means "joining together." Having a religion is not primarily to practice a set of rituals, but to join together many parts of life to form a whole. It may not be a coherent whole, indeed it may contain huge contradictions. But even contradictions help define one's worldview.

Most people are not aware of their worldview. They hold ideals and values unconsciously. Some hold them because they accept what their families believe, or what their teachers hold. Some, because they belong to a certain religious group. I can remember my own mother, brought up in the Anglican Church, puzzling over some doctrines in the catechism. "Isn't it odd, some of the things we believe," she once exclaimed to me. I was amazed that she was not evaluating them in order to accept or reject them. She simply believed them, even though they made little sense to her. Some hold their worldviews more aggressively. There are militant strains of atheism, and there is an aggressive type of Islam, and, to be honest, there are some Christians who make great efforts to browbeat others into their worldview.

Worldviews are not necessarily coherent or logical. Many people hold to bits and pieces of a point of view, even when they do not fit neatly into a system. In that case they don't hold together, at least on the surface. For example, a recent study of religion among American teenagers revealed that a significant number of them held to moralistic therapeutic deism.[1] In this case several different components, not always logically related, are held at the same time. Generally this worldview includes:

---

1. Study conducted by Christian Smith & Melinda Lundquist Denton, *Soul Searching*, New York: Oxford University Press, 2005.

- God, or a god, who exists, who made the world and watches over it.

- This god wants people to be nice, and fair to each other.

- The main purpose of life is to be happy and feel good about yourself.

- We don't need this god very often – usually only to help solve problems.

- All good people go to heaven when they die.

The word "moralistic" simply means being good for the sake of being good, or for a quiet conscience, rather than for the higher purpose of glorifying God. (Of course this is very different from what is taught in the Christian faith.) "Therapeutic" refers to the desire for many in this generation to simply feel good and not offend anyone, rather than do the right thing whatever the cost. And "deism" means believing in a divine force, or god, who no doubt created the world but is not particularly closely involved with it now.

Maybe you don't fit this outlook at all. There are thousands of worldviews. We cannot hope to be familiar with all of them. Yet there are types and classes of worldviews which allow us to boil down the wide variety of beliefs people hold to. What is sure is that you do have a worldview, spoken or not, well-articulated or not.

Only Two, Really

The twentieth-century apologist Cornelius Van Til once declared:

> Apologetics is the vindication of the Christian philosophy of life against the various forms of the non-Christian philosophy of life.[2]

There are many different worldviews, but when you pare them all down to basics, there are only two. The "Christian

---

2. Cornelius Van Til, *Christian Apologetics*, Phillipsburg, NJ: P & R Publishing, 1976, 2003, p. 17.

philosophy of life" is the biblical worldview we have been describing, with God at the center, and then creation, fall, and redemption. The "non-Christian philosophy of life" is in the singular because, if the gospel is true, then you can only be for it or against it. There may be "various forms" of unbelief but what they come down to is a "suppression of the truth," and a denial of the gratitude due our Creator for his generosity and patience (Rom. 1:18-22).

Does this force everyone, like pushing a round peg into the same square hole? In a way, yes. While there is a great variety to the many religions and philosophies, the Bible teaches that they all amount to some form of idolatry. Have you ever thought about idols? Perhaps you have seen them in museums. They are statues which people used to worship, thinking they could find power through these objects. An idol may be a statue or an image. But it also may be a concept, or even a disposition of the heart, such as greed (Col. 3:5). The essence of idolatry is to worship something that is not God. Thus, atheism is idolatrous because it posits a force or principle besides God that explains the universe (chance, material force, survival, etc.). Animism is idolatry because it believes the world is permeated by spirits who control people and events. Greed is idolatry because it prizes something besides God as having the greatest value. This is why several times in the Bible our choice is reduced to only two. Joshua famously said to the people of Israel: "And if it is evil in your eyes to serve the Lord, choose this day whom you will serve" (Josh. 24:15). Or, again, the prophet Elijah at Mount Carmel challenging the people thus: "How long will you go limping between two different opinions? If the Lord is God, follow him; but if Baal, then follow him" (1 Kings 18:21). Sometimes these prophets would taunt the people into making their choice.

Ezekiel told Israel they should go after their idols since they wouldn't listen to him (Ezek. 20:39).

No one put it more decisively than Jesus himself:

> Whoever believes in the Son has eternal life; whoever does not obey the Son shall not see life, but the wrath of God remains on him. (John 3:36)

Along with the great variety of worldviews, only two emerge in the end. There may be many different practices, personalities and aspirations. Still, regarding being right with God, there is only one way. Dear friend, think about it and do make the right decision!

Discussion

1. Are you comfortable with having your philosophy of life described as a worldview?
2. What are the basic components of a worldview?
3. Describe someone you know. Can you identify his or her worldview?
4. Do you agree that at bottom there are only two significant philosophies of life?

Where is God?

Now then, back to basics. We know something about worldviews, and now we want to inquire into the heart of what the Christian faith claims. Does God exist? This is one of the most often asked questions. Three questions, really. First, is there a God? Second, can this God be known? Can he be accessed? And then, perhaps hard to admit, but, Third, do I really want to know him? Is it not safer to ignore him?

Outside

The answers to these questions depend a great deal on how you ask them. Where should I look in order to find God? How will I recognize him? Here are the traditional ways to look, ones that have stood the test of time. First, we can know him from the external world. Just look, and listen, and you will see that God is there. Here is how the great poet, Gerard Manley Hopkins, put it:

> The world is charged with the grandeur of God
> It will flame out, like shining from shook foil

"Charged" sounds like an electrical surge – so powerful you can't miss it. "Shook foil" is a golden foil, something like a crumpled piece of aluminum foil we might open and illuminate with a bright light.[1] Gerard Manley Hopkins' marvelous poem describes a God so great that the world must reveal him. Indeed the world cannot contain this

---

1. The author explains, "I mean foil in the sense of leaf or tinsel ... Shaken gold-foil gives off broad glares like sheet lightning and also, and this is true of nothing else, owing to its zigzag dents and creasings and network of small many cornered facets, a sort of fork lightning too."

flame, this shining. Hopkins goes on to speak of the Holy Spirit brooding over the world, in words reminiscent of the opening lines of Genesis: "And the Spirit of God was hovering over the face of the waters" (Gen. 1:2).

How can we know God exists? For Hopkins and a host of believers, you cannot not know! Sometimes we have trouble finding him because we are trying too hard to have God answer our questions on our own terms rather than letting him tell us on his own terms. Instead of asking, "where should I look in order to find God," a better approach is to ask, "Where does God look in order to find me!" Many philosophers have tried to convince us that God exists because otherwise we could not explain cause and effect, or motion. For example, Aristotle tells us that God moves the universe, but is himself unmoving; and he adds, the way the beloved moves a lover. But often, they end up "proving" that there is a first cause, an unmoved mover, not particularly the God of the universe as he is described in the Bible. Our God is precisely one who is moved: "In this is love, not that we have loved God but that he loved us and sent his Son."[2] While such proofs may have some value, it is much more convincing to move the other way. The fact is, as Francis Schaeffer was fond of saying, God is there. He just is. Of course there is plenty of evidence for his being there, not the least of which is the world's greatness. We can especially look at two places.

- The first is out there.
- The second is in here.

Out there, what do we see? One thinks, first, of the majesty of the night sky, or the glory of a natural landscape. Some of us find the seaside particularly inspiring. Such scenes and many more communicate to us something of the nature of God: his power, his artistry, his imagination. Also, his

---

2. Aristotle's statement is from his *Metaphysics*, 12.7. There is a long history to the *theistic proofs*, including some appropriation of them by Christians, such as Thomas Aquinas. C. S. Lewis calls them "pagan" and suggests the difference with the Christian view, citing 1 John 4:10. See *The Problem of Pain*, New York: Macmillan, 1962, p. 52.

judgments. There is great violence in nature, as well as tranquil beauty. Do you have a pet dog? Or perhaps a cat? Or a bird, or even fish in a tank? If you look closely at these creatures, there is something wonderful about them. They have personalities and they have purpose. Dogs are loyal, affectionate. Cats are mysterious. Birds and fish are often beautiful. They are eloquent about a creator God, one who has a great deal of imagination in making them.

Do you enjoy science class? Not everyone does. But science gives us the opportunity to see some of the intricacies of God's handiwork. When I was a high school teacher, I remember one day sitting in the faculty room (where teachers could take a break before going back to classes), when in walked my friend the chemistry teacher. He called himself an atheist. But that day, knowing, I suppose, that I was a believer, he blurted out, "Bill, I know I am not supposed to believe in any god, but today we performed an experiment which was just, well, marvelous!" He went on to say, "On days like this I find it hard to be an unbeliever!" I am not exactly sure what he saw, but whatever it was rather jolted him into some sort of recognition that there was more to this world than just chemicals and atoms.

Another outside witness to God's existence is history. History is messy. Yet there are abundant examples of God's hand in human history. He is evident when the church has helped dignify the less powerful. In the first few centuries Christians cared far more about children and lower-class people than the Romans. Health care was often promoted because Christians believed they should reverse the ill effects of the fall. In French, hospitals were called "Hôtels-Dieu," that is, "God hostels." Much of modern science was developed by Christians, who believed the earth is the Lord's and the fullness thereof. One of the greatest reformers of all time, William Wilberforce, together with his friends and a newly freed African named Equiano, succeeded in the overthrow of slavery throughout the entire British Empire. The Civil Rights movement in the 1960s in America was largely guided by Christians.

Not only the world of nature, but also man-made things show forth the reality of God. For example, music, at least good music, is often a signal of the divine. One of our neighbors, a marvelous Jewish person, a rather skeptical one concerning religion, once exclaimed to me that he thought the greatest music often came from the creative minds of believers. He happens to love Mozart, Beethoven and Berlioz. Now, as it happens we cannot be very sure of these composer's personal faith. Indeed, Berlioz was known to be quite skeptical about the Roman Catholicism he was born into. And yet they all wrote out of a Christian consciousness. Think of the exquisite *Mass in C Minor* by Mozart. Or Beethoven's *Missa Solemnis*. Or the *Requiem* by Berlioz. Of course, you may get technical and find sub-Christian traits in all this music. And you may, rightly, point out that much of their music was not for the church. My friend, however, was simply saying these glorious compositions came out of a generally Christian culture. At any rate, his doubts about the Christian faith weakened, upon his own admission, when listening to this music.

Architecture can be another indication of the divine. Think of the silhouette of some of the great cities of the world. San Francisco and Miami in America. Or Glasgow, and Edinburgh in Scotland. Or Kyoto and Singapore. Cities are troubled places, of course, but their skylines often resemble musical melodies. Looking at them at night can be particularly moving. The Bible portrays the city as God's dwelling place. The new Jerusalem is God's ultimate dwelling place (Rev. 21:9–22:5). The place is bedecked with jewels and gold, and has tall, beautiful gates, with the river of life, bordered by trees, running down the middle. Our earthly cities are but a pale shadow of this glorious place, but still, they declare the glory of God, just as much as do the heavens (Ps. 19:1).

Inside Evidence

In addition to all of this evidence from outside of the self, we can also look inward, and find plenty of signs of God's reality there. In the first chapter we warned against looking inward. Our culture is so full of solving problems by appealing to "self confidence" or "good self-image" that we rightly worry about such self-centeredness. But now we do want to look inward, not to solve our problems, but to look for traces of God. Where, then do we look?

First, in the fact that I am conscious at all! Neither you nor I could even have a consciousness if there were no God. Think about it. Why are you conscious? Why are you unique? How can you be thinking? Awareness is itself a sign of there being a God. You could not even think if there were not a supernatural being who makes himself known to you. A bold claim, but perfectly evident. Consciousness is a mystery, one that can only be explained if there is an ultimate consciousness who communicates with us.

Second, we have moral sense. No one is without some feeling for right and wrong. You may want to challenge that claim. Have you ever heard someone argue that right and wrong are just arbitrary? Lots of people will say such a thing. But it's not true when you probe deeper. Ask such a person what he might do if someone attacked a baby or an older individual for no reason. Today, few people believe the Nazis were good, nor the perpetrators of the September 11th destruction of the World Trade Towers, nor those who planned the London underground bombings. That everyone has a sense of right and wrong can be proved like this.

Imagine a long line at the post office. (Our family used to live in France where such lines are most annoying.) Imagine you've been waiting for a while and are finally near the top, about to be served. Then someone walks in off the street, bumps ahead of you without any excuse and simply claims an advantage. We would rightly say to that person, "Hey, I got here first, please wait in line." What might this intruder say? Well, let's hope he would apologize. And then perhaps he would have an excuse: he was there before and stepped out for a minute, didn't I see him? Or he might claim his wife is pregnant and he must rush her to the hospital, so please allow this bad-mannered push. What you will not hear him say is, "What does being first in line have to do with the right to be served." Or, you would not hear him say, "Sorry, my name is King George, so do make way!" The point is, everyone acknowledges the rules about lining up. That's the standard. To break with the standard requires special excuses. It's the same with morality. Everyone acknowledges some sort of morality. We're just born with it. If you put it to the test, very few people would honestly favor theft, murder, and the like.

Even people who claim they have no morality, or who claim it is only a convention break down at some point and acknowledge moral absolutes. I once witnessed a discussion between a skeptical, non-practicing, Jew and a Christian. The skeptic was saying, over and over, that morality is just a human convention. "What about criminal laws?" the Christian asked. "Convention," came the answer. "What about property theft?" "Convention." And on it went. Until the Christian said, "and what about the Holocaust, the systematic gassing of some six million Jews by the Nazis?" There was a long pause. "Well, that was evil," said the Jewish skeptic.

A number of young people I have talked with assure me that morality is simply a matter of choice or preference. Heterosexual marriage? A preference. Working for a living? A choice. "You believe what you believe," one of them said to me. "Please allow me to believe what I believe." I finally asked him whether there could be anything, anything at all that was absolutely wrong. He thought a bit, and finally answered, "Cruelty to animals."

It is no wonder each of us has convictions about at least something being a matter of right and wrong, and not simply preference. The Bible affirms this, and gives it a reason. Check out Romans 2:1,15. Paul says that when you pass judgment on someone else, you show clearly that you have a standard for right and wrong. It is written on the heart of all people, whether they come from a biblical tradition or not. The reason for this sense of right and wrong is simply that God has made us to reflect his own character, and he is a supremely moral being. The evidence of our sense of morality reflecting the truth of God's own moral character is loud and clear.

Now, we may be very bold here. The evil in the world is also a proof for God's existence. How is that? Paul explains that the reason things have gone terribly wrong here on earth is human folly (Rom. 1:18–2:10). As a result of all our bad decisions things have gone wrong. And behind that, God is simply angry with humanity. The "wrath of God" is not a very modern concept. But when you think of it, why should God be indifferent to our behavior? Indeed, it is strangely comforting to know that you cannot get away with evil behavior and expect to hide yourself. If there were no God, evil itself would make no difference. How is it that we even can call something "evil" if we do not have a standard to judge the world by?

What if he does not exist? What if we live in a world that simply has no meaning? Why do we sense there is meaning and morality? Where do those notions come from? There is a powerful, disturbing play called *Waiting for Godot*, by Samuel Becket. It features a sparse stage, and two actors, Vladimir and Estragon. For over one hour, they basically engage in trivial conversation, or deeper discussion, play games, sing, and otherwise try to occupy themselves as they wait for "Godot" who in fact never shows up. As is explained during the drama, they try in a hundred ways to "hold the terrible silence at bay." In their conversation the two constantly engage in biblical references, particularly the need for the cross of Christ and for forgiveness. But even though at times Godot seems close, he never appears.

One can give a number of interpretations of this play. At the very least it tells us that in a world without God there is no meaning. Only a terrible silence. It also describes all kinds of ways in which we search for God, and try to make sense of things. But without his being here no such sense is possible. Well and good, you might say, but that is just the way things are. But then, where does our clear sense that there is a God (not Godot, but the true divine being) come from?

One of the most helpful moves in Christian apologetics is to point out the impossibility of living without God. Every attempt to construct a life philosophy without the Holy Trinity as the basis will ultimately end up in failure, precisely because this God is there, and is in fact a Person, and has in fact made the world, and continues to govern it. Not everyone who attempts a world without God will end up quite as bleak as *Waiting for Godot*. But that is where such a position should logically end up.

Again, when I was a high school teacher, I used to have a class on philosophy. One section of the class was about art (aesthetics). I would show the history of art using slides. One morning we were looking at modern art. I showed a particular artist who was very abstract. I had discovered that this painter had lost any sense of the difference between reality and fantasy. The lesson went on to its conclusion. Within a few minutes of the class a young man came to see me in my office. He had a confession to make. He was a Heroin addict. We talked it through, and made the hard decision to tell his parents, and then try to find a rehab center where he could get some help. In the end, it all turned out quite well, after a good many struggles. I asked him at one point why he decided to come and tell me when he did. 'Oh,' he remarked, 'it was that artist.' I asked what he meant. He said that the drugs made him lose the sense of any difference between reality and fantasy, and he didn't want to be there anymore.

For many young people things will not go quite that badly. Still, without God, life is not very meaningful. Suicide and attempted suicide are becoming more and more common in the affluent West. Suicide is the third leading cause of death among teens, after motorcycle accidents and homicide. There are far more attempted suicides than successful ones. They are almost always a cry for help. Among the many causes that can provoke a suicide attempt are divorced parents, lack of success in school, friends turning on you, violence at home, and the death of a friend. Almost always these are linked with depression. Lack of purpose, hopelessness, and anxiety are the major reasons for suicide and suicide attempts. Many teens today feel they cannot get a handle on life, and that instead they are trapped.

I certainly don't want to over-dramatize. We know that plenty of people seem to live happily without God. But sometimes a clear connection can be observed between those who have no hope or meaning and the state of depression; or even suicide. Not the most lovely proof for God's existence perhaps, but still, something to think about!

Special Revelation

So, then, while we may know all these wonderful truths from the world outside and from the world inside, we have an even better way: God has revealed himself in deeds and in words. Because he is all-powerful, God is able to intervene in our world. He did so numerous times by what we call miracles. A miracle is an unusual manifestation of God's power which upsets the normal way the world works. For example, he opened up the Red Sea (Sea of Reeds) for the people of Israel to escape from their Egyptian pursuers (Exod. 14). He consumed the sacrifice and the altar at Mount Carmel, a feat the priests of Baal could not accomplish (1 Kings 18). Jesus took a basket of five loaves and two fishes and fed 5,000 people (Matt. 14:13-21). The greatest miracle of all was when Jesus rose from the dead after lying in the grave for three days (John 20). These miracles are not magic tricks. Each of them reveals something unique about God's plan. The escape from Egypt tells us he frees his people from slavery and the bondage of sin. Consuming the bull and the altar shows how God is utterly more powerful than any idol, and will bring fierce judgment on human substitutes for the true God. Feeding 5,000 people shows how Jesus has come into the world to give his people daily bread, both literally and spiritually. The resurrection of Christ means death is ended, and the doors are open to the new heavens and the new earth.

In addition to always being present, God enters our world in special, visible ways. Known as *theophanies*, or God-appearances, he allows people to see him in palpable ways from time to time. Theophanies are of various kinds. A figure in the Old Testament known as the angel of the Lord shows up in crucial times of Israel's history, often leading them in battle. It is clear he is actually God himself. For example, the angel of the Lord appears to Gideon and tells him how to save Israel from the Midianites (Judg. 6:11-18). Verse 1 calls him the angel of the Lord, and verse 14 calls him the Lord. When Shadrach, Meshach and Abednego were in a burning fiery furnace through the treachery of the king's counselors, they not only survived, but were found with a fourth person in the furnace, one like "a son of the gods" (Dan. 3:25). The greatest theophany of them all is, of course, Jesus Christ, God's Son come to take on human flesh. This was Immanuel, "God with us," the Word become flesh (Matt. 1:23; John 1:14).

And then, very specially, God communicates with us in words, words we can understand. Because he is a Person, God is able to communicate with us. And because he is merciful, he chooses to communicate with us, even when we seek to hide from him. God had always talked with his human creatures, even before things went wrong. He spoke to Adam and Eve in the garden of Eden, telling them how to live, and giving them tasks. Genesis 3:8 even tells us the Lord "walked in the garden in the cool of the day." In the afternoon, after the sun had died down, his people could meet with God. One commentator says, "Maybe a daily chat between the Almighty and his creatures was customary."[3] That privilege was soon taken away, because Adam and Eve rebelled against God. Yet, the Lord continued to reveal himself to them, and their posterity, in words and in deeds. He told them where history would take them next (Gen. 3:14-19). He began to choose people to worship him, and showed them how to do so (Gen. 4:25-26).

Here, then, is the pattern. God allows the sin and suffering of his creatures to go on for a while, and then he takes pity on them. He saves them from their enemies and from his judgments. All the while, he explains what he is doing, tells them what to believe, and gives them wisdom

---

3. Gordon Wenham, *Word Biblical Commentary: Genesis 1-15*, Waco, TX: Word Books, 1987, p. 76.

for living. Not only does Genesis, the first book of
the Bible, record this pattern over and over, but
so does the entire Scripture. Genesis recounts the
story of human sinfulness in the time of Noah
(Gen. 6). Then he explains how he would rescue Noah's
righteous family from a terrible flood (Gen. 7). Finally,
when the flood subsides, he tells this family how to
populate the world again and live according to God's ways
(Gen. 8–9). He does the same with Abraham, whom he
calls out of a place called Ur, and sends over to the land of
Canaan. And he explains what he is doing to Abraham and
his descendents (Gen. 12–24).

This pattern is repeated over and over again, with Moses
and David and Daniel, and their people. Finally when God's
people were living under occupation, having lost the right
to own their land, God himself comes down and becomes
a man, and speaks directly to his people. "The Word became
flesh," John tells us, referring to the Second Person of the Trinity
becoming human (John 1:14).

He became one of us so he could live the life we failed
to live, and then die, taking the punishment we deserved
upon himself. Finally, he rose from the dead so that we too
could live again, forever.

All this is explained in God's Word. The sixty-six books
gathered into one volume, known as the *Holy Bible*, are not
merely human reflections on what God was doing, although
their authors are human. They are specially inspired books,
because their ultimate author is God. Paul tells us, "All
Scripture is breathed out by God" (2 Tim. 3:16). .Peter tells
us, "Men spoke from God as they were carried along by
the Holy Spirit" (2 Pet. 1:21). Of course there is mystery
here. How can a human pen be so guided by God's "breath"
that they are essentially divine even while respecting the
personalities and culture of the human authors? We don't
know altogether, but we are glad it is so. For we would not
want just any reflection on what God has done and what
he requires, any more than we could only trust in one
newspaper or one pundit for the right view of human events.

What we have in the Bible is nothing less than God's own
Word, telling us about his saving grace and how to enter

into it. So, there is a God, and he has a specific character, and he can be found in the world, in my conscience, and, most especially, in the Bible.

Discussion

1. If God is so clearly revealed in nature, why do more people not see it?
2. History shows a considerable influence of Christians for the good. But they not only produced good things, but sometimes dreadful ones. How do you reconcile those?
3. Can you describe one of your favorite cultural evidences for God?
4. Do you have a conscience? How does it work?
5. How does evil prove God?
6. Would we be able to believe in God if there were no Bible?

What Kind of
God is He?

Have you ever tried to imagine God? Many simply think of him as "the man upstairs," something resembling Santa Claus more than the avenging judge of the Bible (Ps. 75:7; Isa. 66:16; Matt. 12:36; Heb. 10:37).

In reality, no one has ever seen God as he is pure Spirit. That may be a confusing statement, since we have just finished arguing that he can be known. Let's put it this way. God is so great, so transcendent, that we cannot fathom him, nor exhaustively know him. Yet, we do know him, since he has gone to great lengths to show himself to us. Both are true, and to deny either one is to fall into either arrogance or false humility. On the one hand, the Bible tells us, "To whom then will you liken God, or what likeness compare with him?" (Isa. 40:18). Job confesses, "Behold, God is great, and we know him not" (Job 36:26). Paul tells us, "[God] dwells in unapproachable light, whom no one has ever seen or can see" (1 Tim. 6:16).

So we would be terribly arrogant to claim we can fully grasp him. On the other hand, this same glorious God has made himself known to his creatures. We humans are called "the offspring of God" (Acts 17:28). And because of this intimate relationship, we really do know him. Even more so do we know him through his Son, Jesus Christ. "Whoever has seen me," he tells us, "has seen the Father" (John 14:9). If we deny this, we become, at best, falsely humble, at worst, vague deists or perhaps even atheists.

This is why it is not only possible but necessary to conceive of God through human concepts and illustrations. He is a shepherd (Ps. 23:1; 28:9). He is a rock and a shield (2 Sam. 22:3). He is "the Father of lights"

(James 1:17). He is a Prince of Peace (Isa. 9:6). He is a warrior (Jer. 20:11). No human image can really represent God fully. This is as it should be, for he is infinite. But these images do tell us a great deal. What does it mean to be pure Spirit? For one thing, it means he has no physical qualities. He is utterly different from the creation. Unlike us, he has no body. The Bible does describe God by using human analogies. If we are made after God's image then it is appropriate to describe God using metaphors, such as he sees and he hears. These are only metaphors, because God does not literally have eyes or ears, and they they are true metaphors, because he really does see and hear. At the same time, the Bible never describes God as having organs, or eating food, or the like. God is a Spirit, and does not need nourishment or oxygen.

That does not mean he is impersonal. God's eyes are toward the righteous and his ears hear their cry (Ps. 34:15). Underneath us are God's everlasting arms (Deut. 27). These are powerful images explaining to us in our own terms how God can be conceived. In reality, God is without form.

For another, it means he is invisible. Occasionally he shows himself in a special way, called theophany. We don't really know exactly what the people saw when they were visited by God: Theophanies are appearances of God. God becomes visible to his people several times, and in dramatic ways throughout the Bible. Supremely, he comes in the flesh, in the greatest appearance of all, when the Second Person of the Trinity comes to the earth, to come into the world (Heb. 1:1-3). God appeared to Abraham to tell him about his children inheriting the promised land (Gen. 12:7). He appeared to Jacob at Penial, whereupon Jacob remarked, "I saw God face-to-face, yet my life was spared" (Gen. 32:24-30). He showed himself to Moses as a burning bush (Exod. 3:2). He came down as a dove at the baptism of Jesus (Luke 3:22). He appeared to Saul on the Road to Damascus (Acts 9:3-7). And there are a few other occasions. Perhaps you can identify them. In each of these cases the invisible becomes visible, but that does not mean God is in himself visible. Even in heaven, when we will be with the Lord forever, we will not see God's very essence.

Again, though, this does not mean God is without content or personality. He has numerous attributes.

- God is all-powerful. He is in control of absolutely everything, from the tiniest subatomic energies and particles, to the giant bodies of the universe. That does not mean we are robots, as we shall see. Still, he does control everything for his good purposes.

- God is all-knowing. Because he controls everything, he is aware of everything. God knows the past, the present and the future. Indeed, he lives above time!

- He not only knows everything abstractly, instantly, but he is perfectly wise. Whatever he does, and all that he knows, are dedicated to doing the right thing. Not always what we might have hoped for but it is the right thing because he is profoundly good. One of my favorite negro spirituals has the refrain: "God don't come when you want him to, but he's always right on time."

As they say, timing is everything. Perhaps you have wondered why an all-powerful God does not just end all injustice right now. The way we look at things, evil has gone on just too long. But the God of the universe knows just how long the world must wait until the day when he makes everything right.

Is God Limited?

So, then, God is almighty, but that does not mean he is capable of just anything. For example, he cannot contradict his own righteousness, or go against his own truth. Do I really mean to say there are things not possible for God? Sure. He cannot, for example, turn into a bad person. Nor can he break his promises. Nor can he make the world with

63

all its patterns and structures and then violate those patterns and structures. He cannot put fish in the sky and birds in the ocean. And here is something else. While he ordains everything that comes to pass, he does not violate our human wills. Divine predestination is a great mystery. It is clearly taught in the Bible (Acts 4:28; Rom. 8:29-30; Eph. 1:5, 11, etc.). But predestination is not the same thing as determinism or fatalism. When I choose which way to go, God is not forcing me, the way a puppeteer would pull the puppet strings. I am responsible. When I sin, I cannot say, God made me do it (or the devil made me do it).

Here is an illustration of the difference. When a determinist falls down the stairs and hurts himself, he says, "Well, I'm glad that's over!" When a predestinarian falls down the stairs and hurts himself, he will say, "That was clumsy of me; still, God can use it for good."

God indeed must remain faithful to his own being and to his intentions. He is a purposeful God. His plans are wise and unsearchable.

> For from him and through him and to him are all things. To him be the glory forever, Amen. (Rom. 11:36)

A Divine Person

He is infinite. Yet, he is a Person. This concept is unique to the biblical religion; God is a Person, with a capital P. What does that mean? Among other things, it means he thinks, he feels, he speaks. We human beings share these abilities with God, although only in a limited way, as you would expect of creatures. Saying that God is a Person, and not just a force, is an all-important part of our faith.

Many religions, instead, have something like an impersonal energy. Think of *Star Wars*. Of course, it's a marvelous series of films. But look carefully at its theological views. The ultimate reality is a force. "The Force be with you," is said by General Dodonna after explaining the Death Star attack plan to the Rebel pilots. And there are frequent references to the Force: Luke Skywalker, Obi-Wan Kenobi., Hans Solo, and others. Even Darth

Vader admits the Force is "strong" in his enemy Luke. Many people today believe in something like a semi-divine force. New Age believers talk about "channeling" different forces or angels or even people. Yet it is all quite impersonal.

Here is how God can be truly Personal. He is both one and three. The technical word for this is the Trinity. There is mystery here, and yet it is a marvelous truth, one that Christians should have no trouble believing and living with. God has revealed himself as One and Three at the same time. For now we won't have to worry about all the details of this amazing doctrine. They have baffled the best theologians and philosophers. But it is essential to a biblical understanding of God. So we must say a few things about it.

In the Old Testament, there are various ways in which we know there is a Trinity. For example, in the story of Moses and the burning bush, we are told that the angel of the LORD appeared in flames from within the bush (Exod. 3:2). The angel speaks with the voice of God (see also Gen. 21:17; 22:15). Most scholars believe this figure is the Second Person of the Trinity, appearing before his incarnation as a man, recorded in the New Testament. Similarly, the Spirit of God is often referred to as God. He hovered over the waters at the dawn of creation (Gen. 1:2). Before the flood the Lord expresses his anger with the human race thus: "Then the Lord said, 'My Spirit will not contend with man forever'" (Gen. 6:3).

In the New Testament, things become much more explicit. Consider the account of Jesus' baptism (Matt. 3:13-17; Mark. 1:9-12; Luke. 3:21-22). Here we have Jesus, God's Son, being baptized. The Spirit of God descends on him, like a dove. And the Father speaks from Heaven. The Letters are full of references to the Trinity. The most memorable is 2 Corinthians 13:14, which we know as the Benediction:

> May the grace of the Lord Jesus Christ, and the love of God, and the fellowship of the Holy Spirit be with you all.

In the end, why does the doctrine of the Trinity matter? Of course, if this is who God is, that could end the discussion.

But the fact that God is One and Three actually explains many things. We know he is Personal because in all eternity, before the world was made, there was the Trinity. In what we call his high priestly prayer, Jesus says some quite extraordinary things:

> And now, Father, glorify me in your own presence with the glory that I had with you before the world existed... Father, I desire that they also, whom you have given me, may be with me where I am, to see my glory that you have given me because you loved me before the foundation of the world. (John 17:5, 24)

Glory and love were there between the Father and the Son from all eternity. Only if there are three divine Persons could such a relationship exist. And Jesus here asks that we, his people, be able to see something of that glory and love.

The Trinity also matters for other reasons. The Trinity is the way God is, and there is no rational explanation for him, just revelation of God's nature. It is also not without significance that the unity and diversity we find in life find their ultimate background in God being both One and Three. We want to guard against pushing such analogies too far, but we can expect to find unity and diversity in the creation because the God who made us is One God in Three Persons. This is who God is. To know him is to think rightly. But it is much more. It is to have life, and to worship the source of that life, God himself, as he is.

God For Us

Christians surrender totally to this wonderful God. When we recite the creed, we are not simply saying something intellectual about what God is like. No, we say we believe in the Father and in his Son, Jesus Christ our Lord, and in the Holy Spirit, the Lord and giver of life. Our joy and our comfort are that we can and do believe in that God, we trust him, and we expect everything from him.[1]

---

1. Herman Bavinck, *Our Reasonable Faith*, transl. Henry Zylstra, Grand Rapids: Eerdmans, 1956, p. 144.

God has acted into our history in a rich
diversity of ways. He created the world. He set
mankind on a journey which, though badly
broken by our folly, has been overcome and set
straight because of God's love. God is the grand architect
of the history of salvation. Although his deeds are
many, there is a fundamental unity to what he is doing.
Creation, redemption, justification, sanctification, and
finally, glorification, are all part of his symphonic plan
to raise fallen creatures to glory and honor. As the hymn
puts it:

> Frail children of dust, and feeble as frail,
> In Thee do we trust, nor find Thee to fail;
> Thy mercies how tender, how firm to the end
> Our Maker, Defender, Redeemer, and Friend.[2]

All of this flows from the unity and diversity of his divine
self. The Holy Trinity is our source, our hope, the ultimate
ground upon which everything rests. More than that, God
wants us to be his friends:

> No longer do I call you my servants, for the servant does
> not know what his master is doing; but I have called you
> friends .... (John 15:15)

What an extraordinary thought. Jesus Christ, God's eternal
Son, calls us his friends. And this, because he has deigned to
become our friend:

> What a Friend we have in Jesus,
>   all our sins and griefs to bear!
> What a privilege to carry
>   everything to God in prayer!
> O what peace we often forfeit,
>   O what needless pain we bear,
> All because we do not carry
>   everything to God in prayer.
>
> Have we trials and temptations?
>   Is there trouble anywhere?

---

2.   Written by William Croft, 1833

> We should never be discouraged;
>   take it to the Lord in prayer.
> Can we find a friend so faithful
>   who will all our sorrows share?
> Jesus knows our every weakness;
>   take it to the Lord in prayer.[3]

Not only for purposes of prayer, but for the deepest meaning in life do we call upon the Lord as a friend. God, indeed, is for us.

> He who did not spare his own Son but gave him up for us all, how will he not also with him graciously give us all things? (Rom. 8:33).

What a gospel!

Discussion

1. What is your favorite image of God? How has that helped you in a particular challenge?
2. What is the difference between predestination and determinism?
3. Is there anything God cannot do?
4. Why does it matter that God is One and Three at the same time?
5. How can God, so transcendent, be truly present with us?

[handwritten notes:]

1 - loving

2 predestination = believe that God has eternal purpose + He is in control

Determinism = believes that all events are determined by previously existing cause.

---

3. *What A Friend I Have In Jesus*, written by Joseph M Scriven in 1855.

Did Jesus Exist?

When I was a seminary professor in Aix-en-Provence, a beautiful town in the south of France, our students decided to conduct a survey. They went up to the main thoroughfare with recording equipment and asked each passer-by, "Who is Jesus?" An astonishing number of people did not know! He is the central figure in all history. The world was forever changed because of him. Perhaps the very most compelling reason to be a Christian is Christ himself. Who, then, is Jesus Christ? Many people feel they can accept some of the broad ideas of the Christian religion, particularly its moral principles, but they stumble at the figure of Jesus. Are we sure he existed? Does he still exist? If so, can we know the truth about him after the many centuries that have passed since he walked on earth?

There are the odd people who think there never was a person like Jesus. G. A. Wells, for example, believes that there was no historical Jesus, but rather that he was invented by people who need the comfort of religion.[1] Others are not so positive. Kenneth Humphreys argues that Jesus never existed at all, but was a figment of the human imagination, one that eventually led, not to comfort, but to atrocities.[2] Such views are extremely rare.

Others, more commonly, think Jesus was a real person, but that much about him was made up. Some say he was invented by the apostle Paul. Or that he was the product of

---

1. G.A. Wells, *The Historical Evidence for Jesus*, Prometheus Books, 1988.

2. Kenneth Humphreys, *Jesus Never Existed*, Historical Review Press, 2005. His basic idea is that people used the idea of Jesus to start wars, to conduct the Inquisition, etc.

the early church. These people believe we can never know the historical Jesus, since he is inaccessible. They say the rise of Christianity is due to factors that have little to do with Jesus himself. They say a wall has been built up separating the real Jesus, whoever he was, from the Jesus of human tradition. Some say the Christian religion is not a product of Jesus' true teaching, but a perversion of it.

You may remember the book, followed by the film, *The Da Vinci Code*, by Dan Brown. Although completely fictional, the basic idea is widely shared: the church and the Romans created a powerful religion in which spiritual authority was vested in a dominant system, held by bishops, cardinals, and Caesars, not in the pure teaching of Jesus. Even the Bible is a perverted form of Jesus' original intentions. Jesus, in this story, was merely a man, a very good man but a man who had a family and whose descendents had to be protected by a group called the *Priory of Sion*. The church and the Romans did not like this view, because without the supernatural Jesus, their chance to force people into submission was lessened. In the end, they find a young woman who might have been Jesus' distant descendant. The story is fascinating. It's an entertaining read. And it feeds into popular resentment of the Roman Catholic Church, or, indeed, of institutional authority itself.

Many other versions of this kind of theory, most of them less fanciful, can be cited. For decades scholars have been on a "quest for the historical Jesus."[3] The fundamental reason for this quest is a flawed worldview. Until about the 18th century few people worried about connecting the "Christ of faith" (the Christ we confess, the Second Person of the Trinity, incarnate, dead and raised again) with the "Jesus of history" (the measurable Jesus, the "real" Jesus in the 1st century). Then, using modern research tools, a quest began to find the real Jesus. And, of course, many people came up short. So they decided to try and go behind the New Testament, using various clues it provides, to find another Jesus besides the one it provides on the surface. The

---

3. An important book by that title, by Albert Schweitzer (1906) summed up the different approaches to the question up until his time.

flaw is to assume our modern, scientific methods make no room for ancient eye-witness accounts.

Naturally, assuming that the portrait of him in the New Testament does not measure up to our standards, each different quest came out with a different theory of who Jesus truly might have been. For example, H. S. Reimarus saw Jesus as a nationalist Jewish leader who had no intention of founding a new religion. Rudolph Bultmann believed that "We can now know almost nothing concerning the life and personality of Jesus." More recent quests portray Jesus as a political zealot, or a magician, a prophet to help the Jews deal with the occupation, or even a law-respecting Pharisee. While often deeply prejudiced, many of these studies have at least some value, since they help us get closer to the world of the 1st century. And since the Christian faith is based on revelation in history that in itself is helpful. But what is not helpful at all is the presumption (a worldview, really) that there must be a gap between the New Testament and what we really need to know about Jesus.

How Can We Know For Sure?

Why does it matter that Jesus should be a real person or not? Why does it matter whether the picture of him in the New Testament is correct and adequate or not? Very simply, because everything depends upon it! If Jesus were not God's Son, come into the world to die for sinners and to be raised up for their liberation, then everything falls to the ground. If the New Testament does not support this, or if it is only a product of Paul or the church, then all is lost. To use Paul's language,

> If Christ has not been raised, then our preaching is in vain and your faith is in vain... If in this life only we have hoped in Christ, we are of all people most to be pitied. (I Cor. 15:15-19)

If this is true, it matters greatly that the historical data support the true Jesus. Of course, it is all important how we interpret these data. If we do so to find another Jesus, one we prefer, then we will not let the Bible speak for itself. So, what exactly is the evidence for Jesus' existence?

 Not surprisingly, direct archeological evidence for Jesus is quite sparse. As we should expect, there is no trace of the actual cross, nor of the house where Jesus grew up, etc. Why should we expect this? Because the most important things Jesus did are not likely to be recorded in stones and artifacts. Some have desperately grasped at possible physical evidence, like the Shroud of Turin. For some time it was thought to be a veil with which Jesus wiped his face during his long march to the cross. Picked up by Mary Magdalene, she opened it and found he had left an imprint of his weeping face as a gift to her. Today we know that the shroud comes from the Middle Ages.[4] Besides, what difference would it really make to have such a shroud, even if it were marked with the imprint of Jesus' face? Absolutely none, since he is now ascended into Heaven and works with his people through the Holy Spirit, and not relics.

If it is unlikely we will find physical evidence for Jesus' existence, is there nothing archeology can tell us? Sure, there is. For example, it can highlight the customs and cultural practices from those times, and then corroborate them with what we find in the New Testament. Clothing styles, dining customs, agricultural methods, financial practices, etc., these can be identified. When they are it turns out they are quite compatible with what we find in the Gospels. The Jewish temple, the Roman presidium, the walls of Jerusalem, etc., these all fit what we read in the Scriptures.

What about references outside of Christian writings? There are only a few references to Jesus in non-Christian texts from the first two centuries. Tacitus, the Roman historian, does give Jesus a walk-on part in his *Annals* (15.44), written around 115 AD. He refers rather briefly to the belief Christians have in Christ's execution, ordered by Pontius Pilate. Another account is by the Jewish historian Josephus, toward the end of the first century. In his *Antiquities* (18.63-64) he refers to Jesus as a miracle-worker who was crucified, and

---

4. See Walter C. McCrone, *Judgment Day for The Turin Shroud*, Prometheus Books, 1999.

gave rise to the "Christian sect." There are a few other ancient writers who referred to him. But why so few reports? Probably because a leader who did miracles and was executed in a remote province of the Roman empire was just not the stuff of headlines!

That all changed when the Christian group became a strong movement. From the second century onward all kinds of writers took notice of Christians and thus sought to describe the founder, Jesus. This included the so-called "apocryphal gospels," including the famous Gospel of Thomas and the Gospel of Judas. While these documents have very little credibility, they did help foster some of the more elaborate stories later embraced by some portions of the church, including the prominent role for the Virgin Mary, and legends about Jesus' childhood. Separating fact from fiction is the major challenge of these books.

Not so the actual four Gospels and the New Testament letters. One of the most convincing aspects of these accounts is their unity and diversity. The four Gospels, Matthew, Mark, Luke and John, all record aspects of the life of Jesus, as well as his sayings, but each one puts a slightly different twist on it, as we have seen. A bit as though several newspapers had reported on the same event. Especially significant is the fact that John's Gospel is so different from the other three, and thus obviously from an independent source. So these four accounts are mutually complementary. All four were written within a few decades of the events they describe. And they all rely on personal memories, eye-witness accounts, oral tradition, and existing documents. There are simply no other ancient documents that come remotely close to this sort of accuracy. Christians understand them to be divinely inspired.

So, then, what do these testimonies tell us? The four Gospels are not biographies in the usual sense. They do report the incidents and sayings of Jesus and others as they occurred. But, as we have mentioned earlier, when discussing the Bible's reliability, there is considerable

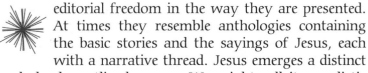 editorial freedom in the way they are presented. At times they resemble anthologies containing the basic stories and the sayings of Jesus, each with a narrative thread. Jesus emerges a distinct and clearly outlined person. We might call it a realistic narrative. The Gospel writers were well aware of their purposes. Yet the overall picture is one of the utter reliability of the historical accounts of Jesus.

Indeed, it was of the utmost importance to these writers that their witness be reliable. Two of them, Mark and John, were actually there. They were with Jesus during his earthly ministry and carefully recorded what he said and did. Matthew records his own call to follow Jesus (Matt. 9:9). He was an expert in the Old Testament and carefully observed how Jesus interacted with the law. He opens with the genealogy of Christ. John several times tells his reader that he was there, and saw these things first hand (John 20:8; 21:24; Rev. 1:9-20). Mark was probably the friend of Peter, and listened carefully to what he said (Acts 12:12). And Luke was a professional historian who wrote "an orderly account" of the things he had heard from the eye-witnesses so that his friend Theophilus could know them for sure (Luke 1:1-4).

There is a fascinating book, by Frank Morison, called *Who Moved the Stone?*[5] Morison, a skeptical lawyer, began by wanting to investigate the evidence for the life and resurrection of Jesus Christ. Convinced at first that most of the evidence was flimsy at best, he proceeded to probe into the case, and emerged with the surprising finding that the data were solid. He wrote chapters entitled, "The Book That Refused to Be Written"; "The Real Case Against the Prisoner"; "What Happened Before Midnight on Thursday"; "Between Sunset and Dawn"; "The Witness of the Great Stone"; "Some Realities of That Far-off Morning"; etc. What began as a skeptic's rebuttal ended up as a believer's substantiation. Jesus exists, and lived, died, and was raised from the dead.

---

5. Frank Morison, *Who Moved the Stone?*, Grand Rapids: Zondervan, 1987.

Discussion

1. How do some people erect a wall between us and the historical Jesus?
2. How do we know the *Da Vinci Code* is fictional?
3. Why does the empty tomb matter? What is at stake?
4. How do the different Gospel writers assure us of the reliability of their witness?

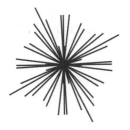

Is Jesus Really God?

But what have we got if we only find Jesus to have existed? Who was he, or, rather, who is he? And why did he have so much influence on the world? One popular view of Jesus is that he was a wise teacher, and a great moral example. No doubt he was those things. But some of his behavior goes way beyond even the best teachers and examples. In fact, some of it is highly inappropriate, unless he was far more than a teacher. For example, Jesus several times simply <u>declared someone's sins forgiven</u>. In a famous example, he was sitting in a crowded room and teaching (Mark 2:1-12) Suddenly a group lowered a paralyzed man down through the roof. At which point Jesus declared, "My son, your sins are forgiven." This was immediately interpreted as blasphemy. To which he said: "Which is easier, to say to the paralytic, 'Your sins are forgiven,' or to say, 'rise, take up your bed and walk'?" A rhetorical question, since neither are possible for any ordinary human being. But Jesus, the Son of God, could do both; and he did.

Jesus told people that unless they followed him and believed in him they would perish. This is not the stuff of a good moral teacher, but rather of a megalomaniac; unless, of course, he really is who he says he is. Indeed, in at least three places Christ is directly called God. They are, John 1:1, John 20:28, and Hebrews 1:8-9. And much of the way Jesus talked about his own identity points to his divinity. His favorite title for himself was "Son of Man." This is a reference to Daniel 7:13, which states that one "like a son of man" came to the Ancient of Days (God himself) and was given "dominion and glory and a kingdom, that all peoples, nations, and languages should serve him ..." Many times Jesus called himself names that could only belong to God. One of the most remarkable is in the Gospel of John, where he affirms his eternity.

At one point he states:"Truly, truly, I say to you, before Abraham was, I am." This is a clear reference to the "I am that I am" passage in Exodus 3:14.

In fact, he often used the identification of *I am*.

I am the bread of life. (John 6:48)

I am the light of the world. (John 8:12)

I am the light of the world. (John 9:5)

I am the good shepherd. (John 10:14)

I am the Son of God. (John 10:36)

I am the resurrection and the life. (John 11:25)

I am the way, the truth and the life, no one comes to the Father except through me. (John 14:6)

I am the true vine. (John 15:1)

All of these claims are rich and powerful. Whatever else they may be, they are not the claims of a good moral teacher. They are the claims of the *I am that I am*! At another point he compared himself to the Father and simply says, "I and the Father are one" (John 10:30).

His enemies, the proud Pharisees, understood what he was saying, and tried to destroy him for reasons of blasphemy. Jesus asks them, "I have shown you many good works from the Father; for which of them are you going to stone me?" (stoning was an approved method of capital punishment within the Judaism of the time; see 1 Sam. 30:6; Acts 7:59). As C. S. Lewis once put it:

> I am trying to prevent anyone saying the really foolish thing that people often say about Him: "I'm ready to accept Jesus as a great moral teacher, but I don't accept His claim to be God." That is the one thing we must not say. A man who was merely a man and said the sort of things Jesus said would not be a great moral teacher. He would either be a lunatic—on a level with the man who says he is a poached egg—or else he would be the Devil of Hell. You must make

your choice. Either this man was, and is, the Son of God: or else a madman or something worse. You can shut Him up for a fool, you can spit at Him and kill Him as a demon; or you can fall at His feet and call Him Lord and God. But let us not come with any patronising nonsense about His being a great human teacher. He has not left that open to us. He did not intend to.¹

Christians understand God, the divine Trinity, to be the Lord of all, the Creator of the universe, and yet utterly above it. Though above, he is also intimately close to his creation. And, he is somehow both one and three. God is one. Unlike many religions, we do not have here "polytheism," the idea of many gods. Yet, at the same time he is three: the Father, the Son and the Holy Spirit. We will never fully understand how God could be a Trinity, as he is called, but we can certainly know him very deeply. So then, Christ is the Second Person of the Trinity. He is God's Son. We don't know how God could have a Son, but he does. If you read through the Gospels, at the beginning of the New Testament, they will describe how God's Son became a human being twenty-one centuries ago. He was called Jesus, which means "savior." And he was called "the Christ," which means God's anointed one, come to lead his people into the way of life. (Matt. 16:16; 22:42; 26:63; Mark 1:1; 8:29; 12:35; Luke 2:11; 4:41; 24:46; John 1:41; 11:27; 20:31; Acts 2:36; Rom. 2:16, etc.)

Jesus Christ came to teach, to heal, and to die for his people. At his death God the Father poured out his anger against him. Why? Because if he had not, then his anger for our rebellion would have to be directed at us. That would have meant we would never know God properly, and, as a consequence, we would be lost forever. But God so loved the world, even in its rebellion, that he provided an amazing way out of our predicament: he would judge not us, but his Son in our place. So Jesus, who did not deserve to die, accepted that terrible doom, because he shared the Father's love for us. After he died, he was raised from the dead and now lives forever. The purpose of his new life is to pour out his love and his power upon believers. He

1. C. S. Lewis, *Mere Christianity*, London: Collins, 1952, p. 54.

sends the Third Person, the Holy Spirit, to guide, direct and empower us with new life. A Christian is therefore one who trusts in Jesus Christ, God's Son, for life, and has power to live it.

Our Only Hope?

One way of examining the claims about Jesus to see if they are true is as we have just done. Look at the hard evidence. But another, perhaps a deeper way, is to ask what difference it would make if Jesus were not truly God? To answer this question we need to look at the big issue behind the assertion of his divinity.

As we said earlier, the world is God's beautiful creation gone terribly wrong. While everything has become corrupted, the deepest level of corruption is a moral one. We, poor sinful creatures, have devised all kinds of ways to offend God and to leave undone what we ought to have done. Our problem is not that we are frail and finite, our problem is that we are morally corrupt. What can remedy our plight? No amount of moral reform will be enough. No amount of good works will be enough. For we have become enemies with God. Or rather, more significantly, he has become our enemy.

The one remedy is the very one God devised: send his Son into the world to take our place. This has two aspects. First, Jesus perfectly fulfilled the divine will. Unlike Adam, unlike Israel, unlike you and me, he was perfect. That does not mean he was boring or straight-laced. As we have shown he was fully human. But he never doubted God, never followed his own way, never sinned. Even when facing the worst temptations he refused to succumb to evil.

Second, he took all of the consequences for our evil-doing upon himself. Altogether innocent, he accepted the call to suffer the death penalty, a very painful one at that, in order that any believer would not have to experience ultimate death. So, what if Jesus were not God? Quite simply, but most profoundly, we would have no hope.

First, if Jesus is not God, then he could never have followed God's will perfectly. But that is the very requirement for us to be reconciled to God. Jesus, our substitute, had to do what we failed to do, obey the Father to the letter of the law.

Second, he could never have born the penalty for our sins. Only God, the Second Person of the Trinity, become man, could have accomplished this extraordinary task.

Technically, we call these two aspects of his work the active and passive obedience of Christ. He actively obeyed the whole law on our behalf. And he passively took the penalty for our guilt.

The Only Way?

Thus, when Jesus said, "I am the way and the truth and the life. No one comes to the Father except through me," (John 14:6) he means quite literally that because of who he is, we may now come back to the Father. He is the way, that is, the means, the path. One cannot come to the Father except through Jesus. Of course there are many ways to Jesus, but only one way to friendship with the Father. He is the truth because he is the ultimate reality, and the one who reveals that reality to us in all its fullness. He is the life because while death has permeated our world, Jesus, by his resurrection from the dead, brings life back to the world, eternal life. If he is not God, then don't bother with him. And don't bother with life, either, for there is no hope for you (or me).

No other religion, no other philosophy, offers anything remotely like the gospel. Hebrews tells us:

> For it was fitting, that he, for whom and by whom all things exist, in bringing many sons to glory, should make the founder of their salvation perfect through suffering ... For this reason he had to be made like them, fully human in every way, in order that he might become a merciful and faithful high priest in service to God, and that he might make atonement for the sings of the poeple ...How shall we escape if we neglect such a great salvation? (2:10, 17, 3)

Discussion

1. What is wrong with calling Jesus just a great moral teacher?
2. Is it arrogant to call the gospel of Christ our only hope?
3. Why did Jesus have to die?
4. So who was, and who is Jesus?

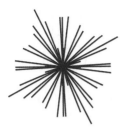

Katherine

Can We Trust
The Bible?

I t is quite common to hear someone ask how a book so ancient as the Bible can be reliable. Indeed, the Bible is not only very old, it was written over a period of at least 1,500 years, beginning sometime around 1450 B.C. and ending near the close of the 1st century A.D. Its books are written in three different languages, Hebrew, Aramaic and Greek, and in many genres, such as poetry, historical narrative, laws, prophetic and apocalyptic literature. The world of today is quite different from the ancient world of the Middle East, so that we may legitimately ask how the writers could have any connection with us.

The Bible and History

Let's begin with a fundamental issue. Is there any historical reliability to the Bible? Many today assume the Bible was written centuries after the events recorded, and that the main reason it was written was to reinforce the ideas they wanted to believe and defend. Even professional Bible scholars question the historical reliability of the Bible, or at least of large portions of it.

There are many questions we could face, but let's just take one or two. Some historical claims are easy to corroborate. For example, the culture of the patriarchs (Abraham, Isaac and Jacob, living between 1900 and 1600 B.C.) as described in the Old Testament, fits what we have been able to discover from archeology. The way of life in the Middle Bronze Age (c. 2000–1550), as set forth by the many discoveries of places and artifacts, fits what the Bible tells us. For example, we can trace various migrations of people such as the Amorites, the Horites, the Hittites and others who were seeking new homes. The patterns of conquests of ancient kings corroborates what we read, for example, in Genesis 14, when Chedorlaomer and his allies defeated the kings of Sodom and Gomorrah in the Valley of Siddim. Travel, trade, commerce, and the customs of the age have been documented on thousands of clay tablets, including rich sources such as the archives from Nuzi.

Other confirmations exist. For example, there is an inscription on the Tel Dan Stele (the Mound of Dan inscribed stone) which records the victory of an Aramean king over his two southern neighbors, the "king of Israel" and the "king of the House of David." We can date it in the 9th or 8th century B.C. This is the first clear mention of King David outside the Bible, and there is every reason to believe it is authentic. It probably refers to the campaign of Hazael, king of Damascus, who defeated Jehoram of Israel and Ahaziah of Judah.[1]

Not everything is so simple, however. Many of the most important aspects of the Bible are very difficult to document. We cannot be sure of the exact location for some of the cities mentioned. Nor the existence of some of the people who are so important in biblical history. One of the more puzzling is the Exodus story. For some time now scholars have questioned the historicity of the Exodus from Egypt. Various reasons are given. For example, Numbers 1:46 tells us there were 603,550 men, plus women and children, who left Egypt and crossed the Red Sea (sometimes called the "Sea of Reeds"). If this number is right, that would mean about two million people were involved. If you count their animals and vehicles you would have to have a group that was 150 miles long. Not impossible, perhaps, but strange that there are no records of these numbers, either of Egypt's population loss or of Canaan's increase. So various critical scholars assume the story is not historically valid, but was probably composed during the Babylonian exile, to encourage the oppressed Israelites.

The story of the Exodus is one of the most often mentioned in the entire Bible. While there can be, to be

---

1. See George Athas, *The Dan inscription: A Reappraisal and a New Interpretation*, London: T & T Clark, 2005, 306.

sure, poetic uses of the Exodus, to remind people of God's power, most of these citations assume it was a real, historical event. One would lose a great deal by putting into question the historicity of the event. It is possible that the 603,550 were families, not just men, in which case the number would have been smaller. But still, we might ask, why is there no record in Egyptian or Canaanite literature of such a huge event. One very good reason is that ancient peoples almost never recorded their defeats, which the Exodus certainly was. We also do possess evidence that there was a Semitic presence in Egypt several decades before the Exodus, although the actual date of the Exodus is under discussion. Furthermore, while we don't have much direct archeological evidence for the event, we can show that the general features of the culture and practices described in the Pentateuch are compatible with a late second millennium world. Finally, claiming that the Exodus was a story created during the exile amounts to saying it is fiction, which goes against the larger arguments in the Bible that God acts into our history with mighty deeds and miracles.

For that matter, whether or not we can corroborate every event and person in archeology, Christianity is a historical religion, and its truth must be grounded in history or all is lost. The final authority for its historicity is not in some "neutral" scientific court, but in God's say-so through his own appointed witnesses. Paul was aware of this when he explained to the Corinthians that not only was Christ's resurrection predicted in the Old Testament, but it was witnessed by the apostles and by over 500 people, most of whom were still alive at the time of his writing (1 Cor. 15:3-7).

The Transmission of the Bible

Another frequently cited dilemma about the Bible is that we do not have the original copies (the "autographa"), that is, we do not have signed copies of Deuteronomy or Isaiah or Matthew. So how do we know what we have now is authentic? If you have ever looked at a Hebrew,

Aramaic, or Greek Bible, you may have glanced at the footnotes. If so, you will have seen that there are different manuscripts from which the editors decided to choose. There are papyri, that is, ancient fragments written on pages from the papyrus plant. There are manuscripts, such as the codex Sinaiaticus, literally found on Mount Sinai, or the "Alexandrinus," or the "Vaticanus," rather complete copies of the New Testament. And there are other fragments. But no original documents. So, you might legitimately ask, how can I know for sure these are true copies of the original?

The transmission of Scripture down through the generations is a fascinating subject. The best way to look at it is to presuppose a God who cares deeply that the events of redemption, grounded in history, also cares that his people will be correctly informed about how to understand those events. Deuteronomy makes this connection frequently: here is what happened, and here is what the future generations need to know (Deut. 31:9-13, 24-29). The prophets needed to have their prophecies written down for the same reason. For example, just to name one place among many, the Lord told Jeremiah (during Jehoiakim's reign) to take a scroll and write on it all the words he had spoken, so that Israel will have the opportunity to be warned and to repent (Jer. 36:1-8). And of course this is abundantly true in the New Testament, where the Scriptures are inspired and written down so that we may believe (John 20:30-31; Rev. 1:11, 19).

Accordingly, we have every right to suppose that there were indeed original texts, signed by the authors, and even though we don't have them, what we do have is very close. So close, in fact, that no important doctrine is even slightly controversial. How did the transmission work? We know that right from the beginning copies were made of the originals to make sure they were preserved. Scribes were meticulous in the task of copying. For example, the Bible itself records the scrupulous care that was taken to preserve the originals. Deuteronomy tells us:

> When Moses had finished writing the words of this law to the very end, Moses commanded the Levites who carried

the ark of the covenant of the Lord, 'Take this Book of the Law, and put it by the side of the ark ...' (31:24-26).

The Levites were given a sacred trust to safeguard the Scriptures. This pattern was repeated over and over again. Joshua, who succeeded Moses, read the words of Moses to the people, and, "There was not a word of all that Moses commanded that Joshua did not read before the assembly of Israel ..." (Josh. 8:35). The Kings of Israel were required to have their own personal copies of the Pentateuch. Later, those who copied the Bible counted every single word, and if the number did not come out correctly they started all over again!

There are some 5,000 manuscripts of the New Testament in existence, many go back to within a few years of their original composition. Compare this to Lucretius, or even Caesar, for which there are less than a score of manuscripts, most dating more than a thousand years after the originals. Without going into great detail, we can say here that hardly any of the variants in these manuscripts are significant. Occasionally there is a small part of speech, an article or a preposition, that might be different from one to another. But almost none of them change the basic meaning of the text. To the surprise of some, there are two longer texts which are not found in the best manuscripts: (1) John 7:53-8:11, the story of the woman caught in adultery, and (2) Mark 16:9-20, the "second" ending of Mark's Gospel. Most scholars would say that while they are probably not there in the original Bible texts, their message is fairly compatible with the originals and certainly not at all controversial.[2]

Why So Many Translations?

We frequently are told that we really don't have access to the real Bible unless we know Hebrew or Aramaic or Greek. Most of us can only read it in translation. And for that matter, there are so many different translations, how

2. One of the most helpful books on this subject is F. F. Bruce, *the New Testament Documents, Are They Reliable?*, Grand Rapids: Eerdmans, 2003.

do we know we are truly reading the Word of God? This is a very good question. The answer may come as a surprise.

It is of course important to have scholars dig into the original text, and try and discover the very best Hebrew, Aramaic and Greek versions to work from. But the Word of God was from the beginning meant to be translated. The plan, from the beginning, was that people from every nation, tribe and language should be saved and worship God and his Son (Rev. 7:9). Somehow this means they needed to understand the saving Word in their own tongue. When King Nebuchadnezzar was converted, after witnessing the three Israelites saved in the fiery furnace, he declared, "to all peoples, nations, and languages that dwell in all the earth…" that they should know about what the Most High God had done for him (Dan. 4:1-2). On the day of Pentecost, the Holy Spirit came down with "tongues as of fire" and gave the apostles the gift of speaking in several languages (Acts 2:1-12). Nothing was lost, as they say, in translation.

Certainly there are weak translations, even bad ones. But in most cases there is no way to miss the central message of the Christian worldview. To put it more positively, the Christian message is the most "translatable" in the world. While different translations of the Bible have their strengths and weaknesses, by and large it is good to have the Bible available in one's own language. So, do get a hold of a good translation of the Bible and do benefit from the message of the gospel that you will find therein. Here is how the renowned scholar, Sir Frederic Kenyon, principal Librarian of the British Museum for twenty-one years, put it:

> The Christian can take the whole Bible in his hand and say without fear or hesitation that he holds in it the true word of God, handed down without essential loss from generation to generation throughout the centuries.[3]

---

3.   F. G. Kenyon, *Our Bible and the Ancient Manuscripts*, 4th ed., (n.p.: Harper, 1951), p. 23.

Contradictions In The Bible?

When I was a new Christian, I met a liberal minister who was quite uncomfortable with what he considered to be my "fundamentalism."
One reason conservative Christian faith could not be true, he asserted, is that the Bible is full of contradictions. So I challenged him to name one. He came up with the following problem: in one passage Jesus says, "He who is not with me is against me" (Matt. 12:30), but in another, he declares, "whoever is not against us is for us" (Mark 9:40). At first, I was rather puzzled by this. It did seem to be a contradiction. But then, when I thought about it, it became clear that these two passages were not contradictions at all. They were saying two quite different things, complementary things, owing to their two contexts.

In the first case, Jesus is simply saying no one can be neutral or sit on the fence. You are either for me or against me, meaning, you cannot just be an agnostic, someone who is not sure. An agnostic is actually against Jesus.

In the second case, the context is about exorcising demons. Apparently someone was driving out demons in the name of Jesus, even though he was not in the official group of disciples. Here, Jesus says, as long as the person is not conspiring against the group, then using the name of Jesus is fine. He's an honorary member!

Does the Christian faith require that we believe in a Bible that has no contradictions? Yes, it does. The reason is that our worldview claims that God breathed out the Holy Scriptures, and that he is incapable of contradiction. Otherwise, the Scriptures could not be, as they claim they are, "profitable" for godliness (2 Tim. 3:16). The Holy Scriptures are able to make us wise for salvation because they tell us the truth about God's ways and about life (2 Tim. 3:15). As our Lord himself puts it, "Your word is truth" (John 17:17). If we only have a fallible revelation how can God's word be truth? And how can we find godliness or salvation in it? Ultimately the inerrancy of Scripture goes back to God's own inerrant reliability.

This point of view does not mean we will never find apparent contradictions. There are several kinds of difficulties with the Bible for any honest reader. And while it is true that we only "know in part" (1 Cor. 13:9) in the present time, that should not excuse us from facing up to some of the challenges of the Bible.

Does God Change?

Some of the most significant apparent contradictions have to do with one of the great mysteries of our faith: the absolute sovereignty of a God who decides all things from eternity, and the real responsibility and significance of his creatures.

Here is one way it plays out in the Bible: can God change his mind? There seems to be evidence on both sides. Throughout, the Bible speaks of God as changeless (the technical word is *immutable*). For example, Malachi 3:1 states, "For I the Lord do not change." Often the affirmation of immutability is made by contrast with how the word and human beings do change. Consider Psalm 102:26-27:

> They [heaven and earth] will perish, but you will remain;
>   They will all wear out like a garment.
> You will change them like a robe,
>   And they will pass away,
> But you are the same, and your years have no end.

Referring to his promises, the Bible is crystal clear: "God is not a man that he should lie, or a son of man, that he should change his mind" (Num. 23:19). The grand statement of his identity in Exodus 3:14 says it clearly: "I am that I am."

Yet there are several places where God does change his mind. One most commonly cited is Abraham bargaining for the survival of Sodom (see Gen. 18:22-33). God has determined to judge Sodom and Gomorrah for their crimes. But in a series of rather bold prayers, Abraham asks him to consider saving the city if only 50, then 45, then 40, then 30, then 20, then 10 righteous people are found there. Each time God says he will. In fact they did not find even 10 righteous people there, but only one, a man named Lot. So the city was judged. But the point here is, God was willing to change his mind.

Another example is this: when the people of Israel sinned in the desert, God determined to wipe them out and start again (Exod. 32:10). But after Moses pleaded for them he "relented from the disaster that he had spoken of bringing on his people" (32:14).

Again, when Jonah preached to Ninevah and they repented, "when God saw what they did, how they turned from their evil way, God relented of the disaster that he had said he would do to them, and he did not do it" (Jonah 3:10). There are several other places where God has decided one thing and then changes his mind.

What is going on here? Does the Bible say contradictory things about God? On the one hand, he cannot change, but on the other he can? That is not possible. Are these statements about God "relenting" simply using human language to explain what appears to be a change? Some have argued that the Bible makes it look as though he had changed his mind by using human language to that effect, whereas in reality this is just an appearance. But this does not take these texts seriously. They really do say he changes!

A better way to look at it is to say that at the ultimate level God doesn't change, nor can he. Yet when he relates to the creation, and especially to human beings, he does change and the change is real. Put it this way: with respect to his being God does not change. What he plans from all eternity will, indeed, must come to pass. At the same time, with respect to his covenant relation to creation the change is real. Yes, he has decreed it. But he has also decreed that the creation be a real place, and that history be significant, and that human decisions matter. These are two realities which we must respect. The one depends upon the other, but it does not make creation and human decision less real. Otherwise, why pray? Why would God care if we make requests of him? Here is another way of stating the paradox: though God is all glorious, we may still glorify him and so add to his glory. How can you fill anything up that is already full? And yet that is precisely what happens when we give glory to God.

This way of thinking is similar to the whole issue of predestination and human responsibility, something we will look into later on. For example, Acts 2:23 says that Jesus was handed over to the Jewish authorities "by God's set purposes and foreknowledge." But then it adds, "and you, with the help of wicked men, put him to death ..." So, you might say, which is it? God's set (predestining) purposes, or human wickedness? The answer is both. God has made the world so that his set purposes include human responsibility. This apparent contradiction, a paradox, really, is found throughout the Bible. Jesus tells his listeners, "No one knows the Father except the Son and those to whom the Son chooses to reveal him." And then he says: "Come to me, all you who are weary and burdened, and I will give you rest" (Matt. 11:27-28).

Can he really be sincere in offering the gospel to anyone who is weary and comes to him, when he knows he will only reveal himself to some? The answer is yes, and it is a wonderful mystery. We are not sure altogether how both God's sovereignty and human responsibility can be true. But to deny one side or the other is certain madness. Paul tells his readers, "Work out your salvation with fear and trembling ...for it is God who works in you to will and to act ..." (Phil. 2:12-13). So, which is it, you might say, my activity or God's? Again, the answer is both.

The Bible As Literature

Other types of apparent contradictions can be found. One important way to address some of these difficulties is by understanding a bit more about the way ancient literature works. For example, we don't want to impose modern standards for accuracy on an ancient text when they do not match the standards of antique literature. That is not to say ancient authors operated on completely different ideas of truth than do we, for if that were the case we could never understand them. Yet it is to say that we owe it to them to enter into their world and to understand their styles if we are going to discover the full riches of their views.

Here is a classic case of an apparent contradiction which can be resolved when we know about ancient writing techniques. How do Genesis 1 and Genesis 2 relate? If you read them straight through you will immediately see a problem. Genesis 1 (well, really, Gen. 1:1–2:4) tells of the creation of the heavens and the earth, with its orderly sequence of the days, culminating in the creation of mankind on the sixth day. Genesis 2 (2:4-25 and beyond) tells about the "earth and the heavens," and explains that at one time there were no plants in the ground because there was no rain and because there was no man to cultivate the land (2:5). The first problem is resolved by the presence of springs of fresh water (which some translations render a "mist" (v. 6). The second problem is remedied by the special creation of a human being, named Adam, whom he placed in a beautiful garden (vv. 7-9). Then, God created a special partner for Adam, named Eve. None of these details are mentioned in Genesis 1, which states instead that God created man in his own image, an image shared by both males and females (Gen. 1:27).

Why such different accounts? They contrast so greatly that some biblical critics have assumed they were written by different authors and then cobbled together by a later editor. Here we have an apparent contradiction in the story of the creation of man, and the two accounts are right next to each other. There is, though, a much better explanation, one that not only dissolves the contradiction but also helps us understand how this part of the Bible is constructed. It turns out that throughout Genesis the expression "these are the generations of" (in Hebrew, *toleh doth*, or, "this is the family history of") is repeated ten times, and serves to divide important portions of the book. In each case, there is a summary story, followed by a more detailed account flowing from that summary. The expression "generations of" serves as a signal marker for the beginning of each section.[4] The first case is here in Genesis 2:4, and it serves

---

4. Most major commentaries describe this literary structure. See, for example, Bruce Waltke, Genesis, op. cit., 17-19. The expression "the generations of" is the heading for the line of the heavens and the earth (2:4-4:26); Adam's line (5:1-6:8); Noah's line (6:9-9:29); the line of

to divide the first text, about the creation, from the second, which is what the creation produced. The next one is "the generations of Adam" (5:1). The next is the generations of Noah (6:9), and so on. The first five *toleh doth* contain the very earliest history of mankind, whereas the last five give more detailed accounts of the patriarchs, Abraham, Ishmael, Isaac, Esau and Jacob.

What the heavens and the earth "produced," then, is Adam, then Eve, the first cultivators of the soil, the first parents of the human race. Tragically, this first couple would also yield to the serpent's temptation and fall into sin, dragging their progeny with them. But then God promised them redemption, and allowed their offspring to continue in his divine purposes, albeit under the curse of sin. These events are recorded in Genesis 2:4 to 4:26. They represent the "offspring" of Genesis 1. The point here is that we have no contradiction, but a literary structure whereby the recounting of the unique creation week (Gen. 1) is followed by a detailed account of the events made possible by that creation week, the "generations" of the creation, Adam and Eve, their calling and their misadventures (Gen. 2ff.).

Genesis 1 and 2 are not the only places in Scripture using such an organizational device. Exodus 14 and 15 tell us the story of the great escape out of Egypt (ch. 14) followed by a poetical rendering of the same story, known as the Song of Moses (ch. 15). Similarly, Judges 4 records the battle fought by Deborah against the Canaanites and the grim account of Jael driving a peg into Sisera's temple while he was asleep (ch. 4), followed by the Song of Deborah which poetically recounts all of these events (ch. 5). These are not exact parallels to Genesis 1 and 2, but they illustrate how the same event can be recorded differently, as narrative history and as poetry.

Writer's Choice

The Bible often uses this kind of complementary editorial technique. The entire Books of 1 and 2 Kings cover much of

---

Noah's sons (10:1-11:9); Shem's line (11:10-26); Terah's line (11:27-25:11); Ishmael's line (25:12-18); Isaac's line (25:19-35:29); Esau's line (36:1-37:1); and Jacob's line (37:2-50:26).

the same material as 1 and 2 Chronicles. Why do we need two different versions of the same thing? The reason is that the Kings tell the story from the point of view of a careful historian who wants to record the specific events and personalities that led from the last days of David to the Babylonian exile, almost four centuries later. When we read this version of the events we realize how much the people of Israel were responsible for God's judgments. The Chronicler, on the other hand, is more interested in recording God's faithfulness to his people, despite the judgments and despite the many ups and downs of Jewish history. Thus, we read a good deal about the great temple, with its joys, its music, and, above all, the presence of God. These two accounts are not contradictory but complementary.

As a matter of fact, the same can be said for the four Gospels in the New Testament. Why do we need four different accounts of the life of Jesus? Matthew is concerned to show how Jesus fulfilled the Old Testament, how he understood the law of God, how he considered the Kingdom of God to have arrived. Mark is concerned to show the immediacy, the authenticity of Jesus ministry. His Gospel is quite brief compared to the other three. But brevity here underscores the authenticity of Jesus' life and sayings. Mark is also concerned to show how Jesus was open to the inclusion of the Gentiles. Luke, who also wrote the Book of Acts, is a careful historian, emphasizing details not found in the other Gospels, for example, Jesus' special attention to children, to poor people, to women. It is possible that Luke was a physician, which would account for his detailed descriptions of healings. Finally, John is quite unique. He is concerned to show how Jesus came to his own people, and how they often did not accept him. His gospel is quite evangelistic, written so that you may believe that Jesus is the Christ, the Son of God (John 20:31).

Having explained these complementary emphases, we still are faced with certain problems. For example, consider the order of events in the three "synoptic" Gospels, Matthew, Mark and Luke. Matthew places the healing of the centurion's servant before the incident where the disciples pick grain on the Sabbath and Jesus heals the man with a withered hand (Matt. 8:5-13; 12:1-14). Luke places the healing of the centurion's servant after the Sabbath incident and the withered hand healing (Luke 6:1-11; 7:1-10). Again, Matthew puts the cleansing of the temple right after Jesus' triumphal entry but before the cursing of the fig tree (Entry-Cleansing-Curse: Matt. 21:1-22), whereas Mark places the cleansing of the temple on the day after the triumphal entry and after the cursing of the fig tree (Entry-Curse-Cleansing: Mark 11:1-25).

Probably the best answer to these apparent discrepancies is that while the general order of events in Jesus' life is respected, the different Gospel writers are not so concerned with strict chronology as they are with topical emphases. Matthew, for example, uses a simple structure for his Gospel: narrative-teaching-narrative-teaching. His Gospel is orderly, organized into seven parts. The introduction tells of Jesus' genealogy (ordered in three groups of 14, a typical Jewish mnemonic device), his miraculous birth, and the beginning of his public ministry (1:1–4:17). The conclusion recounts the Last Supper, the trial, the crucifixion, the resurrection and the "great commission" (26:1–28:20). In between are five parallel sections, each with a narrative on Jesus' actions and miracles, followed by words, or sermons, fitting what the actions suggest. For example, following the story of the calling of his disciples (4:18-25) we have the "Sermon on the Mount" (5:1–7:29). Following the accounts of different reactions to his miracles and teaching, there is a sermon about parables which explains why there are different responses (13:1-52).

So it is safe to say that while Matthew does not carelessly disregard the general sequence of events in Jesus' life, he organizes the material topically, in order to make the point that people respond in different ways to the gospel. Sometimes the Gentiles see it more clearly than the Jews, for example. The centurion understood things better than the Pharisees. The cleansing of the temple was a high priority. Nothing in our doctrine of biblical inerrancy prevents us from saying that these authors could make editorial decisions that were not always strictly chronological.

Other difficulties exist. For example, Mark and John appear to differ on the hour at which Christ was crucified. It turns out Matthew, Mark and Luke use the Athenian or Hebrew timing, whereas John uses the Roman system. Matthew states that Judas hanged himself, whereas Luke says he fell headlong and opened his middle. This one is a mystery. But it simply does not matter much. Sometimes we just don't need to resolve all of the apparent contradictions. In this case we can well leave it alone, and hope that some reasonable harmonization will occur at some point.

The New Testament Use Of The Old

Another series of apparent contradictions occur when the New Testament quotes the Old. Sometimes you might wonder where the New Testament authors get their quotes from, since they can be different from the Old Testament text. For example, Ephesians 4:8 says, "When he ascended on high he led a host of captives, and he gave gifts to men." But Psalm 68:18, which Paul is quoting, says, "You ascended on high, leading a host of captives in your train and receiving gifts among men ..."

On the surface there is quite a difference between giving gifts to men and receiving gifts among men. Interestingly, Paul here is using an Aramaic translation of the Old Testament, called the Targum. Aramaic and Hebrew are very close, but in this case the Aramaic makes an interpretation of the Hebrew term "receive" which makes it say, "receive in order to give." That is, in fact, a perfectly legitimate implication of the Hebrew word, and not a fanciful adaptation. Indeed, as the Bible confirms elsewhere, the whole purpose of Christ's ascension was to receive gifts from the Father in order to give them away to his people (see Acts 2:33; 5:31; Rom. 8:11; James 1:17). There are several cases where the New Testament writers choose a particular version of the Old Testament, such as the Targum or the Septuagint (the Greek translation) for their purposes. Perhaps a more challenging example is when the use of an Old Testament text seems to be novel, or not anticipated by the original author. For example, Matthew describes Joseph and Mary's flight into Egypt with their small child, Jesus, in order to escape Herod's fury (Matt. 2:7-18). He comments, "This was to fulfill what the Lord had spoken by the prophet, 'Out of Egypt I called my sons'" (v. 15).

But if you look up the source of this prophecy, Hosea 11:1, the reference is clearly to God's bringing Israel up out of slavery, that is, the Exodus. Did Hosea have any idea that there would be a child named Jesus who would be hidden in Egypt and then called out when the danger was over? Of course, he would not have known all the details, such as God's only Son, Jesus Christ, going down to Egypt to escape the wrath of King Herod. So, was Matthew inappropriately quoting Hosea here? No, because throughout the Old Testament, including Hosea (not only 11:1 but also 12:9, 13; 13:4) the deliverance from Egypt is considered a picture, a metaphor of the final delivery of God's people through the delivery of their king, the Lord Jesus Christ. Furthermore, Hosea, together with all of the Old Testament prophets, knew there would be a coming Messiah. And while he could not have known all the details of the timing or the circumstances of Christ's coming, he knew enough to be able to trust in God's salvation through the coming Messiah. The statement in Hosea 11:1 is first of all about Israel being delivered in the Exodus. But it functions secondarily as a true prophecy, one whose fulfillment the author could not have known in the detail, but one that Matthew rightly saw as prophetic of events in his lifetime.

Having said all of this, and having put forth some reasonable solutions to these Bible difficulties, our faith in an inerrant Bible does not in the end depend upon our being able to solve all the problems. Rather, it depends on trusting that the primary author, God himself, is utterly reliable, and that he would give us a message that is abundantly clear. What is that message? God created the world, including mankind, made after his image. But we rebelled against his order, plunging the world into a miserable abyss. Yet God loved the world, and planned to redeem it from that curse. After all the preparation, all the seasons of revelation, all of his purposes culminated in the coming to earth of his Son, Jesus Christ. Jesus came, he preached and did great deeds among people, then he died and was raised from the dead. Because of this, whoever calls upon him and asks for mercy, will obtain salvation.

While some of the details of biblical revelation might be up for debate, that central message is not. While it is fascinating to explore the difficulties, don't let the details get in the way of the central message. There is nothing more clear than the essential picture of Jesus and his mission, which emerge on every page of the New Testament. He was and is God's Son, come to preach the reality of the Kingdom of God, and to call men and women to faith and repentance in order that they may enter it. His death and resurrection are the guarantee that if they beg God's help, they will indeed be saved from their sins and be given eternal life.

Discussion

1. What are some apparent contradictions in the Bible that have bothered you? Have you found a way forward?

2. When the Bible says God changed his mind, did he really?

3. Does the fact that the Bible is literature remove from its truthfulness?

4. Do the concerns of different authors destroy the essential unity of the Bible?

5. What if we cannot verify some biblical stories in history? What about the story of the Exodus?

6. We don't possess the "autographa," the original, signed books of the Bible. Is that a problem?

7. Why do we need so many different translations?

8. Do I need to resolve all the problems before I can really trust the Bible?

Is the Christian Faith a Killjoy?

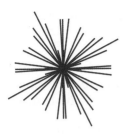

T his may seem a strange question. If God is there, what's the difference? Yet, if we are honest we will realize that coming to know God involves risks. First, if God is who the Bible says he is, he can be scary. God is indeed a God of love. This is abundantly clear from his desiring to save us from death, his patience with us, and above all sending his Son to die and to be raised up for our sakes. But God is also a judge. Some people think it is only in the Old Testament that God is considered a "God of wrath," that is, a God of anger, which he is (Ps. 2:5; Jer. 25:15).

But the New Testament also calls him an angry God, angry against injustice (Rom. 1:18; Rev. 6:16). He is also called "a consuming fire" (Heb. 12:29). There is a touching scene in the Gospels where Peter witnesses a miracle of Jesus. After a frustrating night of fishing without catching anything, Peter and his friends are told the next morning by Jesus to go further out and put the net down again. Understandably puzzled, these professional fishermen nevertheless did what the master said. And they caught so many fish that the nets were torn and the boats began to sink. Now you would think they would rush up to Jesus and thank him. Instead, Peter says, "Go away from me Lord for I am a sinful man" (Luke 5:1-11).

This story goes on to tell us that Jesus told the men not to be afraid, and that from now on they would be fishers of people! But everything here is on Jesus' terms. Notice the order here:

1. Jesus tells professional fishermen to try one more time;

2. They obey, no doubt wondering what was going on;

3. The catch is so great they hardly can handle it;

4. They are afraid.

5. Jesus comforts them and then gives them a greater task, preaching the gospel, of which the fishing venture was but an illustration.

Indeed, these disciples would later go out into the world and proclaim God's truth, and see many people respond. Accepting God on his own terms is a sober thing.

Knowing God is the most important thing in life. Real, deep, intimate knowledge of God means that the fear we have, often connected with our guilt, needs to be removed. Is there a way? Yes, there is. There was for Peter, and there is for us. But not by striving for it or using techniques. The gospel is free, absolutely free. Not only could we not come anywhere close to meeting God's standards, but he is pleased to offer us the gospel as a gift.

Unfortunately the human tendency is to try and earn his good pleasure. We want to achieve peace with God on our own terms. There are lots of ways we try to do this. Social service, generous giving, spending time in missions, pro bono work, and so forth.

The Bible tells us in many places that God is not out to require impossible good works from us, but out to help us. The Lord is a compassionate God, a gracious God, slow to anger, abounding in steadfast love (Exod. 34:6; Ps. 86:15). The ultimate assurance that God is approachable is when we realize we are utterly unable to be good enough. We need forgiveness, not recognition. And we cannot find forgiveness anywhere in ourselves, or in various disciplines. Yet God found a way to forgive us on his own terms. His forgiveness came at an enormous cost, not to us, but to him. When Christ died on the cross he was receiving on himself the anger of God for sins he did not commit. He was being punished for our sins. And when he rose from the dead, that was the vindication for you and me. And now all we have to do is ask God, and believe that he is merciful. Put differently, we must ask in faith. So the Christian faith is free, but it does require for us to give up

trying on our own. That can be very hard. We so
badly want to please him. But as the song says,
"If we tarry till we're better, we may never come
at all."

The Cost Of Discipleship

The second reason many people fear coming to God in order
to know him is sometimes called the cost of discipleship.
One of the most frequently heard objections to the
Christian faith is that it spoils our fun. Put differently, if
you become a Christian you will be captive to a long list
of rules. You won't be free anymore. And you ask, "Will
my friends not like me anymore because I have become
such a straight arrow? Will I be missing some fantastic
experiences in life because I am now a Christian? Will job
opportunities or promotions be denied me because I am a
non-compromiser? Will I have to restrict my entertainment,
whether movies or music, because of my commitment
to Christ?" One of the questions we received fairly often
when doing research for this book went something like
this: "My friend's parents let him go to R rated movies.
Mine do not. How can I persuade my friend that I am
"cool" anyway?"

These are very real concerns, indeed, important ones. It
is perfectly true that being a Christian involves submitting
to certain rules. But not the way you may be thinking.
The Bible favors morality but not moralism. What's the
difference? Morality is the general code of conduct by people
of integrity. Moralism is to be good merely for the sake of
being good. Moralism says, the whole point of religion
is moral improvement, and so if I behave well, I will be
approved by God. That is actually the very opposite of the
Christian religion. At the root, the Christian faith is not
about moral improvement, but about a relationship with
God. The ten commandments are meant to be of permanent
value, to be sure. And if you read carefully through the
New Testament, you will find that the law of God is good,
even holy (Rom. 7:12). And yet the Christian life is a free
gift from God through Jesus Christ. It is an invitation to

become God's friend. If we try to obey our way into the kingdom we will utterly fail. So how do we handle this question of rules?

The answer is that when we become Christians we become new persons. Not that we enter into perfection – that only will occur in heaven. But we have a new orientation, a new direction. Previously we were self-pleasing and were not fundamentally wanting to pursue God. But now we have a new motivation – to do God's will. And, far more, we have new power to begin to walk in God's ways.

Now, let's put this more positively. Christians ought to be the most truly human beings on earth. What does it mean to be human? Many things, and each person is different. Some are funny. Some are thoughtful. Some are athletic. Some, in fact, most, have not yet developed into what they shall be. Adolescence is a time of unprecedented change, and not all of it is pleasant. So, although we may be Christians, we are certainly not everything that God wants us to be. Yet he does want us to be fully human.

The most fully human person ever to walk the face of the earth was Jesus. We may get the wrong idea of his character from some of the traditional paintings of him. They make him look distant, overly serious, his feet not fully on the ground. Or he is portrayed as a sweet and saccharine shepherd, lovingly tending to his little lambs. In reality he was nothing like this. His first miracle was done at a wedding in Cana of Galilee. Although we are not given a great deal of detail, we know these weddings were feasts that lasted several days. Jesus surely sat down (or reclined, as they did in those days) to a banquet with family and friends. What did they all talk about? Probably not wet-blanket "religion." More likely they joked and told stories and remembered the old days. Indeed, things were so much fun they ran out of wine. Jesus changed water into very good wine, so that the hosts need not be embarrassed. Wine stands for joy and celebration in the Bible. Jesus' first miracle was one of celebration!

Other episodes in Jesus' life showed him to be fully human. He could be stern against hypocrisy, as when he railed against the Pharisees for their corruption. He could be kind and compassionate, as when he showed mercy to the handicapped or demon-possessed. He could be dutiful, as when he commended his mother to the care of his friend John, even as he hung, dying, from the cross. He often defended the underdog, as he did with Zacchaeus the tax-collector or the woman who poured ointment on his feet before the scornful scribes. In short, he was fully human. He could experience great pain, as he did many times even before the crucifixion. He also knew great joy, as for example, when he saw poor people coming to the gospel.

To become a Christian is to be increasingly conformed to the image of Christ (Rom. 8:29; 2 Cor. 3:18). Thus, it is to become increasingly human. Now, certainly there are rules to be kept. But we do not keep them out of fear, but out of gratitude. The great Heidelberg Catchism entitles the entire third part of its instruction on the Christian life, "The Gratitude Due from Man."[1]

The Christian life is one of freedom and form. Just as a fire does not do well outside of the hearth, so the flame of our freedom needs to be contained. So the objection to becoming a Christian based on having to learn a new way of life is not persuasive. Of course there will always be people who criticize you or even mock you for your faith. In the long run, however, you will be glad you stayed faithful.

Will I Have To Suffer For My Faith?

Let's examine the cost of discipleship further. Today, surprising as it may seem, some two hundred million people are being denied their religious freedom in some sixty countries. Many of them are Christians. The persecution varies in intensity from place to place. In several parts of China, worshiping the Triune God without registering with the state is a criminal offense. In Iran there is official religious freedom for several faiths, including Christianity, but the revolutionary guard there often bears down hard

---

1. Lord's Day 32-52.

on Christians and the government looks the other way. In the West this sort of overt persecution is unlikely. However, it is well to be warned about how fast things can change. World War II was not so long ago. The unthinkable had occurred: one of the most civilized nations in the world caved in to a brutal and barbaric ideology, promoting the Nazi régime, and then went to war with anyone who did not bow the knee. Particularly heinous was the elimination of over six million Jews, simply because they were not deemed to be fit citizens in the white, Aryan world the Nazis hoped to create.

Persecution can have a softer face. Several young people surveyed in our research for this book told us they felt excluded and were taunted by their peers because they were believers. Going to church is for sissies. Refusing to sleep with your boyfriend or girlfriend is prudish. Daring to criticize evolutionism is murky. Lots in the media implies (and sometimes flat out says it) that having faith is a weakness, or intolerant, naïve, etc. The film _Religulous_ written by and starring the comedian Bill Maher is immensely popular. Pretending to be on a spiritual journey, Maher interviews various types of believers, and comes down hard against most of them. Evangelical Christianity is in for special laughs. Most of the film is so biased that intelligent people, believers or not, can see right through it. But this pseudo-documentary is but the tip of the iceberg of thousands of people who feel basically the same way.

If you are a Christian, or you are contemplating becoming one, will you face persecution? Yes, and that's a promise. The parable of the Sower and the Seed tells us that the Gospel will come to some and be received with great joy, but yet because some hearers have no roots, "when tribulation and persecution arise on account of the word, immediately [they] fall away" (Matt. 13:21). Notice, it does not say "if" but "when." Believers who have entered the Kingdom of God should not be surprised by persecution, but expect it. When the apostle Paul and his entourage were stoned and dragged out of Lystra, they went back, and strengthened the souls of the disciples.

"Encouraging them to continue in the faith, and saying that through many tribulations we must enter the kingdom of God" (Acts 14:21).

Hard persecution in the early church came in waves. Just after the condemnation of Stephen, the entire church of Jerusalem was severely mistreated, causing most of them to be scattered around the surrounding regions (Acts 8:1). The Romans persecuted the church in various episodes until Christian faith was legalized in A.D 313. In all, it is estimated that the church endured at least 130 years of intense persecution. Why? Christians were considered a threat because they sometimes refused to participate in the social system. For example, they refused to perform public sacrifices to the Emperor in order to get a job or receive approval. Pliny, a Roman governor writing around A.D. 110, called Christianity a "superstition taken to extravagant lengths." The term superstition here does not quite mean what we mean by it, but rather means "foreign."

Persecution And Apologetics

Most of us will not be enduring this kind of hard persecution. We live in societies that have achieved a high level of religious freedom. Indeed, our freedom was achieved at a great cost by our ancestors. Instead, we will probably experience "soft persecution," that is, the more subtle kind of pressure to conform or not to appear ridiculous. No fun, to be sure, but far less of a worry than the dangers and threats to life that Christians have experienced through the ages.

While persecution is never pleasant, it can lead to good things. One of them is learning how to defend the faith, to do apologetics. One of the earliest apologists who became a martyr for his faith was Justin (A.D. 100-165). Justin's parents were Greek. He was a brilliant scholar. He was at first what we would today call a seeker, trying out various views, such as Stoicism, Platonism and the philosophy of Pythagoras. At Ephesus he met some Christians, and had long conversations with an older man who persuaded him that Jesus was the fulfillment of Jewish prophecy.

He became a Christian and immediately began to teach from a biblical point of view. He even founded a school for Christian philosophy. At one point he challenged the Cynic philosopher Crescens to a debate. Although he won the debate, someone reported him to the Romans and he was put to death for believing in an unauthorized religion. In the meantime, though, he had been able to write several major statements of apologetics. One was addressed to the Emperor Antoninus Pius and his sons, and another to the Roman Senate. This took considerable courage, particularly as he charged these authorities with their responsibility to be fair-minded toward Christians, which they generally had not been.

There are many examples of Christians standing up to persecution, and producing helpful apologetics. Dietrich Bonhoeffer was a gifted theologian and pastor. He distinguished himself during the Nazis' rise to power by opposing their philosophy on Christian grounds. He had discovered the grace of God through Christ. When the Nazi party began to become a dominant force in Germany, he did all he could to oppose the church's complicity. In 1933 Hitler forced an election of church officers (it was against the constitution for the government to interfere with church affairs in this manner). Sadly, despite Bonhoeffer's pleas, the "German Evangelical Church" overwhelmingly elected pro-Nazi officers. He then led in the formation of an opposition church known as the "Confessing Church." Still, so many Christians acquiesced to Nazism, a discouraged Bonhoeffer went to London, hoping to gather international sympathy for the Confessing Church.

He came back to Germany in 1935 in order to teach in a new underground seminary at Finkenwalde. In 1937, however, the Gestapo closed down the seminary. Bonhoeffer went to the United States, to New York, where he became greatly impressed with the theology and worship of the black church. But he returned to Germany, believing he had important work to do there. He joined the intelligence group *Abwehr* through which he learned of many atrocities committed by the Nazis. He then

decided to join a plot to assassinate Adolph Hitler.
Unfortunately, his part in the plot was discovered
and he was put into prison. He was executed just
three weeks before the capture of Berlin, and then
the end of the war.

Again, though, in the meantime, Bonhoeffer was able
to commit his best thoughts to writing. Among them
are *The Cost of Discipleship* (1937), a meditation on the
Sermon on the Mount, with Jesus' gracious demands
upon all believers; *Life Together* (1939), a study on all
aspects of community life; *Ethics* (collected in 1955), a
series of comments on post-war life and the need to stand
firm against all kinds of idols; and *Letters and Papers from
Prison* (collected in 1953), a series of journal entries and
letters to friends and family from prison, with reflections
on life in prison, and the need to conspire against tyrants.

Facing Persecution

Few of us will be called to make the ultimate sacrifice. But
all of us will face challenges when we will need to choose
between a faithful testimony and conformity to peers.
How can we cultivate the courage to face these tests? First,
prayer. Jesus taught his disciples what we now call *The
Lord's Prayer*. It is the most complete and rich prayer we
could ever have. The very last request is, "Lead us not
into temptation, but deliver us from evil" (Matt. 6:13).
The word "temptation" is the Greek word for trials. So we
could say, "put us not to the test." But if the test comes,
then we ask, "deliver us from evil." One of my favorite
Negro Spirituals goes like this:

> Lord, don't move that mountain, but give me strength to
> climb; and Lord don't take away my stumbling blocks, but
> lead me all around.

So, it is perfectly legitimate to ask God to take the trial
away. But if he decides not to, then ask him for strength
to face it.

Second, by his good Providence, he will indeed give
strength to face it. And he will never ask you to go through

anything that is too hard. Paul tells us (and note the word temptation appears again):

No temptation has overtaken you that is not common to man. God is faithful and he will not let you be tempted beyond your ability, but with the temptation he will also provide the way of escape that you may be able to endure it. (I Cor. 10:13)

This is a wonderful thought. God is completely in control. Whatever it is you are facing, from overt persecution to just the trials of every day, none of them will be too hard for you. And there will always be a way out. The way out may simply be an obvious exit. Turn off the computer, leave the room, flee the party. Or it may be something more subtle. Pay back the debt. Make that phone call. Break up with your girlfriend or boyfriend. Or get married! Some trials we just have to live with. Paul tells us he had an affliction, which he called a "thorn in the flesh," and "a messenger of Satan to harass me" (2 Cor. 12:7). He doesn't tell us what it is, which is probably a good thing. Was it a disease? Did someone literally harass him? Was he poor? We don't know. In any case, he prayed that it would go away. He says he pleaded three times with the Lord about this (v. 8). But instead of removing it, the Lord told him, "My grace is sufficient for you, for my power is made perfect in weakness" (v. 9). So Paul had to live with his thorn in the flesh. He did not simply slump into resignation. He saw it as a learning opportunity. He understood he needed to find power in his weakness, or, more exactly, to see the power of Christ in the midst of his weakness.

God has great patience with shy people! Take Nicodemus, he was a high ranking Pharisee and quite taken with Jesus. He recognized that he had divine authority. So he came to see Jesus. Yet he came to him at night (John 3:2). It seems he did not want his peers to discover him investigating Jesus, as this might have got him into trouble. But throughout John's Gospel, we see Nicodemus gradually becoming bolder. At one point, when there was a heated debate about who Jesus was, Nicodemus stepped in, and said to his colleagues, "Does our law judge a man without first giving him a hearing and learning what he does?" (7:51) Then, when Jesus had died, Nicodemus publically anointed his body with expensive ointments in preparation for his burial (19:39). Although we don't hear anything more about him, we can presume he became a strong believer and contributed to the cause.

If you are reticent about your faith, God will gently lead you until you arrive at a place where you gather more boldness. Expect opposition, for no Christian is ever free of it. But the Lord will work with you and give you the words to say and the decisions to make when the trial comes.

Discussion

1. What is the difference between morality and moralism?
2. Why is it fearful to fall into God's hands?
3. How do we know Jesus wants us to be fully human?
4. Will all Christians be persecuted? Explain the different kinds of pressure we may encounter.
5. What are the benefits of persecution?
6. How can heroes like Justin Martyr and Dietrich Bonhoeffer inspire us?
7. What are the chief weapons we have to face persecution?

What About Other Religions?

4/15
Sarah.

Few questions are more frequently asked than "What about other religions?" If the Christian faith be true, then what of the billions who believe something different? Sometimes it is put this way. There are only about two and a half billion Christians in the world, out of a population of more than seven billion. That leaves about two-thirds of the world population which does not name the name of Christ. There are thousands of different religions on earth, and if you count atheism or even agnosticism then there are even more. Numerically, then, it would seem unfair that one of these be the only true faith. Our world is increasingly interconnected. Because of globalization we meet more people in a single week than our ancestors met in their entire lives. And the people we meet come from a huge variety of different backgrounds, ethnically, culturally, and religiously. How can just this one religion be true?

Wouldn't a good way to approach so many different people be to maintain that most of the world's religions are basically saying the same thing, only using different language, different symbols, or different rituals for it? Many people in fact do contend that most of the religions of the world are about the same. But how can this be? A good Muslim should be insulted when told his religion is the same as, say, Zen Buddhism. Or should he?

One way is to assert that each religion is groping to find the ultimate, and each one has a piece of the truth. A popular image in support of this view is the elephant. Suppose a number of blindfolded people walk down a path and confront an elephant standing before them. One touches a leg, and concludes, this is a tall, tough-skinned object, so it must be a tree. Another touches the tusk, and decides this is a plastic pipe. Still another finds the trunk and thinks it is a large rolled-up blanket.

The idea here is that world religions are like people groping in the dark. They are on to something important, something real, but no one sees the full picture, nor gets even the details quite right. Hindus see one thing, Muslims another, Christians yet another. But no one sees the real elephant! The trouble with this illustration is that it assumes someone knows about the elephant. Who? The story teller. And how does he get away with true, objective knowledge? Why is he not blind along with the rest of them? All the others are but poor, blind seekers who are not even close to the truth, while our narrator has the truth. This is called a self-refuting illustration.

When I was in high school we had a religion textbook entitled *The World's Living Religions*.[1] As a feisty fifteen year old, I wondered who gets to decide which ones are living and which ones are not? The author decided that those who were doing relatively well, and were practicing regularly, were "living." He divided all the religions according to the places where they originated, South India, East Asia, and West Asia. Eleven religions were considered with a chapter devoted to each one. The last chapter is about Christianity. In each case there is an historical description of origins, and then something about the current practice. And then, at the end, the author gives his own evaluation, including the strengths and weaknesses of each religion as he saw them. For example, Buddhism's strengths include:

- The urgency and assurance of its "gospel".

- Its emphasis on a person's inner attitude.

- Certain admirable qualities of its founder, Siddartha, and a number of other strengths.

- The weaknesses include

- Its original atheism.

---

[1] By Robert E. Hume, New York: Charles Scribner's Sons, 1959.

- Its low esteem of human life and the human body.

- Its empty idea of a blissful Nirvana (the ultimate detachment from the present world taught by Siddartha, or the Buddha).

No religion is spared the author's scalpel. Although he taught at Union Seminary in New York, Christianity is also evaluated. It is praised for its concept of a loving God, but criticized for things such as stressing theology rather than ethics, being domineering, dividing into groups rather than heeding the founders' stress on love. Even at a young age I had to wonder, who does this author think he is, pronouncing judgments on each of these religions, including his own. Where does he get his supposed objectivity? Why should we believe him?

Exclusivity, indeed, seems unfair. But it is impossible to get around it. Its supposed unfairness is actually based on a few key assumptions, all of which may be challenged. The first one is that you don't judge the truth or error of a position merely on the basis that the majority rules. Does the existence of a significant population that does not believe in the gospel mean the gospel is not true? Is it unfair that God does not convert everybody? We usually don't settle the most important questions based on how many people believe one kind of answer or another, but by whether they are right. Does the fact that a great number of Germans believed that Hitler was a heaven-sent leader make it so? Does the fact that a majority of the U. S. Supreme Court judges voted in favor of abortion on demand in 1973 make abortion right? If many people split their infinitives (he is going to greatly worry) or confuse their pronouns (this appeals to he and I) make that good grammar? This kind of reasoning is known as *argumentum ad populum*, that is, appealing to the people. But can the people err? Of course they can.

How To Disagree

Why do we feel particularly sensitive about disagreeing with someone's religion? One reason is that we have decided that religion is a private matter. We don't mind if people hold to their beliefs quietly, personally, but religion should not be dragged into the public square. Say you are having a debate with someone over poverty. Many modern people will tell you that's fine, but don't bring religion into it. If you want to build bridges with someone who disagrees, then religion will only come across as the imposition of your personal views. Imposition is just bad.

But when you think of it, this is not right. What if your views on poverty happen to be connected to your religion? And what if your opponent's opinion is based on humanism, the view that claims man is at the center, not God? Do we really mean to say to someone, in effect, you ought to leave behind everything you hold most dear if you are going to have a discussion about an issue like poverty with me? Indeed, this approach actually tilts the balance in favor of the humanist, for humanism appears compassionate on poor people without the trappings of religion. Ironically, though, this view sneaks-in a religion without acknowledging it. For humanism is in fact a kind of religion. Even denying the value of a religion is a form of religion! Why? Because religion is not so much rituals and prayers, but a worldview. As we saw earlier, the word "religion" comes from *religare* which means "to bind together." That is, religion is a worldview which holds everything together, including God (or his absence) and morality. Remember as we looked at worldview we saw that typically a worldview or religion tries to answer four basic questions about the ultimate, human identity, evil and hope. In that sense humanism is a religion. So anyone who tries to outlaw someone else's worldview is gagging the other person, and arbitrarily saying his own worldview is better.

To be sure we are not interested in imposing our views on others. One must be properly civil, and respect one's opponents, as we would expect them to respect us. Some religions have all too often been oppressive. There exist violent extremes in many religions, including Christianity. Anders Behring Breivik, the Norwegian mass-murderer

claimed to be a conservative Christian. We now
have strong evidence that he was no such thing.
The Hutus and Tutsis of Africa are both at least
nominally Christian, and yet they engaged in one
of the worst wars in history. But the heart of the Gospel
is love, and Jesus specifically told his disciples never to use
the sword for the purposes of advancing the Kingdom of
God (Matt. 26:52, see Rev. 13:10).

There is a world of difference between imposing and
persuading. Disagreement with someone, even about his
religion, is a perfectly respectable posture. If we engage in
trying to persuade our friend, using all the gentleness and
respect we can muster, then disagreement is well and good.
In fact, it is a necessity. Christians will and must disagree
with many facets of other religions, because a lot is at stake.

So, What Is The Difference?

Why should the Christian faith be regarded as uniquely
true? Two major issues are at stake. The first is authority.
On who's authority do we make a decision about which
religion is true? Not the authority of "the people" or the
majority, as we have seen. Not because one religion appears
particularly beautiful, of peaceful, or spiritual. Here we
can boldly state that unless God himself has spoken, then
there can be no reliable authority. As in the elephant
illustration, we will only have blind men in a room. But
what if the elephant speaks, as one friend of mine puts it?
What if God tells us not only who he is, but the basics of
the true religion? That is exactly what has happened. God
has spoken. He speaks both in the general way through the
world he has made, in human conscience and in history,
and specially in miracles, in his appearances, and in his
Word, recorded in the Bible.

A person with authority has both the power and right
to command an action or to proclaim a belief. We could
not live without authority. Loving parents have authority
over their children. The government has authority to write
laws which order society. A piano teacher has authority
over the student. Now, all of these human authorities

have limits. Parents may not abuse their children. Government may not be tyrannical. Piano teachers must inspire and not only give commands.

Further, these human authorities have no legitimacy in themselves, but only as they derive their warrant from God (Rom. 13:1).

God, however, does not derive his authority from anyone else. He is God. "I am that I am," he tells Moses (Exod. 3:14). He spoke, and the world came into being (Gen. 1:1; John 1:3; Heb. 1:10; 11:3). He also controls, or governs, everything in the universe (Ps. 24:1). The purpose and meaning of the entire universe is defined in Jesus Christ, the Second Person of the Trinity (Col. 1:15-18). And he will judge the world and make all things new (Rev. 21:5). God is so powerful that nothing can stand against him (2 Chron. 20:6).

A caution here. God also spoke in human language so that we could know for a certainty what we are to believe and what we are to do.

> All Scripture is breathed out by God and profitable for teaching, for reproof, for correction, and for training in righteousness ... (2 Tim. 3:16)

God does not control us as though we were robots. Amazingly, he has built into his creation, and into us, a great measure of <u>freedom and responsibility.</u> The purpose of this is so that we can better know God, and enjoy his fellowship. But the truth actually "sets us free" (John 8:32).

No other religion has authority remotely like this. Either they are atheist, as is Buddhism, or the so-called "New Atheists" or they are based on frail and fallible gods, such as in the case of Greek or Roman polytheism. Or they may have a fatalist, tyrannical god such as does Islamic faith. But the God of the Christian faith is fully authoritative, and yet personal, neither tyrannical nor cruelly empty.

Jesus Would Not Need To Suffer

The second issue is at the heart of the gospel. If Christianity is not true, then we have no hope. Because the biblical view states that God did not simply make the world, and then, when it tried to live without him, walk away from it, which he was fully in his rights to do. No, he had compassion and sent his Son, who became man, and suffered and died for the sake of his people. Again, no other religion has anything like this: a God who so loved the world that he came down and lived in it, and was willing to suffer the extreme torture of a death on a wooden gibbet. Allah is called the compassionate one, yet there is no whiff of an idea that he would die for his people. Buddha (Siddartha) taught detachment, not involvement with the messiness of human life.

Consider how agonizing death by crucifixion is. The Romans perfected it as the most shameful and painful way to die. Shameful, because unlike those medieval paintings where Christ is lifted up high, the victim was just a few inches from ground level, naked, allowing for mockers to stare them in the face and taunt them. "You who would destroy the temple and rebuild it in three days," they said to his face, "come down from the cross" (Matt. 27:40). Painful, because you die of suffocation. As you try to push yourself up to breathe, your legs run out of strength (particularly if the feet are nailed, not tied), and your chest crushes your lungs.

Jesus could easily have come down from the cross and wiped out the crowd with legions of angels. The reason he did not is because he was dying for sinners like you and me, taking away their shame by experiencing it himself.

Stop to consider that this was no ordinary man dying a disgraceful, painful death, but it was Jesus, God's Son (Matt. 27:54). His suffering was far greater than that of any man, because he was abandoned by his own Father.

When he cried out, at the worst point of his distress, "My God, My God, why have you forsaken me?" (Matt. 27:46) he was not only quoting Psalm 22:1, but genuinely asking his Father, why? You rightly wonder, how can the Holy Trinity, eternally One, be divided? There is mystery here, because nothing can destroy God. And yet being fully human, Jesus was in some real way being condemned by his own father. There was the deepest possible agony on the cross.

The reason the Christian faith has to be the only truth is because without this terrible death of Jesus Christ on the cross, followed by his resurrection, there is absolutely no hope for the world. After rehearsing the facts of Jesus' death and resurrection to his Corinthian readers, the apostle Paul says to them, "And if Christ has not been raised, your faith is futile and you are still in your sins" (1 Cor. 15:17). He goes on to say that if we only hope in Christ in this life, not the next, then "we of all people are most to be pitied" (v. 19). Talk of elephants in the room and groping blind men is an affront to this extraordinary answer by the Lord to the devastating problem of sin leading to death.

Wisdom Abroad

Does this mean there is no truth in other religions? Of course not. My high school textbook was on to something important, even though its philosophy was arrogant. Buddhism reminds us not to become attached to this world in an unhealthy way. The god of Islam is very demanding. Our God, the true God, has the highest standards. Indeed, he is even more demanding than Allah. However, at the same time, he is truly merciful and approachable in a way that Allah can never be. New Age reminds us we live in a world where invisible powers are real. Atheism reminds us not to fall back on rituals or superstitions. Because each human being is God's image-bearer, we can expect to find insights, often profound ones, in their views. Jesus once said, "For the sons of this world are more shrewd in dealing with their own generation than the sons of light" (Luke 6:8). Our Lord is not saying that unbelievers are right on all accounts, but that they have wisdom (in a shrewd, not in a negative way) in certain matters beyond that of believers.

The Old Testament recognizes that wisdom can come from places outside of Israel. Even though he became foolish and arrogant, still, the prince of Tyre was called "wiser than Daniel... full of wisdom and perfect in beauty" (Ezek. 28:3, 12). Certain portions of the Proverbs themselves are parallel to Babylonian and Egyptian literature, implicitly approving of the wisdom from outside of Israel. We have several examples of recognizing the wisdom of non-believers in the New Testament. One of the most notable is Paul's quoting the Greek poets Epimenides and Aratus in his speech on Mars Hill in Athens. "In him we live and move and have our being," said the one. "For we are indeed his offspring," said the other (Acts 17:28). Now, Paul deliberately lifts these lines from their larger contexts, in order to make his point. Still, he recognizes the truth of their insights, even though they are not based on a Christian worldview.

In the end, though, while we do find many insights in non-Christian religions, the ultimate foundation for them is utterly different from the gospel. Christianity is a religion of grace, based on the compassion of God who came down to earth in order to pay for our sins. Other religions are based on the principle of works, merit, or discipline. They are humanistic, that is, based on the notion that human beings are the ultimate authority and the ultimate arbiters of the way out of our problems.

Celebrating Diversity

Here are two final thoughts. First, our basic philosophical disagreement should in no way translate into intolerance or misguided fear.

Some of our Islamic friends accuse Christians of "Islamophobia," a fancy word meaning the fear of Muslims. If there is any truth to such an accusation it is greatly to our shame. For we should neither fear, even less, hate, our Muslim neighbors, nor, indeed, anyone from any other religion. Disagreement should never translate to personal antagonism. Furthermore, our public policy should seek wise and prudent ways to insure religious freedom to people of all faiths, including atheists. Immigration policies should reflect the balance of generosity and protection appropriate to each country.

Christians should strive to promote government policies which ensure a high degree of freedom for worship. We are no longer in the Old Testament. After Jesus' death and resurrection, we are now in the time of God's patience (Rom. 2:4). Instead of the sword of Christians (or Jews, as in Joshua's time), it is now only the sword of the civil magistrate which is authorized to enforce justice. We strongly believe in religious freedom, not because we think all religions are the same, but because we understand that this particular period in history, between Pentecost and the Second Coming, is a time when God is guiding seekers to find him (Acts 17:27). And they come to him by faith, not coercion (Rom. 10:13). Let us be known as peacemakers in our generation (Matt. 5:9).

Second, the Christian faith loves diversity. While there are not several ways besides Jesus Christ to be right with God, there are several ways to be introduced to Jesus Christ. To become a Christian is not to have your personality, your culture, your ethnic origins snatched from you. Rather, it is to have these wonderful qualities enhanced and fulfilled. When you walk into a church, you should expect to see significant diversity: age differences, racial differences, economic differences ... After all, the Bible says God has ransomed people "from every tribe and language and people and nations" (Rev. 5:9). One of the main reasons the Christian faith does not advance more than it does, is because we tend to stay within our own tribes. We are uncomfortable with diversity. It's a terrible mistake.

The Christian faith is the most translated of all religions. To date, the Bible has been translated into close to 2,600 languages, and one of the two Testaments into another 1,700, and counting. You might ask, why translate the Bible? Why not make people learn English, or French or some other language into which we already have good translations. The reason is that God loves diversity! He wants people to know him from the heart, and one's language is close to a person's heart. You can find more different countries and people groups practicing the Christian faith than any other religion has, by far. So, the Gospel is exclusive in one way, but in another it is profoundly inclusive!

This is not just rhetorical flourish. "From every tribe and language and people and nations" means just that. The gospel should never be confused with forcing everyone into the same culture or the same customs. Hudson Taylor (1832-1905), the great missionary to China, began to wear Chinese clothes, and combed his hair in a pigtail. His goal was to reach the Chinese by going inland, and not staying on the coastlines. He wanted to affirm Chinese culture, and not impose British Victorian culture on the people. He emulated the apostle Paul, saying, "Let us in everything not sinful become like the Chinese, that by all means we may save some." He was moving in the right direction.

Discussion

1. Why does the exclusivity of the gospel seem such a very hard question?
2. What is wrong with the view that says "every religion is saying the same thing?"
3. What is wrong with the *argumentum ad populum* argument?
4. Is there no truth at all in other religions?
5. What happens to the death of Christ if all religions are basically the same?
6. What is meant by Christianity being the most "translatable" of religions?

What About Evolution?

I n 1859 a momentous publishing event occurred. Charles Darwin's *On the Origin of Species* is one of the two or three books on a scientific topic that rocked the world. Darwin had spent nearly six years traveling on *The Beagle*, and when he visited the Galapagos Islands he became convinced that species were not stable, that is, that the different species, such as the lion, the walrus, the red deer, were not fixed in their boundaries, but could evolve into different species. Darwin was guided by some missionaries on the Tierra del Fuego. He looked at them, compared them to the natives, and decided the missionaries were from a more advanced type of people. Were the missionaries more evolved than the natives? If so, what was the reason?

Here is how Darwin reasoned. When he got home he read Thomas Malthus' *An Essay on the Principle of Population* (1826). The very influential Malthus tried to prove statistically that there is not enough food in the world for the growing human population, and so consequently there had to be a struggle to survive. Only the most competitive people could receive enough food to endure. Applied to wildlife and plant life, Darwin argued that the species were not necessarily created instantaneously, but evolved according to the survival of the fittest. Indeed, the full title of Darwin's book was *On the Origin of Species by Means of Natural Selection, or the Preservation of Favoured Races in the Struggle for Life*.

Part of the shock of Darwin's theory is that it appeared as though miraculous, supernatural causes for the origin of species were not really necessary. Although he made a nod to theologians and philosophers, including Isaac Newton, who saw no real conflict between religion and science, Darwin clearly felt the traditional view of creation by God's direct action was not necessary.

He was not an atheist, but inclined toward Deism, the view that there is a God who may have begun the world and even put its laws into motion, but is now far away and relatively uninvolved. The introduction of the book quotes John Hershel favorably, to the effect that, the origin of species "would be found to be a natural in contradistinction to a miraculous process." Darwin states the essence of his theory thus:

> As many more individuals of each species are born than can possibly survive; and as, consequently, there is a frequently recurring struggle for existence, it follows that any being, if it vary however slightly in any manner profitable to itself, under the complex and sometimes varying conditions of life, will have a better chance of surviving, and thus be naturally selected. From the strong principle of inheritance, any selected variety will tend to propagate its new and modified form.[1]

Although Darwin carefully avoided mentioning human evolution in this particular book, it was clear from his description of plants and animals, as well as from his other writings, that mankind was no exception to the rule of survival of the fittest. He did address the topic of human origins in the subsequent volume, *The Descent of Man* (1871), which also had an enormous impact. Man's own struggle is exemplary, he said, rising up from earlier species, such as primates. The bottom line is that none of this appears to need divine intervention.

Since Darwin's day many different kinds of evidence have emerged that seemed to confirm his theories (as well, it must be said, as some which rather put his views into question). One important development came about because Darwinism was not able to actually prove that major changes could come from natural selection. Darwin believed that given enough time, larger changes could emerge. But there is nothing in this theory to actually

1. *Origin of Species*, p. 1

verify that. Breeders know, for example, that try as they may, they will never come up with a dog that has antlers. So a refinement of Darwinism came along in the early 20th century, usually known as neo-Darwinism, which suggested ways that bigger changes can occur. That is through genetics. Mutations, sudden, spontaneous changes in a cell, can occur, and could account for rather large changes.

One of the most plausible apparent confirmations of neo-Darwinism is from the human genome. A genome is the genetic and hereditary information of an organism, contained in its DNA or RNA. The human genome is thus the complete set of human genetic and hereditary information for humans, stored as DNA sequences within the twenty-three chromosome pairs of the cell nucleus. Though microscopic, the DNA content is enormously complex. Over the last few decades a series of intense research projects have led to the "cracking" of the genetic code. From 1953, when the team of Francis Crick and James Watson deciphered the DNA structure, to 2003 when the sequence of the human genome was unlocked, these achievements are so great they have been compared to milestones in the arts, such as Leonardo's paintings or Shakespeare's sonnets. Those committed to evolution believe such information yields all kinds of data about how the species, including our own, may have evolved.

For Christians, what is troubling about some of this is not that changes that become hereditary can happen: they can, and they do. For example, no one disputes the fact that certain bacteria can learn to resist antibiotics, and pass this ability on to subsequent generations. The problem is when these changes are interpreted as occurring by chance, and are basically purposeless.

Furthermore, many geneticists believe in two things that are unacceptable for Christians.

1. The first is the claim that the similarities humans have with certain species such as the chimpanzees requires that we have a common ancestor. Thus,

the popular language: "man descends from the apes" means that the present monkey and the present human come from the same earlier group of primates.

2. The second is that the human genome, especially the diversity of human genes, according to a number of geneticists, points to a plurality of ancestors at the beginning, not just one. In a word, a unique, historical Adam and Eve would not be possible according to them.

So, what are the options for Christians? Is it either full-fledged Darwinism and neo-Darwinism, or special creation in a short time? That is how some people see it. Even though they are on opposite ends of the spectrum, many doctrinaire Darwinists and a number of young-earth creationists agree at least on one issue. The atheist Richard Dawkins, in *The God Delusion*, asserts that if you are a good scientist you cannot hold to a Creator God, because Darwinian evolution is basically purposeless. That is the view from one side. Australian applied scientist Kenneth Ham believes that if the Bible is true, then any and all of Darwinian evolution is an impossibility. He argues from his interpretation of Scripture that the earth is quite young, and such a view is in direct competition with the prevailing science. So, these men are miles apart in every way. What they have in common is they believe that there can only be two options.

Questioning Assumptions

Must we reject all or most of mainstream science in order to hold to special creation? Let us look at a few of the issues. First, are the findings of mainstream science absolutely locked-in? Is evolution on a large scale an absolutely proven theory? If we distinguish between the overall macro-evolutionary claims of neo-Darwinism and some of the particular pieces, we can make some headway. Christians should have no problem accepting that certain micro changes may occur over time. But it is quite another matter to claim that all forms of life are the result of unintelligent forces at the largest level, which is what most neo-Darwinists affirm. Indeed, at this point we are doing philosophy, not biology or paleontology.

So, then, what about macro, or pure evolutionary theory? Several issues arise.

1. For one thing, so far, the fossil record, which is considerable, does not confirm a slow and steady development toward modern diversity. If neo-Darwinism is true, then we should expect to find all kinds of "links," intermediate stages between species, yet they simply are not there. So significant is this difficulty that the late evolutionist Stephen J. Gould has called it, "the trade secret of paleontology." It has driven him to suggest that large gaps were bridged rather suddenly. He called these "punctuated equilibria." Instead of gradual modifications, species jump to the next stage in rare and geologically rapid changes, called *cladogenesis*. While this suggestion hardly disproves neo-Darwinists' view, it does indicate that there are serious problems with gradualism, and much more evidence will be necessary before we can call the theory confirmed and unassailable (will it ever happen? Christians would say, no).

2. Another issue we should consider is whether the genetic case for multiple human origins is solid. At the moment, scientists disagree over how compelling the case is. While many geneticists do believe in multiple origins for the human race ("polygenesis"), there are significant exceptions. For example, John Bloom believes that some of the studies leading to this conclusion are based on very selective and thus prejudiced methods. Albert Jacquard and a large school of French geneticists have argued that our inter-fecundity (that any human being can marry any other and have children) is an indication of

a common origin. Another consideration, not strictly scientific, but moral, is that if we really come from a plurality of people, and only some survived, what is to prevent racism?

3. The popular view is that there is an unbroken chain between the apes, the early hominids and *genus Homo*, or man. But if the Bible is a true account of the origins of the human race, and of the fall of man, there should be at least one major gap in chain. Of course, the special creation of mankind is difficult, if not impossible to measure scientifically. Certain Christians, including Kenneth Ham, mentioned above, hold that Genesis 1 requires the view that the days of creation are strictly 24 hour days. On that view the earth is only 6,000 years old. He believes there is a scientifically acceptable way other than evolution to explain the amazing diversity of the different species today. His is, in effect, an alternative science, one he claims has a noble tradition. Using the model of "catastrophism," wherein a universal flood radically changed the contours of the earth, Ham believes such phenomena as the Grand Canyon, fossil remains, and caves with stalactites and stalagmites can have the appearance of age, even though they came about suddenly. Other scientists, also evangelical Christians, believe the biblical data can accord with discoveries of the presence of human beings much longer ago than in a young-earth approach. For example, C. John Collins sees no incompatibility between the data that point to human existence, judging from anatomy, as well as cultural factors, such as the presence of art and other human practices, could be present tens of thousands of years ago. A little later we will take a closer look at how the text of Genesis may or may not support either of these views, or others.

4. Perhaps the best advice we could give here is to be cautious. There is a good deal of rhetoric, with more heat than light, which sometimes gets in the way of

objective evidence. Such rhetoric can characterize Christians as well as materialists.
But most often, it is practiced by those who
believe the church is somehow the enemy
of science and progress. You may be familiar with
the Scopes trial. In 1925, at a high school in Day-
ton, Tennessee, a science teacher names John Scopes
had taught the possibility of evolution. This was an
infraction of the state law. A trial was called, and
the media of the day came to the small courtroom
in great numbers. Two famous Americans were
the protagonists: Clarence Darrow, for the defense,
and William Jennings Bryan, for the prosecution.
Darrow was an atheist, and he tried to disprove the
historicity of the Bible by raising some of the more
difficult questions it posed: How could Eve be created out of a rib? Where did Cain's wife come from?
Where is the proof for the Exodus? The trial was
heated and full of innuendos, including Darrow's
statement that, "We have the purpose of preventing
bigots and ignoramuses from controlling the education of the United States." Bryan, the Christian,
was concerned not to force the children to believe
they were descended from monkeys, "and not even
American monkeys!" Although Scopes lost, and
was fined, the net effect of this trial was to make
"fundamentalist" Christians look ridiculous. Still
today, we can hear people saying, ever since the
Scopes trial, modern people know that the Bible is
not compatible with science, etc. Never mind that
the facts were otherwise.

Similarly, we find a good deal of gift-wrapped evidence
out there, which tends to cover up the real issues.

For example, consider the famous illustration of the
tree. If you look at a standard biology book you will often
find "tree" diagrams illustrating the common ancestry,
then the branching out into different species. But the truth
is, based on the data we now have, the diverse species at
the end of the branches could have arisen simultaneously,

perhaps because of a common design, and might not be related historically to the rest at all. We are missing the links. An often cited case in point is that of the lung fish. This creature should be a perfect candidate for an intermediate species between pure fish and amphibians. But in fact none of the lung fish's organs are intermediary.

In our own day a movement known as "ID" (Intelligent Design) is trying to show that the complexity of the species is proof that someone would have had to design the world. Something so intricate, where there is a unique balance of factors, could not have emerged out of chance.

What Kind of Book is The Bible?

If some of the findings from mainstream science should be held with a light hand, we ought also to pay close attention to the Bible and its legitimate interpretation. What kind of book is the Bible, and exactly how do the Bible and science relate? Here, there are a variety of positions, depending on your view of science and also of the purpose of the Bible. The most radical is called NOMA, Non-Overlapping Magisteria, meaning that the realms of biblical material and of scientific information just do not connect at all. According to this view, the Bible discusses spiritual and moral truths, but not scientific data. The story of the creation according to Genesis 1-2 is about big principles, such as God's overall control of the world and human responsibility, but has no relevance to details such as whether it took a long time or a short time to create the world, and whether or not survival of the fittest might have been a factor in bringing the present world about. This is a very attractive idea, since indeed so much of the Bible is about "spiritual" truth and moral issues.

The trouble with this view is that the Bible actually claims to touch on the realms of history and the cosmos. While there is poetry in Scripture, and while as a whole it is not meant to be a scientific textbook, biblical religion claims to be true, because of its origins in God's own character. And this religion is actualized history. The very

essence of salvation is that Jesus Christ came
down into human history and changed peoples'
lives in the rough and tumble of the real world. If
we begin saying that Genesis is an exception, or,
worse, that Genesis 1-11 deals with myth, and not fact,
events that really happened, then we lose the historical
rootedness of the Christian faith. Faith becomes a matter
of pious thinking, unrelated to real life.

So, how may we take the early chapters of Genesis to
be absolutely true, and then relate them to science? We
have already alluded to the young-earth view. According
to this school, Genesis chapter one requires the literal
interpretation that the six days of creation are 24 hours
long. It argues that the phrase, "And there was evening, and
there was morning," is simply the language of the kind of
day we now experience. Adherents regard any other view
as a departure from the literal meaning of Scripture. From
the relative shortness of the time-span in the genealogies
(Gen. 4, 5, 11; 1 Chron. 1–9; Matt. 1:2-16; Luke 3:23-38,
etc.) we must surmise a relatively recent date of creation.
When asked to reconcile that view with science, they either
plead ignorance (a reasonable plea, since we are finite and
mysteries abound), or attempt to engage in alternative
science (like Ham's catastrophism). God, they maintain,
could well have created the world with the appearance of
age. Adam and Eve were made grown-up, so why could
the Lord not have made the universe look older than it
is? What appears to have taken millions of light years for
starlight to get to the earth was made in a simple burst.
The Garden, which appears to be mature and functioning
well, would have needed soil with decaying organic matter
(usually from dead plants, bacteria, etc.), again, appearing
as though a longer period of time had elapsed.

The 24-hour day and mature creationists believe they
are defending the inerrancy of Scripture, by using its
simple language with the simplest application. Attempts
to reconcile the biblical text with mainstream science, they
argue, runs the danger of accommodation, "selling the
farm" in order to appear relevant. We must respect anyone
who holds this view for this kind of motive. Indeed, if it

can be ascertained without a doubt that the text of Genesis requires a creation week of 24 X 6 = 144 hours then responsible Christians must challenge mainstream science altogether, and either remain agnostic or try to construct an alternative science.

Although we cannot go into great detail here, we need to throw up a few important reservations about the young-earth interpretation. First, can we legitimately fit the Genesis account into a chronology of 24 hours, in that the 24-hour day was only officially adopted in the 19th century? There is nothing innately impossible about that, but we should be very cautious not to make Genesis answer all the requirements of our modern minds in the very terms of modern science. Sunset and sunrise may have a much more metaphorical meaning in the Bible than we might imagine. Second, we could ask, why would the Lord make an earth full of records and clues indicating a past event, such as the death of once live plants to make for fertile soil, or the circles inside the trees showing their age in years, if no such a past occurred? And why would he create rocks that appear to have metamorphosed over years and years, when they did not? Or, why would he have built-in measurable signs indicating an older earth, such as the radiometric age dating of meteorite material and analysis of lunar samples, if the earth were really young? Of course, he could have made such a world with the appearance of age, full of clues to the past, without such a past having existed. If that is his method, then we must respect it. But then much of the project of geological, paleontological and astronomical scientific research would have to be abandoned, or at least seriously questioned. But modern science, as we shall see, owes a great deal to a Christian worldview. Parts of it may be misguided, but a radical revision of its entire project would be a drastic measure.

There are a number of alternate views to the young-earth approach, equally held by Christians who believe the Bible to be without error. Many responsible scholars believe that a longer process is perfectly well-matched with the biblical account of creation. Charles Hodge, for example, a most conservative 19th century Reformed theologian, believed that there could be a certain amount of "guided evolution." At the same time he rejected Darwinism, which for him amounted to atheism. Benjamin B. Warfield, who like Hodge later taught at the venerable Princeton Theological Seminary, argued that the biblical genealogies did not require a short history of the human race. Their purpose was not to be exhaustive, but indicative. Warfield was well aware of the challenge of Darwinism, and declared forthrightly that evolution cannot act as a substitute for creation. But he also argued that whereas perhaps on the surface the biblical record indicates a relatively recent origin for the human race, a closer look shows no such requirement. He strongly questions the chronological scheme of Archbishop James Usher (1581-1656) which estimated that the creation of the world occurred in 4138 B.C. Instead, he asserts that the length of time mankind lived on earth is theologically indifferent.

What are the limits, here, and how are we to render the proper respect to these different views, while moving toward discovering our own? First, it must be asserted that Genesis 1 is a unique text, describing the grand sweep of the creation process, not the details of exactly how it all happened to the satisfaction of a modern scientist. Is Genesis 1-2 a scientific text? If you mean, is it true, then, yes, it is scientific. If you mean does it conform to the wishes of a modern scientist to explain every detail of when and how the different parts of creation were made, then, no, at least not fully. Perhaps it is better to look at these days not so much as an exhaustive blow-by-blow account of events that we could have videoed in a purely chronological sequence, but rather as a well-ordered accounting of the general components. Old Testament scholar John Walton sees the days of Genesis picturing the Lord setting down the great functions of the environment needed for human existence. "So on day one God created the basis for time; day two the basis for weather; and day three the basis for food. These three great functions – time, weather and food – are the foundation of life."[2]

---

2.   John H. Walton, *The Lost World of Genesis One*, Downers Grove: InterVarsity Press, 2009, p. 59.

If Genesis 1 is a unique piece of literature, that does not mean we can dismiss it as some sort of mere bit of fanciful poetry. The New Testament authors, including Jesus, assumed the text to be authoritative. But there is still a good deal of room for an honest discussion of what the text really says, and how it says it. At the very least, we can assert that the text is organized into marvelous patterns. One of them is that the creation week is a divine pattern, which human beings would follow when they plan their workweeks. This leads scholars such as C. John Collins and Vern S. Poythress to argue that the days of Genesis 1 could be "analogical" days, rather than "chronological" days. This fascinating view suggests that the days of Genesis 1 picture God as a worker going out in the morning, then resting at night. God worked, and then "rested" from his labors. This is analogous to the way human beings work. Or, rather, human work is analogous to the way God worked (Exod. 20:11). Thus, rather than necessarily being 24-hour episodes, the days represent the events, the panels, the occasions, when God accomplished various tasks.[3]

If this view is correct, then some "evolution" might have occurred. Perhaps it is the "guided evolution" allowed by Charles Hodge. It might be better to drop the word "evolution" altogether, because of its Darwinian associations. Better to talk about "development," which is less fraught with adaptation and survival than is the term "evolution." Such a view allows for some of the tentative conclusions of the study of the human genome, with its indications of limited kinds of changes in recent times. Again, extreme caution is in order. We don't want to yield to an unhealthy pressure to conform to what the latest findings of science might be. At the same time, why could not the Lord have provided for some of these findings to be made by scientists in our time, by his good Providence?

---

3. C. John Collins, *Science and Faith: Friends or Foes?*, Wheaton: Crossway, 2003, pp. 94-95; Vern S. Poythress, *Redeeming Science*, Wheaton: Crossway, 2006, pp. 84-85. See Bruce Waltke, *Genesis: A Commentary*, Grand Rapids: Zondervan, 2001, pp. 56-57.

What is at Stake?

In the end, what we need to safeguard is the positive teaching of Genesis, in harmony with the teaching of the entire Scripture about the creation of the world. What are some of these positive teachings of the Bible we must respect, in order to be faithful to the Scripture's intent? Here are the basic ones. It is crucial to assert that whatever the means he might have used, God created the heavens and the earth (Gen. 1:1). Simple, but profound. The first verse in the Bible is one of the most revolutionary statements in all literature. That biblical expression simply means he created everything, the visible world and the invisible world, the lands, the seas, the plants, the animals, and, of course man. God made it all. Revolutionary!

It is also crucial to assert that human beings were specially created. Genesis 1:26–27, as well as Genesis 2:7, make it clear that man is not the product of an evolutionary process, but that he was made deliberately, expressly, created specially after God's own image. How this fits with the history of various beings from ancient times, some of which seem to have man-like features, we really don't know. Before Adam, whatever they were, they could not have been human. There are other open questions. For example, where did all the people come from described in Genesis 4:14-16, those who pursued Cain. How did so many people get there so fast? We don't know. Perhaps Adam and Eve were fairly prolific. Perhaps the text is just painting the broadest strokes. The text says nothing about how long ago people were created, but it does say they had to descend from Adam, specially created, who was made an adult, and not part of an already existing humanity. At the moment we just do not know exactly what the date of this creation was. It is a subject for further study.

Another non-negotiable affirmation in the early chapters of Genesis is the failure of our first parents to obey God's command to them, and thus the historical moment of the fall. From the upright world of the Garden of Eden to the sin-ridden world of posterity, a massive change occurred. Sin and misery now pervade every part of life.

Only the redemption of Jesus Christ, predicted in Genesis 3:15, finally fulfilled in the first century, can release this world and its inhabitants from the great curse.

What makes someone human is the ability to worship, to think, to love, none of which are easily measured by paleontology. Again, we want to affirm a real, historical first pair, Adam and Eve, who not only were our first parents, but serve as the basis for the unity of the human race. We know this not primarily for scientific reasons (although there is strong evidence for the genetic unity of the human race) but for biblical reasons. As Paul asserts, "[God] himself gives all men life and breath and everything else. From one man he made every nation of men, that they should inhabit the whole earth..." (Acts 17:25-26). Furthermore, Paul presents a very important analogy, between Adam and Christ. Just as Adam was our first covenant representative, so Christ is the covenant representative of the new humanity (Rom. 5:12-17; 1 Cor. 15:45-49). If Adam did not exist, then the analogy breaks down, for certainly Christ not only exists but is our head in the new covenant.

Finally, while it may be acceptable to believe that God used process, including certain developments in the creation of the world, what is not acceptable, as we have mentioned, is doctrinaire neo-Darwinism. If the only reason the species have evolved is because of adaptation, and survival of the fittest, genetic mutations and recombinations, with no divine activity, then we are left with a world that is dog-eat-dog, and not the beautiful, diverse world of God's making, a world which he pronounced "good and very good" (Gen. 1:31). Nowhere in Scripture are we taught that survival based on competition among humans is a virtue.

This view does not preclude some strife and even death in the animal world. While, again, we do not want to turn the Bible into a scientific manual, there are certain indications of animal violence that do not have to come as a result of the fall. Psalm 104, which is a meditation on Genesis 1, tells us that the same God who gave us day and night, made young lions to roar for their prey (104:21).

Job 38:39-41 makes the same point about God overseeing crouching lions and preying ravens. Animal death is of an entirely different realm than human death. So, without wanting to be dogmatic here, we may say that life in the plant and animal world before the fall does not require that there be no death at all. Such phenomena as predatory beasts may bring glory to God by exhibiting his great power.

Among humans the story is different. Indeed, the very character of love, which is the highest value, is not to assert oneself but to sacrifice oneself for the sake of others (1 Cor. 13:4). A loveless philosophy of Darwinian self-preservation is not only undesirable as a theory of human origins, but can become a serious threat to human freedom when applied socially. Although Darwinists will deny it, it is hard not to see some connection between biological Darwinism and social Darwinism of the Nazis.

So, can we match scientific data and biblical data? Since it is the same God created the world and gave us the Bible, in principle we should find no conflict between the theology and science. If we use the tools and gifts he has given us we can, with proper humility, find harmony between what the Bible tells us and what science can discover. Of course, we can misapply those tools. And we can miss data that are in front of our eyes. Yet, while we certainly do not have all the answers to our questions, answers there are! With proper caution about scientific discoveries, and with proper modesty in the way we interpret the Bible, we will make progress. Let's be the first not to accept the heated rhetoric of neo-Darwinians who believe they have more evidence than they do. Let's also be the first not to force the Bible into a certain mold.

The Call to Do Science

One final, related, point needs to be made. It would be a great shame if the attitude of Christians toward the sciences were so focused on the debate about Darwin that we could not see the broader picture. Throughout history, until more recent times, science was not considered a rival of religion but as its natural fruit. Francis Bacon published a landmark study, the *Novum Organum* (1620) which argued for biblical reasons that the experimental method of modern science was better than the more frozen views of Greek philosophers such as Aristotle. In his *Principia Mathematica* (1687) Isaac Newton argued, "The most beautiful system of the sun, planets, and comets, could only proceed from the counsel and dominion of an intelligent and powerful Being." Even today, many great scientists are believers in God, and they do their careful work, not in spite of, but because of their commitment to the Bible.

If you are a young person reading this, then I would urge you to think of going into science as a career. Don't let the loud minority of new atheists or other doctrinaire pundits discourage you from pursuing God's wonderful calling, first addressed to Adam, and now to us in our fallen world which is being redeemed, to understand the way the universe works, for his greater glory, and for the betterment of mankind.

Discussion

1. Why do some people think there are only two options, Godless evolution or 24-hour days in the creation week?

2. What is the difference between Darwinism and neo-Darwinism?

3. What are some of the weaknesses with neo-Darwinism?

4. Could the creation week described in Genesis 1 be longer than 144 hours? Given reasons.

5. What are the non-negotiables from the Bible?

6. Is science our friend or our foe?

Why is There Evil?

lbert Camus was a major spokesman for his generation. Though not a Christian, he often articulated themes dear to those who follow Christ. It may even be that he became a believer later in life. One of his best-known books is *The Fall* (1956). Set in Amsterdam, the famous canals resemble the circles of Hell in Dante's *Inferno*. The story is a series of monologues by Jean-Baptiste Clamence, who is talking with a stranger in a bar. Clamence has a problem. He was a wealthy defense lawyer in Paris, highly respected by his colleagues. The majority of his cases were in defense of widows and orphans (much like the biblical ideal). He was kind to strangers, gave to the poor and helped the blind to cross the street. However, late one night he is crossing a bridge over the Seine, and sees a woman dressed in black leaning over the bridge. He guesses what she is up to but walks on. Then he hears a splash. Then screaming. The screams were more and more distant as the struggling body was dragged downstream. And then nothing. Clamence did nothing. He told no one. But he began to realize what a coward he was.

Here is a man who knows right from wrong. He had constructed an image of himself as a hero, a savior. But the truth is, he cannot come through when it counts. He is selfish and protects himself from any kind of risk. Camus here is speaking of the human condition. Why is it that we know good and evil and yet we ignore or minimize that knowledge when we are put to the test? Is this the way God made the world? If so, is he not the one to blame?

The question of evil, what it is and how it got into the world, comes up over and over in conversations about Christian apologetics. We looked briefly at it in chapter 3, when considering what went wrong. So many other questions are good ones, but this one is the most deeply felt of all. There is an intellectual component to the question: if evil exists, how can God be all-powerful and truly good? If he were all-powerful he would stop evil, or not allow it to begin with. If he were truly good he would not want a world in which evil has a part. But the problem of evil is most often a deeply felt problem, not just an intellectual one. When we see a child suffer, when a relative is afflicted with Alzheimer's, when terrorists bomb buildings and subways, we feel the outrage, and of course, the sadness. When President John F. Kennedy was shot by a sniper in Dallas, the only words recorded out of Jacqueline's mouth were, "No, no!" There is denial, there is defiance, there is outrage. Is there any answer at all to this persistent question?

First, God himself reviles evil. On just about every page of Scripture there is a word of judgment, a word of con-demnation, a word of warning against evil. "[God is] of purer eyes than to see evil and cannot look at wrong" (Hab. 1:12). James puts it most forcefully. One may nev-er say that God tempts him, for God cannot himself be tempted, nor will he ever tempt someone else.

> Every good gift and every perfect gift is from above, coming down from the Father of lights, with whom there is no variation or shadow due to change. (James 1:13-17)

Such statements show that God is holy, and against all wrong. More than that, he grieves over evil. The shortest verse of the Bible, "Jesus wept," comes in the context of Our Lord having lost one of his closest friends, Lazarus, to death (John 11:35). When he came to Jerusalem, the Bible says, he saw the city and "wept over it" (Luke 19:41). When you think of the strategic position of this amazing city, and of its future conflicts, it is poignant that Jesus cries over it.

You might legitimately ask, if this is so, what about the wars in the Old Testament? And what about the "imprecatory Psalms," that is, those Psalms which pray for evil to happen to enemies? For example, David prays:

"Appoint a wicked man against him, let an accuser stand at his right hand. When he is tried, let him come forth guilty; let his prayer be counted as sin!" (Ps.109:6-7)

How can such an attitude harmonize with Jesus Christ telling us, "Love your enemies and pray for those who persecute you" (Matt. 5:44)?

The simple answer is that the time between Joshua and the exile was one in which God used Israel to exhibit both his judgment and his mercy. He told Abraham that his descendants could go and possess the promised land when "the iniquity of the Amorite was full." The inhabitants were so perverse that God decided to judge them. And so he allowed war by a most reluctant Israel on the land of Canaan under Joshua and then the other Israelite leaders. The Psalmist was not praying about his own personal enemies but the cruel opponents of his people, Israel, who represented God. Mercy, because the promised land was a picture of heaven: the temple, the sacrifices, the "milk and honey," all of these were a foreshadowing of heaven, not just for Israel but for anyone who associated themselves with her. Eventually, though, Israel lost its right to the land, because she become perverse. Dispossessed, they had to wait for Jesus Christ, the Messiah, who would receive judgment on himself so that his people could be spared and enter the real and final promised land, heaven.

Second, consistently the Bible points the finger not at God but at human beings as responsible for bringing evil into the world. No one does this more consistently than Paul in Romans 1, where he explains that the reason for the considerable chaos in the world. Very starkly, it is that people suppress the truth. They deliberately hold the truth at bay, when they know perfectly well what it is, and how they are responsible for it (Rom. 1:1:18-19). Paul goes on to argue that God's person and his ways are clearly perceived in the world around us and the world within. But yet still we don't listen. We "refuse to give thanks," that is, we do not acknowledge God in all our ways (vv. 20-21). So, to answer our question, how did evil get into the world? No, God did not make the world this way. It is this way now because of a completely abnormal event, one that is confirmed over and over again by all people. We may call it the fall into sin. The original creation was good, and very good (Gen. 1:31). But evil entered into the world by the will of our first parents. And each of us confirms this will every day. And most often, we know we are guilty, much as Clamence knew.

To boot, it turns out that evil and human suffering may be the strongest evidence of all for a good and powerful God. Many atheists argue that because the world is so cruel and unjust, there can't be a God. But the honest ones will have to ask, where did my idea of injustice come from if there is no God? If you just say it is just a "personal" view, then you have trashed the vary idea of good and evil in the first place. As we saw, the great poet W. H. Auden knew the Germans in the cinema were wrong to call for the death of the Poles. But he could only be sure it was wrong when he connected with an utterly transcendent God who actually defines good and evil. So it turns out that your instinct for good and evil is a powerful indicator that you have rightly squared with the universe, which is directed by a holy, moral God.

Third, and this is the hardest: If God is all-powerful, as well as good, why did he make a world into which sin could intrude? It won't do to say he is not powerful. Some have tried to excuse God by saying that he gave up some of his power in order to give human beings the power of free choice. But if God sheds even a tiny portion of his power, then he is not all-powerful. A God who is less than all-powerful is no God at all. But then, does that not make God responsible for sin? Here is a great mystery. God may be the ultimate cause of sin, since he causes everything that comes to pass. But yet in this case causality does not mean responsibility. God is not in any way accountable for sin. Here is how the Westminster Confession of Faith puts the mystery:

> God, from all eternity, did, by the most wise and holy counsel of his own will, freely, and unchangeably ordain whatsoever comes to pass: yet so, as thereby neither is God the author of sin, nor is violence offered to the will

of the creatures; nor is the liberty or contingency of second causes taken away, but rather established. (III:I)

This is quite a statement. It needs unpacking. The first part of the sentence describes God as utterly powerful. He ordains everything. That's everything! And he does it from all eternity and unchangeably. And he does it freely, from his own will, that is, with no one telling him what to do, and with a plan which he entirely devised by himself. Notice also, however, that God's counsel is not arbitrary or fatalistic. It is a wise and holy counsel. God is a person, not a mechanical programmer.

Now comes an amazing qualifier. Somehow, mysteriously enough, God's ordaining of everything does not make him the author of sin. An author is a creator, much as the author of a book is the creator of the book. In this case the word means the responsible person, accountable for what he made. So God is not accountable for sin. Man is. This corresponds to the biblical data we found, where God is always against sin and of purer eyes even than to behold evil. Is that all we can say? Just put the two statements together, God is powerful, but not accountable for sin, and walk away? There is more. The statement goes on to explain that God guarantees the liberty of his creatures. He does not force them to do anything. Indeed, his very sovereign power is the reason the creature can have that freedom.

Choice Is Real

One of the basic teachings of the Christian worldview is that the creation has meaning and significance. Human beings have real freedom. We don't know how this can be, if God is so powerful. That is because we are used to thinking about raw power, or push-button power. But God's power is something different, something greater than the act of pushing a button. He has been able to make the world outside of himself. Think of it. Pantheism teaches that God is everywhere and that everything is somehow God. Christian faith teaches that God is everywhere and yet that the creation is not to be confused with God. If you care to put it this way, there are two kinds of being in the entire universe: God's being and the creature's being. In theology this is known as the Creator-creature distinction.

So, now, while we don't have a humanly understandable explanation for how a powerful and good God could allow the intrusion of sin into the world, we have almost everything we really need to know. God is all-powerful, so powerful he can give us real significance and real choice. Human beings are the authors, accountable, for sin. They (we) are responsible for evil because in God's created world they (we) have that kind of power. Realizing I actually am accountable for evil is one of the hardest ideas to get across in our times. If this all sounds rather abstract, ask yourself the question, if no one were looking, not even God, would I … fill in the blanks. Look at pornography?; steal a diamond bracelet?; embarrass my friend (or my enemy)?; drink to excess?; any of these or more? If you are honest, perfectly honest, you'll know you have it in you to do these things. Perhaps you are more the moralistic sinner, like the elder brother in Jesus' parable. Your sins are not outside like the prodigal's, but inside, a matter of attitude. You think you are better than others. Or you think you are a victim of society or parents or church.

Evil is not only individual, but collective. This is easily perceived when we look at wars and revolutions. Soon after the opening years of the French Revolution (1789) began the "reign of terror" (1793). Not satisfied with the progress of the revolution the French government put Maximilien Robespierre at the head. His philosophy was that through terror justice would prevail. He allowed just about any method to put down the "enemies of liberty," a vague expression that turned everything into chaos. He once said, "The government in a revolution is the despotism of liberty against tyranny." Heads rolled, houses were burned, churches destroyed (the word "saint" was removed from every street). If you have ever read Charles Dickens' *A Tale of Two Cities* you can get the idea. The same collective violence has been true of the Nazi era and of Pol Pot's Cambodia.

Evil is also ~~structural~~. One of the clearest examples of this coming to light is the international sex trade. Young children are sold into slavery by their parents, seeking to get out of debt. Governments look the other way. Wealthy Western people use these children for kicks. Everyone is involved, not just the cruel pimps, not only the complicit governments, but also the parents and the clients. Less dramatic examples would include corrupt business deals, where money is dealt under the table for work given to cronies, with no contract. The Bible is the most realistic book ever written. It describes individual, collective and structural sinfulness with excruciating honesty. "All have turned aside; together they have become worthless; no one does good, not even one" (Rom. 3:12).Sad, but true.

The "Problem" of Good

Fourth, I said we have almost everything we need to know. There is one thing missing: the ~~good news~~. God did not let the world rot in its sinful condition. He could have. It would have been perfectly fair for him to leave us in our self-wrought misery. But instead, he loved the world and crafted an astonishing answer for the problem of evil. The plan involved coming to earth himself, bridging the Creator-creature barrier, and being willing to live the perfect human life, and die a horrible death, all for the sake of meeting his own standards. He who could not look upon evil became its victim on a horrible cross.

Becoming incarnate as a man, experiencing all of the human temptations in a fallen world, never giving in, dying and being raised from the dead, Jesus was able quite amazingly to triumph over the world. When he announced his departure to the gathered disciples, he told them:

> I have said these things to you, that in me you may have peace. In the world you will have tribulation. But take heart, I have overcome the world. (John 16:33)

This good news becomes the basis for our entire outlook as Christians. When a calamity occurs, such as the Japanese tsunami, or September 11, or my dear friend is dying of cancer, it is right to ask, where is God in all this? The answer is that he is right there. He is in the destructive ocean waves. He was in the fire and rubble in New York City. Even the cancer victim who is not a believer can find God's compassion and the promises of his Word, which could drive him to faith.

> Even though I walk through the valley of the shadow of death I will fear no evil, for you are with me; Your rod and your staff, they comfort me. (Ps. 23:4)

> When you pass through the waters, I will be with you; And through the rivers, they shall not overwhelm you; When you pass through the fire, you shall not be burned, and the flame shall not consume you. For I am the Lord your God, The Holy One of Israel, your savior... Because you are precious in my eyes, and honored, and I love you. (Isa. 43:2-4)

> I have been crucified with Christ. It is no longer I who live, but Christ who lives in me. And the life I now live in the flesh I live by faith in the Son of God, who loved me and gave himself for me. (Gal. 2:19-20)

God loves us so much that he was willing to go through the high waves and the fires with us, even ahead of us. And because of that, though the tragedies are real, their final power is gone. Now, not only do Christ's followers have their own guilt forgiven, but they are given a new lease on life, a mission. What is it? To fight against the evil in this world. So, then, under Christ's leadership, we can fight against our sins, fight against the collective sins of humanity at its worst, fight the structural evils of slavery and corruption and the like, because Jesus is right there, fighting ahead of us and alongside us. The apostle James tells us that at the heart of true religion is the struggle against affliction.

> Religion that is pure and undefiled before God and the Father is this, to visit the orphans and widows in their affliction, and to keep oneself unstained from the world. (James 1:27)

The little word visit means more than a friendly "hello" to a poor older woman. The verse is discussing people who are disenfranchised, barred from legitimate access to power. Christians need to bring redemptive love to people who have been denied their rights, like the little children who are dragged into slavery, or the uneducated, or the hungry.

In the end the problem of evil is not meant to detain us by long philosophical discussions of God's nature and power. It is meant to tell us that something is horribly wrong with the world, but that if you work alongside Jesus, you can have a part in making it right. Today, opportunities abound to act for the emancipation of the powerless. Your church can volunteer for missions either in its back yard or in some of the darker places in the world. You don't have to be a high-profile crusader to do this, just an ordinary Christian doing something for the improvement of your fellow man.

Discussion

1. Is human guilt real, or only a feeling?
2. Can God possibly be against evil and yet somehow command that it should exist?
3. Is guilt only individual, or is it also collective?
4. How does Jesus' death prove God's good intentions on our behalf?
5. What is the answer to the question, Where was God in a particular tragedy?
6. What can you and your church do to work against evil in this world?

Can I Have Real Friends?

In the survey work we did to prepare this volume one of the questions that came up a good deal was about the kinds of friends we may have. One thing behind this question is that many of the "coolest" people in school or in a social group are not Christians. Should we stay away from them? Often, Christian parents are wary of their child hanging out with unbelievers. They fear their child could be led astray. At the same time, Christian children may wonder why there is a problem, since so many unbelievers are apparently good people. It is helpful to remember that the gospel is not primarily about being better, but about being saved. Even some Christian friends may come from more liberal families than yours and may raise questions for you about associating with them. As we mentioned earlier, one assertion we got several times from young people we interviewed is this one: "My friend's parents let him see R rated films, and mine do not. My friend thinks I'm a bit of a prude. How can I deal with that?"

First, the Christian life is not primarily about rules and regulations. It is about living in God's grace, in his glorious light. Paul tells the Ephesians to "[W]alk as children of light...the fruit of light is found in all that is good and right and true" (Eph. 5:8). Being a Christian means living in the heavenly places, where Christ lives. Rules matter, and, in fact, you cannot claim to have fellowship with God, who is light, and walk in darkness (1 John 1:5-6). Furthermore, his commandments are not burdensome to us (1 John 5:3). Still, following the rules alone will not help us. Rules are good, but only if they result from your first love: God himself. Not if they are an end in themselves. Your Christian witness does not first and foremost come down to what kind of movies you look at. That can matter, but what matters first is whether you let your light, a light from God, shine before other people (Matt. 5:16).

Second, God has given us parents as a wonderful gift. The Fifth commandment tells us to honor our father and mother, adding that if we do so we will have a long life in the presence of God (Exod. 20:12; Eph. 6:1-3). Of course, it's a two-way bargain, since parents are told not to provoke their children (v. 4). So, while you are growing into adulthood, and thus into a stage where you will be making more and more of your own decisions, for now you are beholden to your parents. Are parents infallible? No. Do they make mistakes? Yes. In some cases families are horribly dysfunctional, calling for some serious reparations. But in general it is good to remember that the Lord has given you parents for a purpose. They are your first teachers, they love you, they provide for you. So if they forbid you to go to see certain movies, and explain why, you owe it to them to follow their counsel.

Third, true friendship is not based on agreeing about everything, nor doing everything together. True friendship is certainly not based on wearing the same clothes, going to the right fellowship group, or rooting for the same team. True friendship is based on mutual trust and mutual affection. One lesson to learn early in life: disagreement is not disloyalty. Really loyal people are in fact free to disagree with one another, because they have established trust. The proverbs have a good deal to say about friendship. "Faithful are the wounds of a friend," they tell us (27:6). Indeed, in true friendship, "as iron sharpens iron, a friend sharpens a friend" (27:17 NLT). A really good friend, then, knows you, warts and all, and still loves you. St Augustine once put it this way: "They are my true brothers, because whether they see good in me or evil, they love me still."[1]

A Very Good Gift

As such, friendship is one of God's best gifts. Here is how Aelred of Rivaulx, the 12th century English Abbot, put it:

---

1. St. Augustine, *Confessions*, R. S. Pine-Coffin, transl., Penguin eds., X.4.

No medicine is more valuable, none more efficacious, none better suited to the cry of all our temporal ills than a friend, to whom we may turn for consolation in time of trouble, and with whom we may share our happiness in time of joy.

A friend of mine whom I greatly admire once said this:

We all long for ... rich companionship, consciously or not. Friendship is a form of love, and to be known and loved for who we are brings not only deep satisfaction and lasting joy, it makes for a profound, life-changing, and even world-changing experience. And if friendship is risky by its very nature because close companionship can expose us to the core, such rewards are worth both its risks and the effort we need to invest.[2]

Why is true friendship risky? Because if we truly entrust ourselves to another person, he or she will have a certain power over us. Not in a bad way. But when people know things about you that are somewhat private, then only true loyalty will protect your relationship.

There is a dreadful play by existentialist Jean-Paul Sartre called *No Exit*. Actually, in French, it is *Huis Clos*, meaning "Behind Closed Doors." The doors are actually not locked. Three characters are in the room, talking endlessly. The basic plot is simple. No one dares leave, because they fear what the other two might say about them. At one point someone declares "hell is other people." The reason this is so confining is that there is no way to leave the room and not have to worry about the other two. They have too much on you. In the Christian message there is such a way! That way is when Jesus Christ is the one we trust as our ultimate friend. With his friendship we need not fear other people. Because even if they do say bad things about us, we are protected. We are "hidden with Christ in God" (Col. 3:3). Hell is not other people. Hell is the ultimate experience of life without God. There is a beautiful passage in the Book of Ecclesiastes. It says: "Two are better than one."

---

2. J. Douglas Holladay, "Forward," *On Friendship* by Marcus Tullius Cicero, McLean, VA: The Trinity Forum, 2004, p. 5.

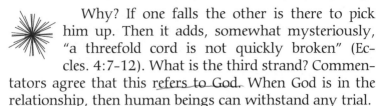

Why? If one falls the other is there to pick him up. Then it adds, somewhat mysteriously, "a threefold cord is not quickly broken" (Eccles. 4:7-12). What is the third strand? Commentators agree that this refers to God. When God is in the relationship, then human beings can withstand any trial.

Not all of our friends need to be Christian friends. In fact, there may be Christians you should not associate with. Paul tells his Corinthian readers, "I wrote you in my letter not to associate with sexually immoral people – not at all meaning the sexually immoral of this world, or the greedy and swindlers, or idolaters, since then you would need to go out of the world. But now I am writing to you not to associate with anyone who bears the name of brother if he is guilty of sexual immorality or greed ..." (1 Cor. 5:9-11). Christians live in the world, and they are obliged to associate with unbelieving people, even grossly immoral ones.

There is a famous friendship in American history. It is between Benjamin Franklin (1706-1790) and George Whitefield (1714-1770). Franklin was a Deist, the author of *Poor Richard's Almanac*, a series of witty remarks about how to get rich, how to stay in good rapport with everyone, and aphorisms such as "God helps those who help themselves." Whitefield was an itinerant evangelist who was arguably the most powerful preacher in North America during the colonial period after Jonathan Edwards (1703-1758). Franklin was worldly, Whitefield was a staunch Calvinist. Yet they enjoyed each other, even loved each other. One reason is that they admired one another's skills. Franklin once decided to measure Whitefield's ability to project. He had been skeptical of rumors to the effect that Whitefield could reach tens of thousands in England. So he went to hear him in Philadelphia, and walked until he was no longer audible, and then concluded he could be heard by at least thirty thousand! He was so impressed by Whitefield that he published several of his tracts, even though he really did not believe in what he was saying. Whitefield felt the same way about Franklin. Franklin noted that after Whitefield's preaching people became

more religious, more charitable, and sang the
Psalms everywhere. They had common interests,
particularly in matters of charity and humility.
They admired one another's generosity. Still,
they were so different. Francis Schaeffer once talked about
the virtue of "co-belligerence." He meant by this that we
could fight for similar causes, even while disagreeing on
fundamentals. Good point. It is fine to be friends with
people who don't accept all of our basic views.

So, where does this leave us? It is not always easy to
deal with what is often called peer-pressure. At times you
will just have to say no to potential friends who want
you to violate your conscience or go against your parents'
wishes. But most times when you make efforts to love
someone, to be there for them, you will be repaid with
real friendship. And you will then be able to explain the
marvels of the gospel to them. At the heart of the gospel is
the friendship we have with Jesus himself.

Discussion

1. How can we keep the balance between having
   good friends and yet establishing limits?
2. Do we have to listen to our parents? Why?
3. Is true friendship risky? Why?
4. Why is it all right to have friends who are not
   Christians (presuming we are)?

1. Say "no" when friends want us to go
   off-limits (violate my conscience or go against
   parents' wishes.

2. Yes, God said so.

3. Yes, they know too much about you. (Private,
   deep, etc.)

4. We don't have to agree on everything
   but trust + respect each other.

Q. who has a good 155 friend who is not
   a christian but she/he knows you are a
   christian?

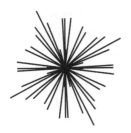

What About
Love and Sex?

Potentially, questions about love and sex are among the most confusing today. But they can also be among the most marvelous, when we fully understand God's plan. Several issues are involved here. Statistics show that, at least in the West, while marriage is generally looked upon with approval by adolescents, a large number believe that cohabitation (living together before marriage) is acceptable.[1] It is not hard to gauge the reasons for this view. Young people would like to be married, eventually, to the same person, for life, and have children and establish solid families. But they are increasingly worried about failed marriages, which they see all around them. They also worry about bringing children into this world, not always to the point of refusing to have them, but to the point of delaying child-bearing considerably. As a result young people are waiting longer and longer to get married. Living together before marriage appears to bring many benefits, while reducing the risks. But does it?

One of the most beautiful stories in the Bible, just at the dawn of human existence, is about the creation of Eve, the first woman (Gen. 2). The setting is important. We start off in the garden of Eden, where trees are pleasant to the sight and good for food. Adam was told to work on the garden and keep it. The one tree that was forbidden was the tree of the knowledge of good and evil. Otherwise,

---

1. See, for example, the yearly *Monitoring the Future* (*MTF*) studies from the University of Michigan, focusing on high school seniors in the United States, conducted by J. G. Bachman, L. D. Johnston & P. M. O'Malley, Ann Arbor: Institute for Social Research. For Great Britain, see A. M. Johnson, et al, *Sexual Attitudes and Lifestyles*, London: Blackwell Scientific, 1994, and updates.

everything in the garden was his. But there was a problem. Adam was alone. Seeing this, the Lord provided a companion for him. He had first created the animals and the birds and now he paraded them before Adam, so that he could name them. But, significantly, the text tells us there was not found an *ezer* for him. This wonderful Hebrew word signifies a helper, or, one who rescues, or one who profits another. None of the animals, none of the birds, were able to fill such a roll, even though many of them were (and are!) quite extraordinary.

And so the Lord God put Adam to sleep, and formed Eve out of his rib. There is a good deal going on in this story. The rib was an ancient Near Eastern symbol of the deepest friendship. That is a point worth pondering. Sex rightly belongs in the context of the deepest friendship. The Hebrew term for wife is *ishsha*, which closely resembles the term for husband, *iysh*. When Adam first saw Eve, he exclaimed "This at last is bone of my bones and flesh of my flesh" (v. 23). His is not the cold, scientific deduction about a similar make-up; his is the delight, the joy of discovering a fellow human being who is yet not a male but a female. Genesis 1 had already explained that the image of God has two versions, male and female (1:27). Here we see this first couple as a family, the founding unit of human society. The author explains:

> Therefore a man shall leave his father and his mother and hold fast to his wife, and they shall become one flesh. (v. 24)

Thus families are meant to grow and proliferate. The expression "one flesh" refers to the extraordinary intimacy between a man and a woman in marriage. It includes the sexual relation, which is considered one of God's loveliest gifts. It also includes the joy, intimacy, security, and love shared by a couple. The physical union is also the means for having children. The chapter recounting Adam's descendants notes that "he fathered a son in his own likeness, after his image, and named him Seth" (5:3). "Seth" means "compensation," although it sounds like the word for "he appointed." Adam and Eve had been deprived of their first two children through a sordid crime of jealousy, one by death, the other by banishment, and so God graciously appointed them another son (4:25).

If sexual union is a lovely gift, it has also become one of the most distorted. As with everything in the fall, the best endowments from the Creator have become the most corrupted and ugly. Although sexual union was to be enjoyed within the safe bonds of marriage, so often the two, sex and marriage, are separated in our fallen world.[2] We imagine that going to bed with our friend does not need to be encumbered with the complication of marriage. And so we become quite casual about sex.

Thus, one of the great problems today is sex outside of marriage. Adultery has become widespread in our society. Technically, adultery refers to sleeping with someone else's spouse. But the term can be expanded to include any kind of unfaithful activity, including sex before marriage, since it is outside of the proper legal bond. Indeed, it can even characterize the attitudes of our hearts. Our Lord, following the Old Testament, declares that even to look upon a woman lustfully is to commit adultery in one's heart (Prov. 6:25; Matt. 5:27-28).

This is one of the tragedies of pornography. This enormous industry has made salacious literature and images available in unprecedented ways. Pornography can be an addiction, just like drugs or gambling. What exactly is wrong with it? Lots. For one thing, it is a business, a huge profit-maker, run by people who use women and men as objects, not persons. For another, it takes all the mystery, and the wonder of spending time with one's spouse away. As one person has commented, the trouble with nudity in pornography is not that you see too much of a person, but too little! They are just flesh, with no soul. Further, pornography creates hopelessly unrealistic expectations about sex, which is patently unhealthy. Finally, it simply

---

2. A recent survey shows 22 per cent of people in the West have had an extra-marital experience. And that says nothing about the thousands of couples living together without the legal bond of marriage.

makes one's eyes wander where they should not. While the enjoyment of a husband or wife in their naked splendor is a rare privilege, a great gift from God, cheating and finding some sort of temporary pleasure in looking at some poor girl or boy on the screen is simply monstrous.

Marriage, Still All Right?

Throughout the Bible, adultery is considered one of the most serious offenses. The Seventh Commandment is stark: "You shall not commit adultery" (Exod. 20:14).

In the Hebrew, it is even more austere: "no adultery!" In the Old Testament a death sentence was attached to this offense, though not always put into practice. Also, adultery is often used as an image for spiritual unfaithfulness. Wayward Israel was often compared to an adulterer (Jer. 3:8-9; 5:7; Ezek. 23:37). The apostle Paul tells his readers that a major reason not to commit adultery is that our bodies are members of Christ, ones which will experience the resurrection. So, joining a prostitute, for example, is equivalent to becoming one flesh with her, and thus denying our union with God himself. Now, be it said that however serious is the offense of adultery, it is a forgivable transgression! God can cleanse you and me from this sin.

Does this mean we should simply become celibates and avoid any sexual union? Some have thought so. It seems some of the Corinthians, so concerned about the dangers of sex, concluded it was best not to have any at all (1 Cor. 7:1). Paul does not accept that answer. Indeed, he says elsewhere that people who forbid marriage and other good gifts have deceitful spirits and teach demonic doctrines (1 Tim. 4:2-3). Marriage between two people is a wonderful calling. Even in a fallen world, this creation ordinance is continued.

It is not the only calling. Celibacy is a legitimate calling as well (1 Cor. 7:17, 25-31). Indeed, people may be celibate for a number of reasons. For some, it is from a desire to expend more energy for the extension of God's Kingdom. This appears to be the case for the apostle Paul. For others, it may be the sad result of not finding the right person. Regrettable as that may be, it is very much a reality both outside and inside the church. For some reason, most often, the church has more single women than single men in its population. In such cases the celibate person must ask God to show him or her how to live fully for the sake of the gospel without necessarily being married. And the church has a special responsibility toward its celibate members. Probably the best is not the traditional "singles group," which only stigmatizes them, rather than involves them.

Marriage is a noble calling. Although marriage is not for everyone, it is God's provision for the many who are called into the kind of companionship and friendship we discussed in the previous chapter, and at the highest level. Even though we live in a sinful world, marriage, with its physical union, is still God's marvelous gift. "Let marriage be held in honor among all," (Heb. 13:4). For Christians, marriage has an even deeper significance. It is a reflection of the union between Christ and his church (Eph. 5:22-33). Imagine! A husband and wife in some mysterious way are an image of Christ, who left the privileges of his glory to become a servant and die for his people (Phil. 2:6; Eph. 5:32).

Marriage has two essential components, a legal one, and an affective one. Both in biblical times and in every society today there is a juridical aspect to marriage. You need a license. You appear before the authorities. One can readily appreciate the reasons for this. For Christians this human contract reflects our upward relationship with God, which is called justification. Justification by faith is the major entry point for obtaining salvation. God declares us just, that is, acquitted of our sins, by imputing the righteousness of Christ to our account. It is a legal status we enter into, and without it no amount of good works could lead to salvation. But there are good reasons for a legal aspect to marriage. Among other things it is a way to maintain the public order. Thus, the marriage contract protects each spouse from possible abuse or desertion. It protects their children as well. But then, marriage is also affective. Nuptials are not just a cold legal contract. We marry for love, or at least we should. The Bible puts them both together. In a reflection on faltering marriages, the prophet Malachi tells us:

...the Lord was witness between you and the wife of your youth, to whom you have been faithless, though she is your companion and your wife by covenant. (Mal. 2:14)

Similarly, in a exhortation against folly, the author of Proverbs taxes the adulteress as forsaking the companion of her youth, and forgetting the covenant of her God (Prov. 2:17). Covenant companionship! It's a wonderful thing. Christians ought to be the first to hold marriage in this kind of honor. Certainly things can go wrong, for Christians as well as for unbelievers. The Bible makes many provisions for addressing troubles. There is much wisdom in Scripture for solving problems, working through issues and allowing love to prevail. Our Lord even allows for divorce under very exceptional circumstances (Matt. 19:9). But in the best of circumstances, marriage ought to reflect the love and faithfulness of God for his people.

So, Who Is Mr. or Mrs. "Right"?

How do you know who should be your life's partner? There is no rule book, other than the clear indication that Christians should marry Christians (1 Cor. 7:39).[3] In our Western culture, there is a good deal of freedom here. If you are a typical young person, you should be thinking about what kind of person, and at what stage of life, you should marry. It is possible to rush into it without enough forethought about whether you are actually compatible, or can provide for one another. It is equally possible to delay too long because of alleged obstacles, money, job, lingering doubts. No one marries someone exactly like them. Every marriage requires give and take. Older? Younger? What about marrying outside of ones class or even racial group?

---

3. If a believer is married to an unbeliever that is not a mandate to divorce, although divorce is permissible in such rare circumstances (1 Cor. 7:12-16).

There is nothing wrong with this.[4] Indeed, cross-cultural or cross-racial marriages have the potential for great enrichment, just as when any two cultures meet. At the same time, it is good to go into such marriages with your eyes open. Without knowing it certain assumptions about roles coming from your particular culture are brought in to a marriage, which can present serious challenges. Are women meant to be in the kitchen? Or are they just as qualified for working outside the house as their husband? Such issues enter into a marriage early on.

It is just as well to talk these things through before rushing into marriage. Here it can be enormously helpful to have the right kind of advice from the right kind of counselor. Many churches provide such guidance. Parents should have a special say in these matters, as they know you best. Not that we should slavishly obey them when our conscience tells us otherwise. But most often it is wise to listen to their advice. A marriage, after all, is not only between two people, but between two families.

Finally, how far can you go, physically, before marriage? This question came up time and again in our research. There is no rule book. Petting? Kissing? Mistakes are easily made, even when courting one's future spouse. Because of the fall we are often not in control as we should be. Paul reminds his younger colleague Timothy that "God gave us a spirit not of fear but of power and love and self-control" (2 Tim. 1:7).[5] Those three virtues do not appear to go together, at first. Power, here, means authority, strength to accomplish godly goals. Love is the supreme value, our generous self-giving to God and to others. Self-control refers to sobriety, being of sound mind, focused. Those three virtues should characterize our attitudes

---

4. Only recently have our societies begun to accept interracial marriages. For an interesting history of the laws in America that have yielded to the validity of interracial marriage, see Fay Botham, *Almighty God Created the Races*, Chapel Hill: The University of North Carolina Press, 2009.

5. Many commentators argue that the word spirit should be capitalized: Spirit. That would mean God has given Timothy, and us, the Holy Spirit's enabling of power and love and self-control.

toward sexuality, even in courtship. We will never regret a proper exercise of self-control, and we may well regret its neglect. While we are not disembodied spirits, with no feelings, we should be careful, respectful, considerate of the other person. Even within marriage, where, of course, physical relations are meant to be enjoyed, there is never cause for debauchery or uncivil behavior.

If younger Christians can have this whole area of sexuality and marriage in the right perspective, that could be one of the most powerful persuaders in the present, very confused generation. The challenges are great in our permissive culture. But God gives special strength to face them. There are lots of creative solutions. Go out in groups, not just two by two. Turn on the filters on your computer. Tell your youth leader to address these questions. Confide in trusted peers who will keep you accountable. Read Shakespeare's love sonnets! Stay close to the Lord in prayer.

Discussion

1. What's wrong with cohabitation?
2. What are the main purposes of marriage?
3. How does marriage reflect the big picture of Christ and his church?
4. Is celibacy a legitimate calling?
5. How does your church help young people deal with sexuality?

Does God Love Gay People? *Yes*

— Does God approve the gay lifestyle or not?

The issue of gay orientation is fast becoming one of the most volatile and most challenging for Christians in our times. Often there is much more heat than light. A few years ago this would have been a simple matter. "God is against gays," was the common thought. In most countries it was not only frowned upon, but actually illegal to be a practicing gay. Homosexuals had to live clandestinely, hoping not to get caught. When I was a young man, one of the worst insults one could launch against a fellow human being, was that he was a fag, or a pansy. In the boarding school which I attended, to be gay was simply… yuck! Today we have a greater understanding of homosexuality and other gender-related issues. Many have come out of the closet, forcing us to reassess our views. At the very least, we should be deeply sorry for having insulted and hurt a fellow human being, often demonizing him, regardless of the reason.

Christians who take the Bible seriously are in a hard place. The Bible clearly forbids physical relations between members of the same sex. Unless you engage in the most fanciful exegesis, several passages simply settle the question. Leviticus 18:22 states "You shall not lie with a male as with a woman; it is an abomination." Leviticus 20:13 adds that the appropriate sanction for homosexuality is the death penalty. It would be tempting to say this legislation is just for the Old Testament. But then we find Romans 1:26-27, which mentions both male and female homosexuality as "dishonorable" and "shameless." Two other New Testament texts describe homosexuality as a practice now abandoned by Christians (1 Cor. 6:9; 1 Tim. 1:10). There have been various attempts to make

165

these texts say something different. One popular view is that these authors are not condemning true homosexuality but unnatural relations. Thus, if you are gay and turn heterosexual, that is just as wrong as being heterosexual and turning gay. This kind of interpretation is simply not credible.

Today, though, to disagree with homosexuality is often regarded as "homophobic" (the fear of gays) or gay bashing (hate against gays). Although the data show the actual number of practicing gays living in the open is quite low, they are a minority with a good deal of clout.[1] More and more legislation is being written based on "hate crimes," including what appears to be crimes against gender identity, sexual orientation, or disability. One such example from the United States is the so-called *Matthew Shepard Act* (2009) written in response to the murders of Matthew Shepard and James Byrd, Jr., who were both brutally murdered based on prejudice, Shepard, because he was gay, and Byrd because he was black. Supporters of the bill argued that, psychologically, hate crimes are more serious than ordinary crimes. It takes victims far longer to recover from assaults based on hate than other kinds of attacks. They also note that in the aftermath of the Shepard case many gays went "back to the closet," not only fearing for their safety, but experiencing self-hatred, often leading to depression and post-traumatic stress disorder (PTSD).

Emotionally, it is difficult not to sympathize with this kind of legislation, and the reasons behind it. How could anything be more clearly unjust than to murder someone because of race or sexual orientation? There is simply no defense for such brutality. At the same time, we want to be very careful not to move too fast here. At the very least, we should be careful not to lump all prejudice into the same bag. Sexual prejudice and racial prejudice are not exactly the same thing. Prejudice is always wrong. Making "pre-judgments" based on someone's sexual orientation or someone's race

---

1. Statistics are difficult to determine. The U. S. Department of Health and Human Services has estimated America's gay, lesbian and bisexual population at around 8.8 million, which would be less than 3 per cent of the population. Other researchers, such as "Gay Demographics" puts the number at 1.6 per cent.

is simply immoral. But homosexuality is actually forbidden in Scripture, whereas racial diversity is celebrated. So to disagree with the homosexual lifestyle is not prejudice, whereas disagreement with racial diversity is.

This is a critically important point. I can disapprove of a gay partnership, based on biblical teaching. But I cannot disagree with racial equality. In many countries darker skinned persons have suffered unspeakably because of their skin color. I must fight such prejudice with everything I have. Of course, gays have also suffered. When they have been persecuted for being gay, I also must fight against such prejudice. Gay bashing has nothing remotely Christian about it. Nor does homophobia. And yet I must be allowed to express my philosophical opposition to the gay lifestyle. There is a saying attributed to the French Enlightenment skeptic, Voltaire (though it was probably voiced by his defender Evelyn Beatrice Hall). He said "I disapprove of what you say, but I will defend to the death your right to say it."

This distinction appears very difficult for modern people to grasp. Existentially the distinction can work just fine. I have a very small group of truly best friends in the world. They are people who have supported me, shared in my struggles, people I have worked with side-by-side. I believe I would literally be willing to die for any one of them, and they for me. One of them is gay. He knows two things. First that I care very deeply about him and would do anything to support him. Second, he knows that I profoundly disagree with his lifestyle. We have had long discussions about this, and both of us have learned a lot about each other's position. I have remained unyielding on the fundamental issue, but have a much better understanding of the reasons that led my friend into this commitment. Best of all, it is no stumbling block to our friendship.

What Does The Gospel Say?

So, does God love gays? If you put it this way, the answer is simple. God loves everyone. He loves every kind of person. He loves every kind of sinner. "God so loved the world,"

John tells us (3:16). "Every family in heaven or earth is named from the Father" (Eph. 3:14). It does not get more inclusive than that. But, of course, what is probably meant by the question is whether God approves the gay lifestyle or not. The Bible clearly forbids homosexuality, as we have seen. It is sinful behavior.

So, we may ask, what kind of sin is it? And is homosexuality worse than other kinds of sins? The passages we cited certainly qualify it as a serious sin. They use words like "abomination" and "dishonorable." There is no question that homosexuality represents something fundamentally amiss in human relations, since heterosexual marriage, as we saw, is such a fundamental pillar of society. Yet, as you look at the context, you will observe that a number of other sins come in for the same kind of judgment. Idolatry, incest, murder, and many others are in the lists. So we mustn't label homosexuality worse than all other offenses.

Furthermore, as the gospel states so clearly, homosexuality is a forgivable sin. Paul states in 1 Corinthians 6:9–11 about homosexuals and other kinds of sinners, that "such were some of you." But now, he says, "you were washed, you were sanctified, you were justified in the name of the Lord Jesus Christ and by the Spirit of God." After all, our Lord Jesus Christ was the friend of sinners, and even some of the worst kinds of social outcasts felt they could confide in him. So should they feel about us. David Powlison, a counselor whom I greatly admire, discussing sexual sins, says this:

 Jesus Christ comes to those who have pursued unholy pleasures. He who hates the gamut of perversities [listed in previous paragraphs], is not ashamed to love sinners. He does not weary in the task of rewiring sexuality into a servant of love. He is not only willing to forgive those who turn; he takes the initiative to forgive, and to turn us, and to give us countless reasons to turn. He says, 'You need mercy and help in your time of need. Come to me. Turn from evils, and turn to mercies that are new every morning. Flee what is wrong. Seek help. Everyone who seeks finds. Fight with yourself. Don't justify things that God names as evil. Don't despair when you find evils within yourself. The only unforgivable sin is the impenitence that justifies sin and opposes the purifying mercies of God in Christ. Come to me, and I will begin to teach you how to love."²

Some Tough Questions

One thing I like to tell my teenaged friends: God heartily approves sexual desire. It is his handiwork. But he has an even better way for you to express it than in a same-sex relationship. Heterosexual marriage is his marvelous provision for your desire. However, with gay people certain special issues may complicate things. What are the practical implications of this disapproval plus this grace extended to gays? Several distinctions should be made.

First, if a gay person is not a believer the first priority is not to get rid of that lifestyle, but to accept the gospel. In practical ways, that means we can approach gay persons as we would any unbeliever: with respect for their dignity as God's image-bearers, and the hope that they can embrace the good news. Gays, like everyone else, need resurrection power today, which is a foreshadow of the resurrection life of tomorrow.

Second, if the gay lifestyle is not biblically sound, is the answer for every homosexual to become heterosexual? As we learn more about this condition we realize that there can be a number of causes for homosexuality. Undoubtedly, some of it is learned behavior. The friend I mentioned had a very bad relationship with his father. He also had a favorite relative who was his mentor as a young man, and wielded an enormous influence on him. Following this relative, my friend chose the gay lifestyle. There may have been a predisposition, but some of his reasons for turning gay were learned. Then there are clearly some people who are gay not from learned behavior, but by natural inclination. Perhaps they are born with a predisposition toward same-sex attraction. Just as some people are predisposed toward

---

2. David Powlison, "Making All Things New: Restoring Pure Joy to the Sexually Broken," [http://www.ccef.org/making-all-things-new-restoring-pure-joy-sexually-broken].

anger, or fear, or, for that matter, toward good things, like affection or optimism, so it is certainly possible to be predisposed to a homosexual orientation.[3] When this is the case, even if the person is a Christian, it may not be the best idea to force them into a heterosexual marital relationship. Sometimes it can work, but one should proceed with great caution. I have known of cases where marriage was entered into hastily and much wreckage followed. (Of course this can happen between heterosexuals as well.) As we mentioned above, celibacy is a legitimate calling for some. And it could be far better to choose celibacy as a gay person, and keep those inclinations under control, than to force oneself into a marriage that is not likely to survive.

Third, can a gay person be a church member? Church membership is for those who have received Christ and resolved to follow him. A gay person needs the gospel as much as anyone else does. The gospel should be offered freely, with no strings attached. The New Testament never says, I will let you into my Kingdom as long as you give up this particular sin. Jesus often did say to those who sought him out, "go and sin no more." But that is quite different. Nor did he say, "if you do sin again, you've lost your chance!" Church membership is for all believers, whatever their backgrounds.

True, once you are a believer you have responsibilities to work toward change. All of us are told to "[W]alk in a manner worthy of the Lord, fully pleasing to him" (Col. 1:10). When a gay person accepts the gospel, while it does not mean that overnight a complete transformation will occur, anymore than for the rest of us, it does mean that there is a new willingness to follow Christ and conform to his will. A part of his will is to work toward sexual purity. Such a person, one who is on the path to sexual purity, has every right to church membership. Only a person who refuses in principle to submit a particular area to Jesus ought to be scrutinized, and asked what the problem is.

---

3. Gay persons are bound to be offended by this comparison. But if we are consistently biblical then the analogy is just, since we are not talking of a neutral "orientation" but of a perversion.

One does encounter the odd Christian who tells you he (or she) is convinced the gay lifestyle is compatible with the gospel as long as you live faithfully with your partner. We may have no doubt that such a person is truly a Christian. Here, a great deal of patience is called for. In the end, though, we will want to persuade the brother or sister that the Word of God says otherwise, and do the serious work together of interpreting the biblical text.

Fourth, what about leadership in the church? Many of us know that in some of the larger, mainline denominations today, one of the most volatile issues is their decision to ordain practicing gays. Leaders (elders, bishops, deacons, etc.) are meant to be "above reproach," and "the husband of one wife," with his house and children under control (1 Tim. 3:2, 4-5, Titus 1:5-9). The central idea here is that leaders should be models. They are due special respect, because they are charged with keeping watch over our souls, for which they will render account (Heb. 13:17). In view of the high regard for heterosexual marriage in the Bible, going back to the creation of Adam and Eve, evangelicals have been rightly offended by moves in some churches to ordain practicing gays.

Does this mean no celibate person can be an elder? Not at all. By the way, the expression "husband of one wife" translates the Greek, "a one-wife man," that is, a man who, if married, must be loyal to his wife. But that does not mean only a married man can be an elder, nor for that matter does it have to be a man with children. The apostle Paul himself is considered an elder (Acts 15:22) and was no doubt a single man (1 Cor. 7:8). The level of the elder's integrity in the Christian life must be high indeed. Does it mean that a gay person who does not practice, but has his life under control, can be an elder? I do not see any clear prohibition of it in Scripture. Only this person, as should any other elder, must exhibit all the virtues listed in the New Testament:

> "sober-minded, self-controlled, respectable, hospitable, able to teach, not a drunkard, not violent but gentle, not quarrelsome, not a lover of money..." (v. 3)

What About The Public Square?

A final crucial question for us today is how to treat gays in public life.[4] Christians greatly value civil rights. The history of the concept of civil rights is deeply rooted in Western culture, and owes a great deal to a Christian awareness, with some Enlightenment consciousness mixed-in. The basic idea of civil rights is that human beings, simply because they are human, should be protected from discrimination. Being God's image-bearers should come with equal protection under the law. Most modern societies recognize their right to life, property, free speech, religious freedom, freedom to associate, access to a fair trial, ability to participate in a political process, and the like. For these privileges it should make no difference whether a person be white, black, male, female, heterosexual, gay, or any other characteristic. The only time someone's civil rights may be removed or limited is when they have engaged in criminal activity and been proven guilty. The right to form partnerships for all kinds of purposes, legal, financial, religious, or other, belongs to all human beings. Legally, homosexual people should neither be given special benefits nor special prohibitions based on their sexual orientation.

Is marriage a civil right? Most countries have provisions in their statues for marriage, its status and protection. However, marriage is not simply a civil right. It is a creation ordinance. Marriage is a sacred institution, as we have argued above. Marriage is meant to be heterosexual and life-long. Procreation should be within the bounds of a family, rooted in marriage. Children and their parents are thus assured institutional protection.

Homosexual partnerships do not practice the kind of sexual relations (technically coitus) which have the potential for life-generation. Therefore, we should not call such partnerships marriage, nor capable of family life in the biblical sense. Nor should the state attempt to redefine marriage in order to include gay partnerships. That is both a philosophical and an empirical mistake. Indeed, public law does not create marriage

---

4. In what follows I will generally agree with the position espoused by the Center for Public Justice. See [http://www.cpjustice.org/content/homosexuality].

or the family. God does. In recognition of this, the law ought to protect marriage and family. They are essential for a healthy society. Of course, a number of governments have instituted marriage for same-sex partners. So what do we do? In a democracy there is still opportunity to try and change things. If that does not succeed, we must honor the law, while disagreeing with its content.

Again, that does not mean gay people who are in partnership should have no rights. Any legitimate partnership should be afforded basic civil rights. I would favor considering health benefits or retirement benefits to various kinds of legitimate domestic partnerships, as long as this is not a way to specially benefit gay people. I know of an elderly brother and sister who never married, and decided to live in the same house and own property together. I cannot think why they should be denied such things as health insurance. It would be discriminatory to single-out one kind of non-marital partnership for privileges normally accorded to a husband and wife, while denying such privileges to other kinds of partnerships, such as the brother and sister, or friends. Put simply, we are not defending the civil rights of gay people specially, but of any lawful partnership generally. We should be happy to uphold the civil rights of all citizens, even when we disagree with their lifestyle. We should be the first to defend the civil rights of all peoples, and of all legitimate partnerships. We should do everything we can to prove to gay people that we are neither homophobic nor gay-bashers, but that we are willing to defend their rights as people in public life, and more than willing to bring the gospel to them.

Questions abound. Should the state require that every free association, such as the church or a business, grant entry to gay people? In advanced Western societies the "right to assembly" is fundamental. That is why they are called free associations: they decide what criteria for entrance best suits their purposes. So, if the church decides (hopefully based on Scripture) that practicing gays may not aspire to office, the government has no right to tell them otherwise. If a school decides it cannot hire a practicing gay person because that would violate its mission, it would have to carefully defend that position, but in the end that would be its right. The same goes for the military. It has to decide whether practicing gays make good soldiers or not.

One of the most difficult challenges facing Christians is the one of opportunity. There are ministries to schools and universities which have been told that if they disagree with homosexuality they are no longer welcomed on campus. What should they do? Face the music and leave? Or keep silence and preach the gospel? These decisions require much wisdom.

Pastoral Care

Christians need to be very careful here. While we cannot approve the practice of homosexuality nor the legitimacy of a civil marriage of two gays, yet we should have a very real pastoral concern for many who are struggling with this lifestyle. This is not patronizing, but a biblical calling. Throughout the Scripture, believers are enjoined to rescue the vulnerable (Job 31:16-23; Matt. 25:31-46; James 1:27). Today there are a number of ministries actively helping gays find a way out and discover freedom in the gospel. They stress that many gays are struggling with their condition. Sexual brokenness is hardly restricted to gays. Everyone, to some extent, is afflicted in this area. Yet gays have had an especially hard time. The church should reach out to them and find ways to minister to their deepest needs.

Discussion

1. Why is the issue of homosexuality so volatile?
2. What are some of the mistakes conservative people have made in relation to gays?
3. Where does the Bible prohibit homosexual practice?
4. What is the Christian's responsibility toward gay people?
5. Should all gays who become Christians get married to someone of the opposite sex?
6. How should the civil law treat gay people?

Does God Love Racial Minorities?

One of the stumbling blocks to evangelical Christian faith often is the imagined attitude in the Bible against minorities. There are many different types of minorities, of course, and they are not all strictly the same. The expression "minority" does not have to mean exclusively numerical minorities, but any kind of excluded people. Two major categories can be considered here: ethnic minorities (blacks in South Africa, Jews in Europe, Turks in Germany, non-Han Chinese, etc.); and gender (women in most countries). Let's look at ethnic issues here.

One of the most heinous forms of race prejudice is that of lighter skinned people against people of color. Many people prejudiced against blacks have tried to justify it from the distortion of a Bible story. An ancient book known as the Babylonian Talmud states that three in Noah's ark were punished for sexual impurity, a dog, a raven, and Ham. Ham's punishment was to be "smitten in his skin."[1] Later commentators explain that Ham's skin was darkened. All his descendents would be black people and would be accursed because of it. Ham was the youngest of Noah's three sons, and the father of Canaan. According to the biblical text, Noah got drunk and lay down naked, and Ham "saw the nakedness of his father" (Gen. 9:22). We are not altogether sure what Ham's misdemeanor was. This could mean simply that he saw his father in a state of undress, and instead of discretely covering him up he went and gossiped about it to his brothers. When Noah woke up and realized what had happened, he put a curse on Ham's descendents, the Canaanites: "Cursed by Canaan;

---

1. Talmud Bavli, Sanhedrin 108b.

a servant of servants shall he be to his brothers" (v. 25). It is not clear why Noah cursed the son rather than the perpetrator. In that culture the next generations are considered to be strongly tied to their ancestor. In any case the Canaanite people were indeed subjugated to Elam, Shem's son, and perhaps to others down through history (Gen. 10:22, 14:4).

The point is that many have associated being dark skinned with the sin of Ham. During the slave trade in the 17th to the 19th centuries, this argument could be heard repeatedly.[2] It was reinforced by interpretations of other parts of Scripture. For example, in Deuteronomy 20:10-11, the Lord allows Israel to enslave their conquered enemies. Colossians 3:22, 4:1 enjoins slaves to obey their masters in all things according to the flesh. Paul in the book of Philemon actually tells the slave Onesimus to go back to his master, who is told to treat him kindly. These were taken as a justification for slavery by European and American Christians. The problem is that the biblical text says nothing about Ham's skin color, nor does it ever link slavery to someone's racial origins.

To these fables were added arguments from divine providence, most often conflated with natural law. One of the more articulate spokesmen in favor of Southern American slavery was the Anglican bishop Samuel Seabury. He writes, in 1861:

> I have defined a slave to be a person who is related to society through another person—a master—to whom he owes reasonable service for life and from whom he is entitled to receive support and protection. This definition I believe to be in accordance with facts; in other words, I believe that those persons called slaves in our Southern States are persons born on the soil and under such circumstances (circumstances not of our choosing but of God's ordering) that a debt of service is the very condition of their life.[3]

---

2. See David M. Golberg, *The Curse of Ham: Race and Slavery in early Judaism, Christianity, and Islam*, Princeton: Princeton University Press, 2003.

3. Samuel Seabury, American Slavery, distinguished from the Slavery of English Theorists, and justified by the Laws of Nature, New York: Mason Brothers, 1861, abstract.

Arguments for Apartheid in South Africa had a similar hue. One of the most eloquent spokesmen in favor of Apartheid (the separation of the races) was professor J. D. Du Toit, who affirmed that God is a "great divider." Just as he divided light from darkness, heaven from earth, and man from woman, he ordained the separation of one nation from another. His key biblical proof-text is the story of the Tower of Babel (Gen. 11). He concludes from the confusion of languages that races must have been defined at the same occasion, and therefore, what God has separated, let no man join together.[4]

Not only are these views completely unfounded, but they are highly destructive, blasphemous, even. Yet racism rears its ugly head in a variety of circumstances. And certainly there are many arguments for the inferiority of certain races other than those coming out of biblical culture. And there are far more varieties than based upon skin color alone. Often they mix class with racial traits. For example, in traditional Hinduism we find a rigid system of dividing humanity into castes. There are four main castes and several subdivisions within them: The Brahmins (priestly, ruling class); the Kshatriyas (warriors); the Vaishyas (merchants); and the Shudras (laborers). A subdivision of the Shudras is the Shandalas, known as the "outcastes," or the "untouchables," because their very presence is considered a pollutant. The caste system became rigid and inflexible based on the dharmashastras (law books) of the post-Vedic era (after 500 B.C.).

Basically, racism is an ideology which favors the domination of one ethnicity over others. According to William Julius Wilson, this ideology involves two components: (1) beliefs that a designated racial group is either biologically or culturally inferior to the dominant group, and (2) the use of such beliefs to rationalize or prescribe the racial group's treatment in society and to explain its social position and accomplishments.[5] In the

---

4. See his *Holy Scripture and Race Relations*, Potchesfstrom: Pro Rege, 1960

5. William Julius Wilson, *The Bridge over the Racial Divide: Rising Inequality and Coalition Politics*, Berkeley: University of California Press, 1999, p. 14.

past racism has been predominantly biologically-based. In the 19th century, for example, black people were often considered incapable of the same kind of accomplishments as white people for biological reasons. In the United States, right after the Civil War (1861-1865) an era known as Reconstruction, popularly known as the Jim Crow era allowed for various practices based on racism including the belief that schools should be segregated because black people learn more slowly than whites. Interracial marriages were not allowed until the 20th century, because of the belief that "mixed blood" was bad for the development of humanity. Health care was denied or at least limited for people of color, because it was believed they were physically less resilient than whites.

Skin color was not the only basis for race prejudice during those years. Jews, for example, whether white or dark-skinned, were considered a threat to the "Aryan" societies of Europe. Whereas during the Reformation oftentimes Protestants were persecuted by the Roman Catholic Church, it could happen the other way round, as it did in North America during the nineteenth century when the predominantly Protestant society made it difficult for the Roman Catholic immigrants to fit into the mainstream. Although it is hard to give grades out, perhaps the anti-Semitism that led to the unspeakable horrors of the holocaust qualifies as the worst in history. It grew incrementally. In the 19th century, the German journalist Wilhelm Marr published a pamphlet which translates this way: "The Victory of the Jewish Spirit over the Germanic Spirit" (1873). The main argument is that Jews, or "Semites," as he called them, represented an ethnic group that was busy infiltrating German culture. In 1879 he founded the *League of Antisemites* which encouraged Germans to resist the Jews and deport them whenever possible. Anti-Semitism has several types, depending on the time of history and the culture that nurtures it. It is often economic and political, that is, fearing the Jews will "take over" by their shrewdness. It also can be nationalistic or racial. That is, believing that Jews have certain characteristics such as greed and arrogance, which make them unworthy of full citizenship or membership in various institutions. Or, it can be religious. Some Christians have believed that the Jews were the ones primarily responsible for killing Jesus Christ. Some would add that this is the reason they have been condemned to wander and be persecuted.

Today biological racism is rare. Very few people will say they believe you can rank the races according to achievement, capacity, innate virtue, etc. And yet many of our cultural institutions are still racist. This can apply to businesses or schools or clubs. Recently, an experiment was carried out in France. A research group was allowed to make up credible sounding job application forms and send them around to different companies. The so-called candidates all had good backgrounds and good records. In many cases where the applicant had a European sounding name (Dupont, Bernard, etc.) he or she was invited to come in for an interview. But in almost every case where the applicant had a Muslim or North African sounding name (Mohamed, Hasan, etc.) the candidate was never invited to come in at all.

Causes And Cures

Racism begins in the heart. One of the books in the Bible that most clearly deals with prejudice is James. Among other things it denounces the type of discrimination that belittles the poor person. "Let the lowly brother boast in his exaltation, and the rich in his humiliations,"(James 1:9-10). James warns against seating rich people in prominent places and pushing the poor to the side (2:1-7) The root cause of prejudice is "bitter jealousy and selfish ambition in your hearts" (3:14). The reason people quarrel and go to war is that we "desire and do not have..," (4:2). The cure is also spelled out.

> "Religion that is pure and undefiled before God and the Father is this," he tells us, "to visit orphans and widows in their affliction..." (1:27)

From the heart, then, come not only jealousies and unfulfilled desires, but the creation of organizations that institutionalize prejudice. Even though never condoned by the Bible, several types of racism were around in biblical times. For example, there was hatred between the Samaritans and the Jews. The Samaritans claimed they were true descendants of Jacob, whereas the Jews developed separately. Thus, when the Jews returned from their Babylonian captivity and found Samaritans populating their former lands they were greatly peeved. Later, the Samaritans helped Alexander in his conquests, for which he rewarded them with a temple built on Mount Gerizim, a rival place to Jerusalem. Remember, though, that Jesus showed compassion on a Samaritan woman whom he met at a well at midday, the only time she dared draw water. Remember, too, the disciples were told by the risen Lord to preach the gospel in all parts of the world, including Samaria (Acts 1:8). And, indeed, the churches in Judea, Galilee and Samaria had peace and were built up (Acts 9:31).

Race-based or ethnicity-based prejudice is often more subtle than we may think. Here, briefly, are three (among many) manifestations of prejudice, and some suggested cures.

Ignorance is often accompanied by fear. Lack of information is often coupled with selective perceptions, stereotypes, and false beliefs. For example, a common perception of Asian people is that they work harder than others. And of Africans, or African Americans, that they are lazy. A careful look shows that no people group is innately harder working than another. What is deceptive here is that circumstances may have a good deal to do with these surface appearances. Many Asians immigrate voluntarily to the West in order to find a better life. Asians are just as sinful as anyone else, but they often work very hard, and endure parental pressure to succeed, in order to achieve a measure of accomplishment. On the other hand, many Africans often came to the West involuntarily, as slaves. This tends to sap anyone's motivation. Because of severe color-based race prejudice, black folks have been kept from succeeding by all kinds of invisible ceilings (or even quite visible ones, such as segregated schools and neighborhoods). Caricatures are easy to form if one does not know how to observe properly. For example, people who casually visit certain African countries and see women bearing burdens while men talk for hours on a street corner may come to the hasty conclusion that they are indolent. We cannot rule out a certain amount of injustice here. But the fact is, Sub-Saharan culture often promotes getting things done by conversation, story-telling and the like, rather than simply pushing a plow or carrying a load.

One remedy for ignorance is deliberately to cross racial divides and make friends with people outside of your own racial group. When was the last time you invited a Muslim into your home? When did you share an activity with a person of color? I have the great privilege of working in a band that is racially mixed. In our more relaxed moments we share experiences about how we perceive one another. One of the black members told us that occasionally, when walking down the street, people coming in the opposite direction clutch at their purses or pick up the pace. Another told us how they hate it when someone says, "you're such a good friend, I don't even see your color anymore." This is highly insulting to someone who is proud of their color and the history of their race. It can work the other way as well. I have been told that as a white person I cannot really play jazz! Blindfold tests have consistently shown you cannot tell whether a musician is white or black by the way he plays; but the prejudice is still around.

The Bible never asks us to airbrush our ethnic differences, but to work together for mutual enrichment. When Paul says that when we have put on Christ, "There is neither Jew nor Greek, there is neither slave nor free, there is neither male nor female ..." (Gal. 3:28), he surely is not saying that backgrounds and gender differences don't matter. He is saying that the gospel is an equal opportunity plan of salvation. Ideally we should strive to have churches that are racially mixed, and that demonstrate great respect and mutual love between the races.

Related to ignorance that leads to caricature is *ethnocentrism*, and its counterpart, *xenophobia*.

These are big words signifying something simple. Ethnocentrism says, my race, my people group, my ethnicity is better than yours. There are many variations. Euro-centrism argues that European history and values are superior to other people's. Afro-centrism argues that being from Africa is superior than being from other places. These attitudes are often unconscious. But they are very destructive.

The Protestant Palestinian writer and culture critic Edward Saïd famously demonstrated that many Europeans or North Americans look at Middle Eastern cultures as uniform, and in most cases inferior. He called it "Orientalism." But this approach justifies the worst kind of prejudice. Here is how he characterizes that unfairness:

> So far as the United States seems to be concerned, it is only a slight overstatement to say that Muslims and Arabs are essentially seen as either oil suppliers or potential terrorists. Very little of the detail, the human density, the passion of Arab-Moslem life has entered the awareness of even those people whose profession it is to report the Arab world. What we have instead is a series of crude, essentialized caricatures of the Islamic world presented in such a way as to make that world vulnerable to military aggression.[6]

Saïd's point of view is admittedly strongly stated, but has he not put his finger on the way we often look at cultures we don't know very well?

The second term, xenophobia, simply means a fear of strangers. From two Greek words, *xenos*, meaning "foreign," and *phobos*, meaning "fear," it means to worry inordinately about people from another culture or race. For example, during World War II many Americans developed a fear of the Japanese, and in some cases of any Asian. Conspiracy theories are often based on xenophobia. This was surely the case with the European prejudice against the Jews, which we have briefly discussed already. When I was growing up, during the Cold War period, "the communists" were poised to take over, infiltrating every

---

6. Edward Saïd, "Islam through Western Eyes," in *The Nation*, April 26, 1980.

institution in the free world. It led us to fear the
Russians. The school I attended offered courses
in the Russian language, in part to "be ready for
the worst." This is not to deny the evil intentions
of worldwide communism. History has too often proven
those fears to be well-founded. But the way in which our
fears were nurtured was alarmist. The world was divided
into good guys and bad guys. Thus, anyone with lightly
left-leaning political views was deemed a communist.
There is a short distance from this stereotyping to scape-
goating. The problem in our society is … them!

The fear of strangers is especially heinous in that the
Bible everywhere insists upon welcoming the stranger,
breaking down the wall of separation, sharing our goods
with those who have less. As in the first case, one remedy
to ethno-centrism is to visit other places, fraternize with
people who are different, learn about other cultures. One of
my colleagues who works in a strongly Hispanic section of
Philadelphia, is always urging us to "sit at the feet of your
neighbor's culture" in order to learn. The ultimate model
for us in this expression of racial reconciliation is Jesus
Christ himself, who left the security of his heavenly glory
to become… a first-century Palestinian Jew! Yet he opened
up the gospel to all people, including the Gentiles. When he
issued the Great Commission, recorded in Matthew, to "Go
therefore and make disciples of all nations," a few hairs
may have bristled. The word "nations" is *ethnos* in Greek,
a word used in much of the Old Testament for non-Jews!

No doubt progress has been made in racial relations.
But it is not enough to settle for laws that prohibit discrimination. There needs to be positive teaching and then
practice before we can claim we have achieved something
important. And clearly, the church is the best place to begin. Why not teach classes on ethnicity? Why not learn
songs from other cultures? Why not elect leaders from a
diverse population so that the people from various backgrounds truly feel represented?

Exploitation. This is another variation on the theme that
one group, the dominant people, considers it their right to
abuse another, the less powerful group.

There are obvious cases, such as slavery, discussed earlier. But there are less obvious ones as well. Being from a certain family, having lived in certain places, attended a particular university, these can feed one's pride to the point where we may unwittingly deny lesser people certain privileges. Without wanting to overstate things, there can be different kinds of entitlements which are never questioned. You may land a good job through networks which not everyone has. As the old saying goes, "it's not what you know but whom you know" that counts.

Often exploitation is simply driven by economics. It is simply cheaper to "outsource" your work, no matter how hard that may be on the people close to you who would require more benefits because of laws protecting workers. We justify such practices by telling ourselves the menial worker in Africa or India is "better off" than he could be in his own country because wages are so low there. So everyone wins. Everyone, that is, except for the laborer in our own back yard. At its worst, raw, unbridled capitalism is exploitative because it assumes the little person will benefit from the wealthy person by a kind of "trickle-down" economics.

Not Always Easy

I don't want to give the impression there are easy answers to all of these issues. Socialism, the opposite of raw capitalism, which tries to force equality on everyone by law, almost always backfires. Surely the answer is to practice justice and equal opportunity rather than try to make everyone the same, rich or poor.

Here we are only addressing the question, does God really love minorities? The answer is a thousand times yes. There is a surprising amount of material in the Bible on ethnic prejudice, its causes and cures. One of the most prevalent in the New Testament was the "wall of separation" between Jews and Gentiles. From the time of Abraham, the Jews were the chosen people. This was never meant to be to the absolute exclusion of everyone else. Isaiah tells us Israel was called to be a light for the nations (Isa. 42:6; 49:6). Still, they were the people through whom the Messiah was to come (2 Sam. 7:11; Ps. 110; Isa. 9:6-7). The Gentiles were unclean (Lev. 15; Isa. 35:8; Acts 10:14). When he did come to the Gentiles, they were declared "clean." Still, many of Jesus' own people did not receive him (John 1:10). The gospel was then fully opened up to the Gentiles (Rom. 11:11-13; 15:9-18). But meanwhile not all Jewish Christians could accept this.

Peter in particular, who had been a good Jew, struggled to accept Gentiles as believers. In one dramatic episode the Lord revealed to him in a special dream that Gentiles were on equal footing with Jews. He was told to preach the gospel to Cornelius, a God-fearer (Gentile admirer of Judaism). On the way, he had a dream in which a table descended full of "unclean" foods, formerly forbidden to Jews, and he was told to eat. At first he would not, but he was told that God had made these foods clean (Acts 10:15). He had to be told three times before he realized that it was all right to preach to a Gentile. When he did, and Cornelius responded Peter understood that the gospel was opened to the Gentiles, without barriers. He reported this to the hierarchy and from then on it became clear that Jews and Gentiles were on equal footing. This acceptance did not come easily. For example, according to Paul, in the Galatians, Peter came to Antioch and became afraid of eating with the Gentiles. Paul had to admonish him for forgetting their equality (Gal. 2:11-14).

Paul, indeed, makes a huge point out of the good news being a way to tear down barriers. To the Ephesians he writes, "For he himself is our peace, who has made us both one and has broken down in his flesh the dividing wall of hostility..." (2:14ff.; see Col. 1:21). In the gospel, then, there is no place for race prejudice. Every knee shall bow and every tongue confess that Jesus Christ is Lord (Phil. 2:10-11). If this be so, then there is no room for showing partiality based on ethnicity.

"Blessed are the poor in spirit," Jesus taught in the very first Beatitude, "for theirs is the kingdom of heaven"

(Matt. 5:3). The expression "poor in spirit" is not meant to exclude people who are economically poor. Jesus constantly lifted up the lowly, the powerless, the economically poor. He praised the widow who gave only a penny, her entire substance, to the temple treasury whilst the Scribes gave out of their abundance (Mark 12:43). But the point of this Beatitude is to stress that unless any of us stops being self-reliant we cannot inherit the kingdom. The kingdom is God's gift to those who know themselves helpless and without the needed resources to get in. Minorities are often more aware of their need than others. God does not love the wealthy person who surrenders to him any the less. He simply reminds them that to whom much has been given much will be required (Luke 12:48). And what is required is proper humility. Race prejudice is incapable of humility by very definition.

Remember that God loved the Jews in a special way, and they were a tiny minority. Why did he choose them? There is mystery here, but it has to do with the nature of love, which is not based on the object's potential or loveliness. "The Lord your God has chosen you to be a people for his treasured possession, out of all the peoples on the earth. It was not because you were more in number than any other people that the Lord set his love on you and chose you, for you were the fewest of all peoples ..." (Deut. 7:6-7). So surely God loves minorities. He does not exclude the rich and powerful; not at all. But he enjoys calling those who are not wise or rich in the world's eyes because they exemplify his meritless free grace (1 Cor. 1:26-31).

At the heart of the gospel story Jesus Christ, "though he was in the form of God, did not count equality with God a thing to be grasped, but made himself nothing, taking the form of a servant ..." (Phil. 2:6-7). Jesus became an oppressed minority on our behalf!

Discussion

1. Define racial prejudice.
2. How have people used the doctrine of providence to justify race prejudice?
3. What is the difference between biological racism and institutional racism?
4. Of the three causes of prejudice, ignorance, exploitation/xenophobia or exploitation, which have you observed most in your own community?
5. How can the gospel be a cure for racism?
6. Is your church involved in any activities to restrain racism?

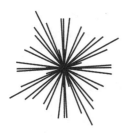

Are Women Human?

This is the provocative title of a book by Dorothy Leigh Sayers which unites two essays on gender.[1] Sayers was a lay theologian and Christian apologist who participated in the Inklings, the literary fellowship in which J. R. R. Tolkien and C. S. Lewis participated. She wrote mysteries, plays, translations (notably of Dante's *Divine Comedy*), poetry and novels. While it is a rhetorical question, Sayers argues that many barriers exist which say something different. She does not consider herself a feminist, but does ask for fairness in debates. For example, she says:

> The question of 'sex-equality' is, like all questions affecting human relationships, delicate and complicated. It cannot be settled by loud slogans or hard-and-fast assertions like 'a woman is as good as a man' – or 'woman's place is the home' – or 'women ought not to take men's jobs.' The minute one makes such assertions, one finds one has to qualify them.

This is wise counsel. As we look at the second category of minorities, women (not numerically minoritarian, but often excluded from privilege), we would do well to follow Sayers' directives.

It should apply first to those who find in the Bible disturbing texts which seem to indicate the inferiority of women to men. Here is a brief list. Leviticus 12:2, 5, a mother was considered ceremonially unclean twice as long for the birth of a daughter (80 days total) as for the birth of a son (40 days total). In 2 Samuel 1:26 David laments the death

---

1. Dorothy L. Sayers, *Are Women Human?*, Grand Rapids: Eerdmans, (orig. 1938) 1971, 2005.

of his best friend Jonathan and declares, "Your love to me was extraordinary, surpassing the love of women." In the New Testament several things Paul says appear rather disparaging of women. To the Corinthians he writes, "As in all the churches of the saints, the women should keep silent in the churches. For they are not permitted to speak, but should be in submission, as the law states" (1 Cor. 14:33–34). Similarly, he tells his young disciple Timothy, "Let a woman learn quietly with all submissiveness" (1 Tim. 2:11). Peter seems disparaging as well, as when he calls women the "weaker vessel" (1 Pet. 3:7).

Can we really follow Dorothy Sayers' advice here and qualify such statements? Let's admit that some of these texts are not easy to square with biblical norms for justice. And it needs to be said up-front that the church has often been slow to recognize the true equality of men and women, and then to apply it. By misusing some of these texts, Christians have often got it dead wrong. Thomas Aquinas, for example, once declared:

> As regards the individual nature, woman is defective and misbegotten, for the active power of the male seed tends to the production of a perfect likeness in the masculine sex; while the production of a woman comes from defect in the active power...[2]

Where he got this idea from we don't know, but such statements have done a great deal of harm. As a result of this kind of attitude women have been denied all kinds of rights. In many countries they may not have access to the same education or career opportunities as men. Their right to vote was a hard fought battle, one that was waged not so long ago. Domestic violence is far more widespread against women than men. Still today in various countries baby girls are rejected or put to death simply because they are not baby boys.

What do we say to these injustices? How does the Christian faith help, rather than hinder the true dignity of women? Before we take a closer look at those passages,

2. Thomas Aquinas, *Summa Theologica*, Q92, art. 1, Reply Obj. 1.

let us first look at the many affirmations of true equality. Right at the outset, the Bible points out that men and women are equally God's image bearers:

> So God created mankind in his own image, in the image of God he created them, male and female he created them. (Gen. 1:27 NIV)

Furthermore, we are, men and women, redeemed into the image of Christ, together (1 Cor. 15:49; 2 Cor. 3:18). It would be hard to overstate this. Yes, there are differences. Yes, there is complimentarity. But at the most basic level, to put is as does Dorothy Sayers, women are indeed fully human.

But we can go further. Women are often the great heroines and examples not only in the Bible but throughout Christendom. We are not saying this to "throw them a bone," but because it is abundantly true.

It was the courage of the Hebrew midwives that saved male children from Pharaoh's infanticide (Exod. 1:15-22).

It was Ruth's remarkable faith that would not let her widowed mother-in-law go alone to her homeland, which then led her to Boaz. This honorable man recognized Ruth's virtue, married her and begat a famous child, Obed, who would become the ancestor of King David, and of King Jesus.

Queen Esther was brave enough to risk a forbidden audience with King Xerxes to disclose to him a plot to kill off her people, the Jews.

The Proverbs warns the young sage against the wiles of the forbidden woman (folly) but then likens God's wisdom to a great lady (Prov. 2:16; 3:13-18; 31:10-31). And, of course, Jesus Christ was the best friend a woman ever had. He met the Samaritan woman in the heat of the day since her shame forbade her to come to the well at any other time (John 4:1-45). In front of the scolding dinner guests, a woman anointed Jesus with expensive ointment, he declared, "she has done a beautiful thing to me." She had understood the implications of his death way before the men at table (Mark 14:3-9). It was the women who came to the empty tomb first on Easter morning (John 20:1-2).

Two Biblical Priorities

So, then, how do these teachings on the fundamental equality, and indeed of the prominence of women, compute with the passages mentioned above where they seem to be belittled? We certainly cannot solve all of the issues of interpretation here. But the general direction that makes the most sense to me is to recognize both the equality and the complementarity of men and women. Equality as to being made after God's image, and co-heirs of God's grace for salvation (1 Pet. 3:7). Complimentary as to having overlapping but different responsibilities in the social network. So, then, to some of the tough passages.

Why in Leviticus ceremonial uncleanness took longer after the birth of a female than a male is probably linked to two things. The first is the importance of the number 40, the total number of days the mother was unclean after the birth of a male. This number occurs throughout the Bible. For example, Noah waited 40 days after it rained before he opened the window of the ark. Moses was on Mount Sinai 40 days. And the second to "primogeniture," the idea in ancient societies that the male is the principal heir, leading to subsequent generations. Thus it was important to "rush" a little boy to circumcision, in a way that was less urgent for a little girl, who did not undergo this rite. Today we do not have to practice traditional primogeniture, since much of that in the Old Testament was in anticipation of Christ, God's firstborn. This does not mean today that there is no room for male leadership in marriage, or there is no freedom for some countries to allow legacies to first-born males.

In any case, the different waiting period had nothing to do with any supposed superiority of men over women. (The mother, not the newborns, was unclean until the purification.)

When David calls his love for Jonathan better than the love of women, we probably have a hyperbole. Some commentators have found in this verse evidence of homosexuality. That would be quite unthinkable. David's friendship

with Jonathan was typical of what we might
call "male bonding" today. They were warriors.
Jonathan had stopped believing in Saul, his father, who had dedicated himself to fight against
David, the true anointed one of the Lord. David recognized
his loyalty. Jonathan saved David's life from sure destruction by his father. As devoted friends in battle do, they
developed a deep affection for one another. David grieved
bitterly when Jonathan died (1 Sam. 20; 2 Sam. 1:23-27).
The love of women is different. It has to do with affection,
sexual attraction, the friendship of a life's companionship,
the admiration of motherhood and of a woman's beauty.
David is trying to express how extraordinary his love for
Jonathan was, and could find no better comparison than
the love of husband and wife. He is hardly assigning a
superior value to male friendship.[3] Today many people
would be reticent to express such affection for a friend of
the same sex, which is a shame.

What about Paul's teaching on the silence of women in
1 Corinthians 14 and 1 Timothy 2? It is fair to say these passages are not easy! We must be careful not to accommodate
our interpretation of them to a non-biblical agenda. Those
who don't like the implications tend to downplay or relativ-
ize what Paul is saying. Those who like it too much tend to
make him sound stricter and more all-encompassing than
he really is. Still, we can assert a couple of things. Surely
Paul is not recommending the total gagging of women in
church. If he were he would be contradicting himself. Earlier in 1 Corinthians he gives instructions of the protocol for
women who prophesy or pray in church (11:5, 13). While
scholars differ on the meaning of the "veil" here, the point
is women spoke and prayed in the church.[4] This is in keeping with all of the Bible where there are numerous examples
of women leading in worship and in speaking the Word of
God in different places.

---

3. See Markus Zehnder "Observations on the Relationship between
David and Jonathan and the Debate on Homosexuality," *Westminster
Theological Journal* 69/1, 2007, pp. 127-74)

4. Some would argue this passage is not about the church. But that
is clearly not the case (v. 16).

For example, citing the Prophet Joel, Peter explains, in the great sermon at Pentecost, that the day has come, foretold long ago, when male and female servants will receive the Holy Spirit and will prophecy (Acts 2:18). The tradition of women prophesying goes back to ancient times.[5]

Miriam, Aarons's sister, was a prophetess. On one occasion she sang a special song in celebration of the exodus (Exod. 15:20-21).

Deborah was a judge, and also a prophetess. In the time of the Judges, she actually led an army against Sisera. Even though she remarked that being a woman would deprive the warrior Barak of all the glory, she went and she conquered (Judges 4).

Huldah, a contemporary of Jeremiah and Zephaniah, had a significant part in raising the young Josiah, who would become one of the great reformer kings. It was she who, echoing the newly rediscovered book of Deuteronomy, foretold of the destruction of God's disobedient people, a destruction which was delayed because of Josiah's reforms (2 Kings 22:14-20; 2 Chron. 34:22-28).

In the New Testament women often play a prominent role in promoting the kingdom of God. When the Holy Spirit directed Paul to bring the gospel for the first time to Europe, it was Lydia, in Philippi, who, along with several other women gathered to hear the apostle speak, making it possible for a successful (though stormy) visit to the city (Acts 16:11-40). That women had leadership roles in the New Testament is undisputed. They were disciplers. Timothy learned the Bible from his mother and grandmother (2 Tim. 3:14). Paul greets women first in the long list of friends he asks the Romans to salute. Phoebe is referred to as a "deaconess" and a patron (Rom. 16:1-2). Priscilla and Aquila are his "fellow workers in Christ Jesus" (1:3-4). Among other things, they had corrected and improved the theology of Apollos, a prominent preacher from Ephesus (Acts 18:24-26). Then there is Junia, possibly on the front lines as a messenger of the gospel (Rom. 16:7). The same

---

[5.] There are seven prophetesses mentioned in the Old Testament: Sarah, Miriam, Deborah, Hannah, Abigail, Huldah and Esther.

is said of Euodia and Syntyche, whom Paul notes "have labored side by side with me in the gospel" (Phil. 4:2-3). John writes his second letter to "the elect lady and her children" (2 John 1:1). We are not exactly sure who she was, but from the personal tone, and the greeting at the end from the children of her "elect sister," we can be nearly certain she is a real person.

So, then, if women could be vocal, fellow workers, able to prophesy, correct men, how is it that Paul tells them to keep silent in the church (1 Cor. 14:33-34, 1 Tim. 2:11)? There are several possibilities. The most likely one is that Paul is bringing into the discussion the larger picture of the biblical worldview, which says that there is a complementarity between men and women, equality but not uniformity. While women are equally made after God's image, and are honored throughout the Bible, that does not mean uniformity across the board. Equality does not mean uniformity. Paul goes to some lengths in 1 Corinthians 11 to explain the diversity yet unity of men and women (11:2-16). Paul's argument may sound strange to us today, since he appeals not to general principles of justice, but to the Law (1 Cor. 14:34—presumably the Pentateuch) and to the story of the creation and fall, and Adam and Eve's roles in both (1 Tim. 2:13-14). According to his reasoning, the fact of Adam's being created first, and then of Eve's being deceived, helps explain functioning in particular roles when the church meets officially. While perhaps foreign to us, this kind of argument, based on the larger picture, is found whenever he discusses the genders. For example, when he describes marriage he calls on the wife to submit to her husband as the church submits to Christ (Eph. 5:22-24). He further directs husbands to love their wives as Christ has loved the church (5:25-33).

So, Paul is not saying women should close their mouths, but he is referring to occasions where, for various biblical reasons, speaking out may be inappropriate. In the formal meeting of the church it was not proper for women to be in a leadership role. They could pray or prophecy but not without signs of their place in the community. The Greek word *sigao* ("silence") does not mean "never talk," but most often means "hold your peace," that is, for a particular issue proper quiet is called for. Earlier in 1 Corinthians 14 Paul orders someone with the gift of tongues who has no interpreter to stay silent, rather than alienate the audience (v. 28). He also tells a brother who is speaking to defer in silence to someone with a more current revelation (v. 30). Thus, verse 34 does not gag women from any speech, but tells them to speak only according to their proper position within the church and within the family.

By the way, when Peter calls a woman the "weaker vessel" he is not referring to a physical or emotional weakness (1 Pet. 3:7). That would be absurd, since often women show great stability and strength (Would a man would have the strength and endurance to give birth to a child!). Arguments for role differences based on physical constitution rarely succeed. Rather, he is saying that society has put women in a subservient role and so men should recognize that and honor them the more, that is, lift them up. And, as we have seen, he adds an ultimate reason: "since [women] are heirs with you of the grace of life." (Furthermore, neither Paul nor Peter are commenting on the wider context of society, where presumably these role restrictions apply differently: women may govern the state or run a company.)

Biblical Justice And Practice

So, then, can this biblical larger-picture way of arguing be fair at all? Especially since, as we all know there is an equal distribution of talent among men and women. So why should (properly gifted) men be given the leadership role in church and in family when many women are equally gifted but are not? If we only had the fact of gifts to go on, then it would not be just. If gift equals office then wherever someone is more gifted, be it a woman or a man, then the office of leader (elders in the church, husband in the family) should be open to the most gifted. But biblical reasoning is quite a bit broader than that. It is based less on merit than on analogy. People are in places of authority not because they are qualified humanly, but because they reflect the way God governs. That is why Peter tells us to "be subject for the Lord's sake to every human institution" (1 Pet. 2:13). Women don't rule in church because Eve should not have led Adam astray (1 Tim. 2:14). Husbands should love their wives as Christ loved the church (Eph. 5:25). People must obey the civil magistrate because they are God's servant for good. Indeed there is no authority not instituted by God (Rom. 13:1-7).

We should add the important qualifier that government and authority are not meant to be harsh or arbitrary. For example, if male leadership in the family is meant to be Christ-like, look carefully at Jesus' leadership style. He took the form of a servant (Phil 2:7). He washed the feet of the disciples (John 13). Sure, he was a leader, and at times could be quite forceful. He was angry at the Pharisees for their lack of mercy (Mark 3:1-6). He violently overthrew the money tables in the temple (Luke 19:45-46). But he always comported himself with a marvelous combination of authority and servanthood.

It should be the same for church elders and husbands. Likewise, when womanhood is healthy, there should be a beautiful combination of diligence and grace (Prov. 31; 1 Pet. 3:1-6).

In the end, this pattern of analogy is actually more liberating than rule based on talent or qualification. How so? Because it eliminates wrong-headed competition. It eliminates disloyalty. Granted, there is plenty of homework to be done on the texts to make sure we have correctly understood their meaning and application. But the simple existence of teachings we struggle with is not proof of a fallible Bible. Rather, it shows us being in the hands of God is not always safe (to echo Mrs. Beaver's statement in the Narnia stories about Aslan not being safe, but instead being good). As Tim Keller puts it:

> To stay away from Christianity because part of the Bible's teaching is offensive to you assumes that if there is a God

he wouldn't have any views that upset you. Does that belief make sense?[6]

The historical fact is that no religion or philosophy has been so supportive of women's rights than the Christian faith. The push of the early church for women's dignity has been well-documented. Historians have shown that the Christian commitment to being joint heirs of God's grace led to a new-found worth for women. The moral code prohibiting polygamy, divorce and infanticide practiced by Christians helped women to enjoy the same well-being as men.[7] Down through the centuries Christian leaders have advocated the right of women as well as men to be educated. Missionaries, in places like India and China, advocated the right of women to be educated, often in the face of considerable opposition.

In the 19th century a number of extraordinary Quakers, many of them women, found themselves defending women's rights, especially the right to vote, based on the analogy of the evils of slavery. Among them are the Grimké sisters, Sarah and Angelina. Despite their father's arch-conservatism, they managed to educate themselves and became major intellectuals in the defense of women. For example, Angelina Grimké argued that men and women were utterly equal before God. Against the usual argument that Eve was weaker than Adam, she noted that she had succumbed to a supernatural beast, the serpent, while he had succumbed to a mere human being![8] Both sisters affirmed the egalitarian nature of the image of God. Another fascinating Quaker woman, Lucretia Coffin Mott (1793-1880) worked tirelessly against slavery. But she and her colleagues were also ardent defenders of women's rights. In 1848 Mott and her younger friend Elizabeth

---

6. Timothy Keller, *The Reason for God*, New York: Penguin/Dutton, 2008, p. 112.

7. Although he states this a bit too strongly, Rodney Stark has helped rectify certain false impressions about the subjugation of women in the early church. See, *The Rise of Christianity*, San Francisco: HarperOne, 1997, pp. 95-128.

8. Agelina Grimké, "Letter XII Human Rights Not Founded on Sex," October 2, 1837, pp. 194-8.

Cady Stanton organized the first American
women's rights convention at Seneca Falls, New
York, which passed the resolution of the "duty of
the women of this country to secure themselves
the sacred right of elective franchise (the vote)." Much of
the rhetoric behind this kind of movement was gospel-
driven.

There is still much to be done. But the clear biblical
answer to the question, "Are women human?", is overwhelmingly yes.

Discussion

1. Give an example of gender-based prejudice
   from your own experience.
2. Do you agree with the dual principle, equal but
   not uniform? Discuss.
3. Does the idea of justice based on a divine pattern
   in the creation and the fall appeal to you, or
   not? Is the Bible fair to women?
4. Who is your favorite Christian woman in history, and why?

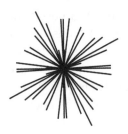

When Will The World End?

A surprising number of young people asked us about the end times. They wanted to know how and when the world will end. And they wanted to know what would happen to each of us after death. While this may seem to have little to do with apologetics, actually it does, very much so. Death, after all, is the last enemy, the very thing Christ has overcome, which is "the hope we have" (1 Pet. 3:15). And, after all, our understanding of the end times is what explains the Christian faith as grounded in history.

Have you been to a funeral where a child wants to know, where will grandma go now? Or are you simply a bit concerned about how things will pan out in the end? Or, do you simply want to know more about heaven and hell? Do you remember any time at which it became clear you were going to die? In my own case I remember it as though it were yesterday. I was attending a conference on genetics, of all things. The speaker was one of the leading experts in the world on genes and DNA. I don't remember most of what he said. But I do remember somewhere in the lecture he said this: death is imprinted on our genetic makeup, each of us. I probably phased out. It suddenly dawned on me that I (me, of all people!) would die sooner or later. Death, of course, is the great leveler. As the classical poet Horace reminds us, death beats both at the poor man's cottage door and at the palace of kings.

Young people usually have little sense of their own mortality. Why should they? They are in their prime, Death is for older people, not me! Well, there is bad news and there is good news. The bad news is that you will no doubt grow older and you may die in an accident or by disease. In North America, 64 teens out of 100,000 die every year. Causes vary: suicide, car crashes, youth violence, cancer ... So, you are going to die. The good news is that death is not just a statistic. Death is a foreign intruder, an unwanted enemy. Why is that good news? Because it means death is not normal. It is bound up with human guilt. And, as we have seen, that guilt has been removed for all who believe in Jesus Christ. At the end of the world, we who are perishable shall put on immortality, and "Death is swallowed up in victory" (1 Cor. 15:54).

This being true, when is the end of the world? The Bible gives us tremendous assurance that the end will come, but not a huge amount of detail. What it does tell is what we need in order to conduct ourselves properly before the end. So, what can we expect?

If we die before Christ returns (the Second Coming) then we will be immediately ushered into the presence of the Lord. We will be a disembodied spirit. We are not given many details about this state. That believers go directly to Paradise is assured by Jesus' answer to the thief dying on the cross next to him. When he asked, "Jesus, remember me when you come into your kingdom," the Lord replied, in the midst of his agony "Truly, I say to you, today you will be with me in Paradise" (Luke 23:42–43).

How? What would the man look like? We don't know. In Revelation 6:9–11 we are given a glimpse at the condition of martyrs who died for their faith. They are called "the souls of those who had been slain for the word of God and for the witness they had born." Apparently they are conscious, because they can articulate a concern: how long before you avenge our blood? To which they are told simply to put on a white robe (signifying their righteousness), and to rest a little longer until their fellow martyrs should all be brought in. So, based on this sparse evidence, we can know those who die in Christ are at rest, and are conscious. We don't know if the dead have any specific knowledge of what happens on earth.

The Judgment

What happens to unbelievers who die, and where do they go? Much is not clear. We do know that a major event attends every person who has died and gone on to the future state. That is the judgment. There will be an accounting for all we have done and said and thought (Rom. 2:6; Ps. 62:12; Prov. 24:12). There is no hiding. This event will occur, and cannot be displaced (Acts 24:25; Heb. 9:27; 2 Pet. 2:9). What we have said and done and thought in private will be shouted from the rooftops (Luke 12:2-3). The Bible indicates that the judgment will be handled by Jesus Christ (John 5:27; Rom. 2:16; Acts 17:31). One of the important implications of this is that we will not be able to say, "O God you are so lofty, so far away, you can never understand my plight or my struggles." No, but Jesus will say "As a matter of fact, I was tempted in every way as were you and I intimately understand the human condition." As it might be said today, "been there—done that" (see Heb. 2:14-18). Another implication is that those who have greater knowledge will be condemned more severely (Matt. 12:41-42; Luke 12:48).

The Book of Revelation pictures a "great white throne" and the judgment of all people "according to what they had done" (Rev. 20:11-13). We may think of those great paintings about the last judgment, such as Hans Memling's 1473 depiction, or Michelangelo's Last Judgment where Christ is at the center, banishing the lost to eternal suffering and welcoming the saved to the new heavens. Is this simply old-fashioned mythology? No, it is utterly sacrosanct. If there were no judgment, no accountability, then anything goes. Why not sin? Why not go on a rampage? Instead, we are told that our actions, words and thoughts, really count. As the Creed tells us: "He shall come to judge the quick and the dead." That is those that are alive and those that have died.

But, aren't Christians forgiven? Acquitted? Justified? Certainly. "There is therefore now no condemnation for those who are in Christ Jesus" (Rom. 8:1). So, are they not spared the judgment? We will indeed all stand before the judgment seat (Rom. 13:10). Yet believers will not hear the angry words of conviction. The very reason they have been saved is to be exonerated from this terrible, though deserved, condemnation, and to pass on into life eternal because of God's free gift. That is why in one way we long for death, to "depart," since it will put us in the presence of Christ forever (Phil. 1:23). At the same time, our lives, even as Christians, need to be evaluated. Today, we aim to please the Lord, for tomorrow:

> We must all appear before the judgment seat of Christ, so that each one may receive what is due for what he has done in the body, whether good or evil. (2 Cor. 5:10)

A sobering thought. We, Christian believers, will be judged, not on matters of eternal life or death, for that has been settled, but on matters of service to the Lord. So, let's get this straight. There is no condemnation, not now, nor later at the judgment, for those who are in Christ. Yet there is an evaluation of what we have done. What difference will it make if we have done well or less well? Again, details are scarce, but Paul alludes to those who work well, building on the foundation of Christ with gold or silver, and those whose work is less enduring (1 Cor. 3:12). When the judgment comes each person's work will be submitted to the test of fire, and will endure or fall short accordingly. Good work will receive a reward. What kind of reward? Perhaps being entrusted to rule over various cities in the new heavens and new earth (Luke 19:11-19). Yet whatever the case, one's work does not affect our salvation (vv. 13-15).

Heaven And Hell

What will heaven be like? At one level, the answer is simple. Heaven will be unspeakably wonderful, for the reason that Christ is there at the center of it. The king of kings who struck down the nations will rule in the peaceable kingdom where his saints shall dwell with him forever (Rev. 19:15; 21:22). What will happen at the end is nothing short of a new cosmic order, ushered in by Jesus Christ. Death will be no more, nor sorrow, nor pain (Rev. 21:4). The New

Jerusalem will come out of heaven like a bride
(Rev. 21:2). And we will dwell in that city with all
of God's people forever and ever.

Some people picture heaven as a rather boring
place where disembodied spirits play their harps and float
around on clouds. The Bible gives a far more robust view. We
will not be ghosts but "spiritual bodies" bearing the image
of Jesus Christ, the man of heaven (1 Cor. 15:44, 49). The
resurrection joins soul to body so that without our physical
self there is no resurrection. What is a spiritual body, you
rightly ask? It is our physical selves, so full of the Holy
Spirit that we will be far more, not less, than our former
selves. If you want to try and imagine this, consider Jesus
after his resurrection and before his ascension into heaven.
Though he could eat and drink, yet he also could appear and
disappear whether or not inside a building (Matt. 28:8-10;
Luke 24:30-31). He was recognizable and yet sometimes
veiled from his friends (Luke 24:16). His hands, feet and side
had the scars from the soldiers' spear, yet he was alive and
could never die again (John 20:24-29).

There will be singing and worship and all kinds of joy in
the presence of the Lord (Rev. 19:1-5). But there will also be
cultural activities, learning, science, the arts, and every task
we now have, yet immeasurably enhanced (Rev. 21:24-26).
Apparently there will even be eating at a banquet table
(Luke 14:15; Rev. 19:9). There will also be something like
politics. Faithful people will be entrusted the rule over cities
(Matt. 25:14-30; Luke 19:12-26). And we will recognize
each other. In his powerful gospel song, *Twelve Gates to
the City*, the Reverend Gary Davis describes the beauty of
the New Jerusalem. And then he adds:

> If you see my dear old mother
> Won't you do this favor for me
> Won't you please tell my mother
> To meet me in Galilee
> Well, it's twelve gates to the city, hallelujah

For him, and for most African-Americans who came to
Christ out of their oppression, heaven is not a foggy,
faraway place, but it is the earth remade.

How can God raise us up? What about those who were cremated? Or died at sea? We really don't know. That there will be a resurrection is absolutely certain (Dan. 12:2; John 5:25-29; Acts 24:15). He should have no problem reassembling the molecules and knitting anyone back together! And that God watches specially over his departed saints is also sure: "Precious in the sight of the Lord is the death of his saints" (Ps. 116:15; Ps. 72:14). One of the most marvelous thoughts from the Book of Revelation is:

> Blessed are the dead who die in the Lord from now on...
> that they may rest from their labors, for their deeds follow
> them. (Rev. 14:13)

They rest from the struggle of living in a fallen world. But their rest is not inactive. Heaven is real, not static, full of learning and growth and enjoyment!

What of those who don't believe? Do they get a second chance? No, for this is the time and the place to decide where they will spend eternity. This is not a pleasant topic. We casually say of someone who died after much suffering, "it was a blessing." But those who are outside of Christ are no longer blessed. Rather, they are lost, forever. The prophet Daniel speaks of two kinds of resurrection, the one group to "everlasting life" and the other to "everlasting contempt" (Dan. 12:1-2). Jesus himself describes Hell as a place of darkness and punishment, of weeping and gnashing of teeth. It is where the Devil and his cohorts, together with all evil-doers, are sent (Rev. 18; 20:7-10). Again, we are not given great detail. Authors and painters have used their imaginations to depict the place. Perhaps the most significant description of Hell is just to say it is "outside" of the city of God's dwelling (the word *Gehenna* which is the Greek term we translate Hell meant the garbage heap outside of Jerusalem). You don't want to be there. Right now is the best time to ask Jesus into your life so he can spare you being lost or outside.

What about those who never heard the gospel? What happens to them? This question is often asked. Here's the best way to answer.

First, God is a loving God, who takes no pleasure in the death of a sinner, but that he may turn and be saved (Ezek. 18:23). God is not "out to get us," but rather "out to save us." He is a merciful God. Nothing he does is cold or arbitrary.

Second, while not everyone has heard the words of the gospel, everyone has heard of God's reality, his holiness, his goodness and kindness. Absolutely no one is with without clear knowledge of God and his requirements (Rom. 1:18-21). The universal law is that if we do good, we will have eternal life, if not, we deserve judgment (2:6-8). To be sure, no one is righteous enough. But it is not a case of unfairness, since it is we, not God, who choose to do wrong. Today, we all know enough so that our consciences will agree with God's revelation on the day of judgment (2:15-16). Are there no exceptions? It would be wrong to speculate. The Reformed Confession known as the Westminster Confession of Faith allows for two possible exceptions: infants and handicapped people ("so also are all other elect persons who are incapable of being outwardly called by the ministry of the Word" X.3). Beyond that, we dare not go. If you are very concerned about this issue, consider becoming a missionary!

The Calendar

When will the end occur? Many people, many generations, have wanted to know. It is characteristic of cult leaders to predict the end times. Charles Taze Russell, the founder of the Jehovah's Witness movement thought that Christ had come, but invisibly, in 1874, and then would appear visibly in 1914. When it did not happen, the Jehovah's Witnesses then decided that it would be "very soon." More recently Harold Kamping, the owner of a large network of Christian radio stations, decided that the end would be in 1994. Then, May, 2011. When it didn't happen he changed it to October 21, 2011. After vain attempts at calling these appearances "spiritual," he finally apologized to his constituency, to his credit. If there is one clear teaching in the Bible it is that we do not know the day or the hour.

> But concerning that day or that hour no one knows,
> not even the angels in heaven, nor the Son, but only
> the Father. (Mark 13:32)

Even Jesus, in virtue of his humanity, did not know. It's not for want of asking that Christians do not know. The disciples asked the resurrected Jesus. He simply answered, "It is not for you to know the times or seasons that the Father has fixed by his own authority..." (Acts 1:6-7).

Christians disagree on how to put together the data from the Scriptures which would indicate any kind of timetable. We certainly cannot settle the question here. But we can state a few matters with certainty. First, and foremost, the Lord Jesus Christ will return, personally, visibly, physically and audibly. "They will see the Son of Man coming on the clouds of heaven with power and great glory" (Matt. 24:30). And "Every eye will see him" (Rev. 1:7). This is all that matters. Jesus, the one who set us free, is the one we long to be with forever. That is why we sing,

> Come Thou long-expected Jesus
> Born to set Thy people free;
> From our fears and sins release us,
> Let us find our rest in Thee.
>
> Israel's strength and consolation,
> Hope of all the saints Thou art;
> Dear desire of every nation,
> Joy of every longing heart.

Second, there will be two kinds of scenario before the end. The first is a time of God's patience, a time of quasi-normalcy so that several of God's purposes can be accomplished. Most important, the gospel will be preached far and wide, "to the whole world" (Matt. 24:14). We don't know how much of the planet that will include. Here we are 21 centuries after the commission to go and make disciples of the nations was given, and apparently the job is still not done. Also, to some extent, life will go

on as usual. Jesus says there will be eating and
drinking, marrying and giving in marriage, to
the extent that the end will come as a surprise
(Matt. 24:38). The second scenario is the pressure
of evil and persecution. "Lawlessness will increase,"
Jesus tells us (Matt. 24:12). There will be a redoubtable
man called the "anti-Christ," sometimes called "the man
of lawlessness," or simply "false Christs" (2 Thess. 2:3;
1 John 2:18, 22, 2 John 7; Matt. 24:24, etc.). There has
been considerable speculation on who this murky figure
might be. Most likely it could be any sort of dangerous
leader who makes life particularly odious for Christians.

Third, the end will be a complete transformation of the
entire cosmos. Again, details are not certain. But many
biblical scholars believe that the new heaven and new
earth will be just that. This place, made-over, cured of
sin and evil. Questions abound. Will the new planet Earth
be large enough to contain all of the believers from the
earliest times till the second coming? Will all those people
live in the New Jerusalem? We just don't know. What we
do know is that God will be at the center, and we will be
perfectly free from sin and misery and will perfectly be
able to worship him, to have fellowship with him, and to
enjoy reconciliation across the board. "And I heard a loud
voice from the throne," John tells us, "saying, 'Behold,
the dwelling place of God is with man. He will dwell with
them, and they will be his people, and God himself will
be with them as their God. And he will wipe away every
tear from their eyes, and death shall be no more, neither
shall there be mourning nor crying nor pain anymore,
for the former things have passed away'" (Rev. 21:3-4).
Compared to this reality, nothing else matters much.

Discussion

1. Why does the future life matter?
2. Will Christians be judged?
3. What will heaven be like?
4. When will Christ come again?

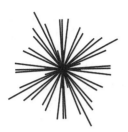

Christian Apologetics

After all these considerations, all the issues we have covered (and there are no doubt many more!), it is time to think more directly about Christian apologetics. But why should we? The name is deceptive. It does not mean to apologize! We are not sorry for our faith, but rather we give good reasons for it. Christian apologetics is a discipline that has its origins in the Bible. Apologetics is meant to equip us to deal with some fairly hard questions. If you are at all honest, you will admit that such questions are real, and even at times quite disturbing. We are encouraged throughout to do apologetics. A verse that summarizes the call to give answers to hard questions is 1 Peter 3:15, which states:

> [...] in your hearts regard Christ the Lord as holy, always being prepared to make a defense to anyone who asks you for a reason for the hope that is in you ...

The expression "make a defense" here is an English translation of the Greek word, apologia, which, you can tell, is behind our word apologetics. It has the term logos in it, which has to do with reasoning, thinking things through. Basically apologetics means to commend the Christian faith in a reasoned or thoughtful manner.

Apologetics is more than simply a defense, though it certainly needs to include arguments which reply to hostile attacks. But the best defense also needs to be positive. Apologetics, when it is well done, is a presentation of the reasons for our faith. Here Peter says to explain the hope you have. Hope is more than just a bare statement of the gospel. It is an entire outlook, a worldview which begins with God's creation, recognizes the devastation of the fall into sin, and then centers on Jesus Christ and the salvation of his people, bringing them to the new heaven and the new earth. Notice how the verse begins with worshiping Jesus Christ!

So, how do you do apologetics? This book was meant to help you explain the basics of the Christian faith to friends around you, or even to yourself. The chapters we have read contain some answers to some of the most frequently asked questions about the faith. Of course, sometimes the questions are not actually asked, but are still there, deep down, since we often doubt things secretly, or unknowingly. At the same time, no one wants to read a very long book that claims to have answers for everything. So the chapters have been brief. Such a book could never exist, actually, because there are always new questions, and new twists on old ones. Therefore, you will find here not only a few specific answers to questions, but also patterns. We do need to learn a number of basic answers so we can help people who have different questions, but, just as important, we need to learn to "read" our friends, and find out what may be behind their questions.

Let me explain. I once sat in on a discussion between a believer and an unbeliever. It was all about the virgin birth of Christ. Christians understand Christ, the Second Person of the Trinity, to have come into the world through a mother who was a virgin, in other words, who had not yet had a sexual union with her husband.

Many unbelievers reject this idea. No one has ever seen such a thing, and today, if a woman gets pregnant, the chances are 100 per cent she has been physically one with a man. Well, in the discussion, the Christian and the non-Christian were arguing about the virgin birth. The discussion went back and forth, and at times got fairly heated. Some of it went like this:

"Women don't get pregnant without a man."

"But in this one case it happened, because that's the only way God could become a man."

"That's absurd, no one has ever witnessed such a thing."

"Yes they have, in the first century A.D."

"Well, that was a long time ago, and people were

superstitious. With science today, we know better."

"It depends what you mean by science. As a total system with no recourse to the supernatural, science becomes another religion. But if it is humbly trying to apply rigorous research methods to predict results, it should not rule-out any possibility, even miracles, at the outset."

"Christians always look to miracles when they run out of explanations."

"What's wrong with miracles?"

"They are a cop-out…"

And so it went. Things weren't going anywhere, until suddenly the believer said this:

"Of course, if you are a materialist, a virgin birth is impossible. But I challenge your materialism. You don't act like a materialist when you fall in love or get carried away with music. The Christian view is that we do not live in a purely materialist world, but in a supernatural one. That is, God is there, and has in fact made the entire universe. And continues to intervene. If he created the human birth process in the first place, why is there a problem believing he could make an exception in this one case, for a special purpose?"

The discussion stopped. They had gone far deeper than simply bits and pieces and had looked at presuppositions. Each of us carries around deep assumptions about how life works. Whether we can express them or not, we have these patterns, sometimes called a worldview. (See p. 43) This particular man was a materialist, although he had never said so in so many words. According to him, reality was simply atoms governed by chance, but there could be no God. What you see is what you've got, he thought. Even if you challenge him with eye witnesses, evidences, even detailed ones, it wouldn't matter, as he will always try to fit things in to his materialist views. He might think he is being scientific, but won't admit that science is not neutral. His science was obviously agenda-driven. So he needed to be challenged at the deepest level: his assumption about reality need to be put into question.

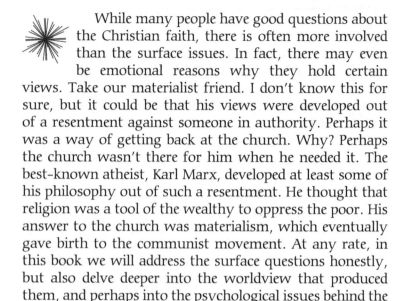

While many people have good questions about the Christian faith, there is often more involved than the surface issues. In fact, there may even be emotional reasons why they hold certain views. Take our materialist friend. I don't know this for sure, but it could be that his views were developed out of a resentment against someone in authority. Perhaps it was a way of getting back at the church. Why? Perhaps the church wasn't there for him when he needed it. The best-known atheist, Karl Marx, developed at least some of his philosophy out of such a resentment. He thought that religion was a tool of the wealthy to oppress the poor. His answer to the church was materialism, which eventually gave birth to the communist movement. At any rate, in this book we will address the surface questions honestly, but also delve deeper into the worldview that produced them, and perhaps into the psychological issues behind the worldview. Don't worry, though. You won't need to be a professional philosopher or psychologist to do this!

Are Words Important?

Some people don't like apologetics. Why do we need words, they ask? Why cannot people be won over simply because of the inherent beauty of the faith and the example of those who proclaim it? The answer is actually not as obvious as it might seem. Many people are not particularly drawn to folks who have all kinds of reasons why the Christian faith might be true and yet whose behavior is not particularly attractive. They would rather be drawn to it by the lives of those who believe it. And they have a point. How often do we hear it said, "he talks the talk, but doesn't walk the walk." Actions matter enormously. Who wants to be barraged by someone who knows it all but is not especially winsome? Jesus himself often won people over because he was such an authentic human being, so loving, such a defender of the weak, very kind to children, and the like. In my own experience of coming to faith the attractiveness and integrity of those who proclaimed it had a very important part to play. So why do we need words?

Let's be careful here, however, not to overstate things. Sure, Christians should be winsome, and they are not always so. However, there are plenty of winsome people around who represent other religions or even no religion at all. Does their winsomeness make their point of view true? Of course not. To put it the other way: although we sincerely could wish that believers were all attractive, to be honest, they are not. We are not! I once saw a bumper sticker that read: "Jesus, save me from your followers." A bit cynical, but you know what is meant.

Well, words do matter, as well as actions. Truth needs a proper defense. Not an aggressive defense, but a persuasive one. Unlike the Scarecrow in *The Wizard of Oz*, we have been given brains. We have been given the gift of language. We are rational creatures who need to think. Indeed, our life depends on it. That means we need not only actions but answers. The verse we mentioned above, 1 Peter 3:15 stresses the need to have logical, rational reasons for our faith. The word *apologia* in this verse contains the idea of "logos," from which we get the idea of reason and logic. Words matter because we are made to operate with logic. Without words our belief might just be purely emotional.

Today, many people have a serious problem with rational thought and logic. They don't trust words. Perhaps they have been disappointed in people who use empty words. They want authenticity. In many studies about young people suspicion of words and verbal arguments have been a constant theme. We mentioned that there can be emotional reasons for believing or not. Take the case of June (the name is made-up, though the person is real).[1] She met her now ex-husband Nick when she was seventeen, at a Pizza Hut. They "hooked up" and began to live together. June got pregnant and they married. But then Nick started abusing her. Pretty badly. She left him several times but became "codependent," meaning she couldn't quite live without him. She eventually divorced and went on to live

1. Christian Smith and Patricia Snell, *Souls in Transition: The Religious and Spiritual Lives of Emerging Adults*, New York: Oxford University Press, 2009, pp. 21-25.

a very rocky life. When asked where she thought she belonged, she answered that it could not be with Christians. When she drives by a church she cannot imagine going in. Why? She has been let down by the very people who are meant to support her, she decided. Did she give Christianity a chance? Not really. But her inability to trust others, anyone, Christian or not, is a roadblock to faith. To get through to June Christians will have to be very sensitive to her fragile personality. And surely, talking the talk will not be enough. Yet, surely, there will have to be talk at some point.

After all, the most clear form of God's revelation is in words. Specifically, it is in the Bible. While God does reveal himself in events, and in pictures (think of the decorations in the tabernacle and the temple, meant to symbolize various truths about him) the primary way he makes himself known is through the Word. There are many reasons for this choice.

First, God is a God of speech, a God of communication. The Son of God is identified as the Word (in Greek it is the *logos*, the same term we encountered in describing apologetics, see John 1:1-2, 14).

Second, having been made in his image, we human beings are also speaking creatures. There is an enormous difference, of course, between God's speech and ours, and yet there is a likeness between the two. Third, the Bible often tells us that God uses speech to communicate with us. Many of the prophetic books begin with such phrases as:"The word of the Lord came to me" (Hosea 1:1; Micah 1:1; see also Ps. 19:8).

The good news is we don't have to choose. Words and actions both count. Hearts and minds! The Apostle Paul says it well when he writes to the Thessalonians in his first epistle "… our gospel came to you not only in word, but also in power and in the Holy Spirit and with full conviction." (1:5)

He goes on to remind them of the integrity, even under much pressure, of his evangelistic team, when they came to preach the gospel to them. Thus it should be with us. We ought to strive for using the right words, and the right authority, and the right integrity. Notice he even adds that God's Holy Spirit was there with them. We need that too.

Why Defend The Gospel?

The Christian faith is worth defending. Why? First, it contains what you might call explanatory power: it can answer the most important questions anyone would want to ask. It addresses the most crucial issues anyone will ever face. It responds to our deepest aspirations. The right words help us find out life's meaning. That is why the prophets of old, and Jesus Christ himself, were great wordsmiths. Prophecy was not primarily about telling the future (fore-telling), but about interpreting the times by the light of God's truth (forth-telling).

Second, it can answer the deepest questions people will have, including ourselves. Before I was a Christian people gave me books on apologetics. Quite frankly very few of them got through to me. But once a believer, such books became quite helpful. Non-Christians and Christians alike will legitimately ask about the kinds of questions we are dealing with in this book, and many others: If there is a God, where is he? What about Islam? Did Jesus exist? What about other religions? What about evolution? Are there contradictions in the Bible? How can God be good in the face of so much evil? Apologetics not only begins to answer these issues but places them in the deeper context of personal aspirations and matters of the heart.

Third, it is simply a great privilege to be able to articulate matters of such importance. Doing apologetics is not a luxury or a hobby. To put it dramatically, it is a matter of life and death. What an honor it is to be entrusted with the task of defending and commending the Christian faith. As you move from childhood into adolescence, and then on to adulthood, you will find that these questions are not merely entertaining. They are crucial for your own growth and for the flourishing of human society.

For all these reasons, and more, the calling to engage in Christian apologetics is a noble one, and a most fascinating one. Being in God's world, we have nothing to fear. We can say with great confidence that "He who did not spare his own Son but gave him up for us all..." will also with him "graciously give us all things" (Rom. 8:32). This includes understanding our faith to the point where we can defend it before others. In this book we have looked briefly into some of the most important questions that arise in a young person's quest for understanding. I do hope you have been encouraged and challenged along the way. May the Lord bless you and keep you.

Discussion

1. Define apologetics in your own words.
2. Why are presuppositions important?
3. Do we need words, or do they just get in the way?
4. How would you encourage your friends and your church to engage in apologetics?

Appendices

In this section we wish to consider certain apologetic issues too specialized to include in the main body, but yet of significant interest and importance.

New Age

Just so we can know a bit more how a worldview works, let's take one. Actually, it is quite a diverse group of beliefs and many people who might not actually call themselves "New Agers" would still fit into its broad contours. New Age is a non-institutionalized movement, or ethos, which encompasses several themes. It has ancient roots in the esoteric mystics of the 18th and 19th century. Emanuel Swedenborg (1688-1772) was a Swedish scientist who believed he could travel back and forth from Heaven and Hell, and commune with angels and demons. The first to use the term "new age" was William Blake, the 19th century romantic poet who was in fact influenced by Swedenborg. Blake believed mankind would evolve into a more spiritual being in the New Age. This is all rather esoteric. But New Age became quite trendy in the 1960s and spread considerably among all kinds of people. The musical, *Hair* with its opening song, "Aquarius," helped propel New Age thinking into popular culture.

New Age draws on a combination of ideas. It is open to Asian spiritual traditions such as Buddhism. But it also incorporates distinctly Western views such as self-help techniques. New Agers claim that the mind and the body and the spirit are all interrelated. Accordingly, they are more open to soft medicines, like homeopathy, over the more aggressive medical approaches which use drugs. So far, nothing alarming about any of this. But wait, there is more. The practice of "crystal healing" comes out of the New Age mentality. It involves placing crystals in the room, or around the body in order to create an energy grid with healing powers.

One of the common observances of New Age is called "channeling." Channeling, or "mediumship" cultivates methods of communication with people, spirits or events from the past or from faraway. This supposedly allows someone to have access to lost or forgotten persons, and even to benefit from them under the right circumstances. There are various ways to practice channeling. Some believe they are specially gifted to contact angels and thus benefit from these heavenly beings. Others believe they can actually leave their own bodies and travel to places or persons who have answers to their questions.

Celtic Culture

To accept New Age does not necessarily mean you commit to these bizarre practices. Many people dabble with aspects of New Age, without worrying about specific doctrines or rituals. The recent fascination of many, including some Christians, with Celtic culture, may have overtones of New Age thinking. The Celts are a very ancient group, having occupied lands all over Europe. Although we have few accurate records of their culture and history, distinctive artifacts and languages are coming to light. Ireland has numbers of Celtic archeological sites which are being explored. They show a fascinating mythology as well as building technologies and artistic output. There were gods representing the sun, fertility, rivers, and so forth. The Celts were fascinated by numbers and riddles. For example, the *triskel* is a figure composed of three spirals, and was meant to represent three layers of the human soul. The number five signifies family order, and has led to the five provinces of Ireland as well as five rules to guide the provincial kings.

Christianity became integrated into Celtic culture and gave birth to a number of combinations. The most important was literacy. In his delightful book, *How the Irish Saved Civilization*, Thomas Cahill shows how the development of literacy, using both Latin and Old Irish, made possible the spread of both the Christian faith and a high civilization throughout Europe. There was also artwork. Some of it is very beautiful. *The Book of Kells* is an illuminated manuscript of the four Gospels plus some commentary. It is in the style called insular art (from the Latin for "island," meaning the British Isles). The style is full of energy and departs radically from the classical art Europe had inherited hitherto. Celtic crosses had a distinctive shape, and have become quite popular in recent times.

So, is anything wrong with this fascination about the Celts? Not necessarily. Where you need to be discerning is in the way sometimes this fascination can be mixed-in with New Age nonsense. Often people romanticize the Celts and in the process unthinkingly mix Christian faith with the more dangerous elements of this rival worldview. Year after year thousands visit the Scottish island of Iona, believing it to contain the remnants of the monastic culture of the Celts, and believing that they can find spiritual peace in this faraway mystery land. But the truth is, although in the past Iona played a role in the development of Celtic Christianity, today it has become a place for New Agers and others with a mix-and-match kind of spirituality.

There is often a disconnect between what we imagine about the Celts and the reality. For example, many people believe the ancient Celts were way ahead of their time on ecology. The reality is quite otherwise. The Celts had ways of dominating nature with little regard for anything like the ecosystem (which is a modern concept anyway). Another view is that the Celts were truly egalitarian. In fact, however, they were hierarchical and had a low view of women. Saint Columba forbade cattle on Iona because he believed where there were cattle there would be women, and women brought trouble![1]

Where Do We Find It?

So, here we have one case of a worldview, New Age, penetrating movements and cultures. New Age melds in with many other groups and interests besides Celtic

1. See, Ian Bradley, *Celtic Christianity: Making Myths and Chasing Dreams*, New York: Palgrave Macmillan, 1999.

culture. One of the more strange developments in recent times is the EST seminars. They were founded by Werner Erhard, and are meant to increase human potential. Typically a group meets over the weekend, having spent a considerable amount of money to get in. Then they spend most of the time trying to get "it." But no one really knows what "it" is. This may seem bizarre, but the EST seminars are wildly successful, even in the business community, where you would least expect it. One reason for the success is that EST is built on the principles of Zen Buddhism, which radically denies anything like reason or logic. Erhard used to say, "In life, understanding is the booby prize." These programs began in California but gradually spread over the Western world. Here, then New Age takes modern business seminars and turns them into a mystical experience.

Yet another example of mysticism related to New Age is yoga. While yoga as simply a form of exercise may be harmless, or even beneficiary, what many people do not know clearly is that there is behind the movements and positions in yoga a philosophy which promises freedom from our basic problems. Here, for example, is the claim of a scientific magazine defending yoga:

> Whether or not you believe in past lives, you certainly carry imprints from your childhood, your adolescence, and the culture you grew up in. We're skewed toward certain behaviors because our past choices have laid down grooves that keep sending us down the same pathways of thought and action. But yoga rejects karmic determinism. Not only is change possible, but many of the practices of yoga—including, especially, pranayama, mantra repetition, and meditation—are designed specifically to burn away the residues of karmic patterning, including stored patterns of guilt. Yoga's all-purpose prescription for cleaning up lingering guilt is *tapas*, or sustained, effortful practice. Tapas literally means "heat," or "friction." In the same way that we think of a fever burning away sickness in the body, the heat generated when you do intense pranayama or mantra practice burns away the

hidden memories that create toxic guilt. Along with the inner practice, it's important to do karma yoga. A person who feels guilt over having taken things that don't belong to him, for example, could make a point of giving away possessions or making donations to people who need it. The ultimate guilt-busting strategy is saying, "I'm sorry." When the guilty feelings are deep and lodged in the past, you may not know what you're asking forgiveness for. But the person from whom you're asking forgiveness is always yourself. You might think of this as asking forgiveness from your higher Self, your divine Self, your inner Buddha, or your inner child. What is important is that you direct your request inward.[2]

This approach to forgiveness, which directs the request to be forgiven inwardly, is absolutely baseless. Repetition of a "mantra" will only numb your mind, not give it relief from guilt. Only God can do that. Thus, if we direct our requests outward, to the God of all love, he will make your guilt go away.

Before you say, "I can't see how these strange practices affect me or my friends," you might want to look around. Have you heard anyone say, "I am spiritual, just not religious?" Or, "I think I can connect with the sacred, I just don't like the institutional church (or 'organized religion')?" Such pop mysticism is actually quite close to New Age, even though it lacks the specific fascination with Iona or EST. Mysticism really belongs to the same family.

So then, how is New Age a worldview, and is it really so dangerous? Remember we enumerated the various concerns shared by most worldviews:

- An ultimate power
- Human identity
- Why things went wrong
- How to live and be happy.

Does New Age Believe in an Ultimate Power?

Yes, although it is vague and elusive. Somewhere in the universe there is a spiritual force which is not personal, nor does it hold anyone to account. It gives you a way to have your cake and eat it too: you can be spiritual without having to be tied down to a church or a set of doctrines. Such an ultimate power is very perilous, because it pulls you in without challenging you to recognize your sins and shortcomings. And because of that you will not feel the need for a savior. The God revealed in the Bible is a Creator God, all-powerful, and yet compassionate, close at hand. He is Personal. We are accountable to him, and will be judged by him. He is ever present to guide us and show his love to us.

What Does New Age Say About Human Identity?

That I am capable of self-improvement simply by practicing certain disciplines, such as channeling, or meditating on "it." You are basically a passive person, needing to allow various forces to control you. This has the trappings of spirituality but none of its real content. Instead, the Scripture describes you as God's image-bearer, responsible for your calling. You are also a sinner who has turned from God and need forgiveness and reconciliation to God. If you turn to him in faith, then the work of Christ, his death and resurrection, will make you into the person you are meant to be.

What Does New Age Say About What Went Wrong?

If it says anything, it is that we are distant from the healing energies of the universe that could do us some good. People are in conflict because they are not submitted to these forces, and until they learn whatever "it" may be, they will be confused and divided. Again, the Bible tells quite a different story. The problem humanity faces is not distance from a vague healing force, but being in moral revolution against

God. That is what is wrong with the world: not that it is finite, but that it has turned against God morally.

What about Living?

New Age tells us we can float from one kind of power to the next. If we want to improve we may learn the art of channeling and such things, or we may simply drift around, hoping some force for good will come into our life. In reality New Age is profoundly self-centered. The Christian worldview, in contrast, believes that although sin has entered the world, yet through Jesus Christ sin can be forgiven and its pollution can be reversed. We who are believers can live the good life not in our own strength but in the power of Jesus Christ.

The next time you read something or meet someone who has a worldview different from yours, think about how they answer these four questions. Perhaps not every view can be put though this grid, but many can. See what you find out.

Discussion

1. What is New Age, in your own words? How is it a worldview?
2. Do you know anyone who falls into the general category of New Age thinking?
3. What explains the Christian fascination with New Age or Celtic culture?
4. What is meant by people who want to be "spiritual" yet not "religious?"
5. What are some of the specific points on which New Age and the biblical worldview differ?

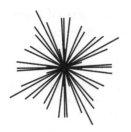

Is Islam the Same as Christianity?

s we said, there are many different religions. Surely, in the scheme of things, Islam must be considered one of the most significant religions. One of the great surprises of modern times is the rise of Islam. Of course, Islam has been around since 622, when Muhammad fled to Mecca with his followers. But recently the West has been caught off guard by so many manifestations of Islam coming into the limelight. From the Iranian Revolution of 1979, to the various attacks on Western targets in the name of Allah, we have suddenly been confronted by Muslim rhetoric and claims. Today, mosques are being built all over the West, and thousands of Muslim are immigrating. It is common to see veiled women in public places. Large sections of major cities are inhabited by Muslims.

Many countries struggle with how to accommodate Muslims. In France, for example, the government enacted a law forbidding certain veils in public places. The Burka, a garb fully covering a woman, except for the eyes, has been outlawed. Paranoia? Anti-religious? Intolerant? The French assert it is about security and the protection of women. Great Britain is more flexible, though hardly without problems. There are far more Muslims in Great Britain than in most other European countries. And they come from various backgrounds, unlike France, where most are from north Africa. In some cases, this means they bring their own conflicts among themselves into Britain. There is considerable pressure in a number of host countries to change the law in order to accommodate Sharia law, the basic Islamic code.

Where do we begin in order to assess this phenomenon we call Islam? The first thing to observe is that it is vast and complex. We often narrow our view of Islam to the Middle East. But did you know that the population of Islam is around 1.6 billion? Did you know that Muslims live on all five continents? This is over one fifth of the world's population. And did you know that about 60% of these live in Asia, while only 20% are in the Middle East and North Africa (although these two places have the highest number of officially Muslim countries)? China has more Muslims than Syria. India has the third-largest Muslim population worldwide. The first is Indonesia.

Besides all this, we find considerable diversity of expression among Muslims worldwide. The three major groups are the Sunnis, the Shiites, and the Sufis. The Sunnis, representing the vast majority of Muslims, believe that the four major successors of Muhammad (known as Caliphs) and their followers are the true Islam. This reign was interrupted just after World War I, at the break-up of the Ottoman Empire. The event was catastrophic, requiring reparations. Osama Bin Laden was a Sunni, and his attacks on the West represent this sentiment. The Shiites are a much smaller group. They believe that only one Caliph, Ali and his followers, are the legitimate successors to Muhammad. That rule ended in 931 when a great Imam (a teacher and political leader), disappeared. Shiites believe reparations began with the Islamic Revolution in Iran, 1979, when the Ayatollah Khomeini took over the government. Hezbollah is primarily Shiite. Sufis are a more mystical group which practices detachment from the world and travel into the presence of the divine. The "Whirling Dervishes" practice spinning around endlessly in order to banish earthly thoughts and concentrate on God.

Having said all this, in point of fact, most Muslims, whatever their school or history, believe very similar things. Very simply, Muslims believe in one God, called Allah, who is supreme, eternal, infinite, mighty and compassionate. To be a Muslim means, literally, to submit to Allah. He does not expect anything from human beings, although he requires that they obey his will. Muslims further believe that Allah sent numerous prophets, all of whom are mortal. They include Noah, Abraham (Ibrahim), Moses, Jesus (Issa) and Muhammad. Islam is a reform movement. Muhammad (570-632) believed that Judaism and Christianity are true, but that Jews and Christians have corrupted the original purity of those faiths. Muhammad led a great movement to reform pagan and lapsed Jews and Christians and revert them into pure monotheism, that is, the doctrine of God's oneness. Any idea of the Trinity is considered blasphemous. Muslims consider the claims that Jesus is God's Son to be utterly sacrilegious. Their holy book is the *Qur'an*, which they believe was revealed to Muhammad by the angel Gabriel (Gibral) and then written down by various successors. Finally, there will be a judgment when all accounts will be settled, followed by the afterlife, heaven and hell.

It is convenient to summarize Islamic practice with the "Five Pillars." They are: (1) The testimony of faith (the *Shahada*), which is "There is no God but Allah, and Muhammad is his prophet." (2) Prayer, which good Muslims should practice five times per day, often called from the minaret, the special tower erected in the center of a town or village. (3) Alms giving (*Zakat*) to support the needy, in specified amounts. (4) Fasting during the day in the month of Ramadan, the ninth lunar month. (5) Pilgrimage (the *hajj*) to Mecca, at least once during one's lifetime, if physically possible.

Folk Islam

All of this is official, orthodox Islam. However, the actual practice of Muslims is often quite different. While no Muslim would deny the official doctrines, yet the real world for him or her is a kind of folk religion that has little to do with these lofty concepts. For example, Muslims believe in the reality of the spirit world. There are many spirits in the invisible world, which exercise a certain influence. Ancestors become ghosts and can have an impact on our lives. There are curious figures known as *Jinn*, both good and bad. They are genies made of a smokeless flame. Angels and demons exist as well. Geographical locations can have special spiritual significance. Graves, holy cities, shrines, can give blessings to those who visit. Days and weeks too. For example, Friday is a good day, Wednesday is not. When someone takes ill, while you might want to visit the doctor, it is best to contact a medicine man or a witch, who can invoke special powers on the sick person.

Muslims often do not think Allah is really concerned for their daily lives. He is too far removed. So in practice, they try to engage various powers in order to succeed in life. Whether it be passing an exam, or meeting one's spouse, or having a career opportunity, Muslims will try to find out how to access some of these special invisible beings and get them on their side. It is most important to realize that most Muslims live on these two levels, the official, doctrinal level, and the folk religion level. One of our friends rents an apartment to a highly educated, highly sophisticated Muslim tenant. He is a prominent student in business, and attends one of the most prestigious graduate schools. Our friend told us about an incident which rather surprised him. He was finished doing the dishes and poured some very hot water down the drain. "Stop!" the tenant exclaimed. "You might disturb the *Jinn*." Apparently he was sure these smokeless flames tended to live in dark places such as drain pipes, and did not want to provoke them.

How They See Us

Before we discuss how to reach Muslims with Christian apologetics, it might be helpful to ask how they see us. After all, regardless of the issues, perception is enormously important. Only when we are truly sensitive to their perception of Christians can we hope to establish true communication with them. So, how do they see us?

First, many Muslims believe the Christian faith is vastly too complicated. Islam, by contrast, is simple. Only five pillars; only one God, not three Persons; and no real contact between Allah and us, certainly no incarnation.

Jesus may have had a virgin birth, but in no way was he God's Son, for Allah is not a man that he should have children. Second, Muslims often deeply resent Christian culture, particularly as it is manifested in the West. They have a long memory about what happened at the Crusades. They resent European colonialism of their homelands. They take exception to being excluded during the Cold War, when only two superpowers, the communist and the free world, called the shots. Most especially, they are shocked by popular culture. From the entertainment industry to the way people dress in public, popular culture is most disturbing to them. They find a phenomenon such as Lady Gaga to be appalling. The amount of skin shown in the streets and in the media is profoundly upsetting. And third, perhaps most concerning of all, they do not believe Christians care about their real needs. Christians are good at debating them, but they do not develop friendships, they are not supportive of legitimate concerns such as trying to have children or living with little money.[1]

Are these perceptions true? They are certainly not entirely false. Yet Christians would want to dissociate themselves from most of them. So, how do we then engage in meaningful conversation with our Muslim neighbors, considering these perceptions? Here are a few suggestions. First and foremost, an approach which is very simply human, though commended in Scripture, is to cultivate friendships with Muslims. Spend time together. Invite them to your place. Bring gifts. Not as a means to an end, but as an end in itself. Surely friendship is one of God's greatest gifts. And friendship also tells people something of what we value. Our Lord had friends. Think of Lazarus and his family. Think of John, the beloved disciple (John 20:2). Only when we meet Muslims in a non-threatening context, can trust be established, and then significant conversations can occur. When we lived in Southern France we had numerous opportunities to get to know Muslims, who were there to

---

1. For a number of these points I have benefitted greatly from the insights of the Rev. Daniel McBride, who spent 18 years in Dar es Salaam, Tanzania, with his family.

study or to find work. We found all of them quite open to talk about religion, unlike many French people.

How to Engage Muslim Friends

Second, what might we discuss, and what are the pitfalls? It is important to know that Muslims don't mind talking about religion, the way many of us do. Once trust has been established, it is fine to discuss theological matters. However, there are wise places to begin, and wise places to avoid, at least at first. For example, it is usually a mistake to attack the Qur'an. And it is a bad idea to put into question Muhammad's integrity. These are not good places to begin, although eventually they may figure in. Certainly there is nothing wrong with examining doctrines and identifying the key differences between the two faiths, Islamic and Christian. Indeed, we must get to those matters at some point. But we ought to make sure that at the same time as we underscore doctrinal differences, we care for the needs and aspirations of our friend. Do they need help guiding their children in school? Can we recommend a good doctor to them? Do we know a good grocery store? If many Muslims feel Christians do not care about their needs, we should look for opportunities to show them how we do care.

We also might demonstrate to our Muslim friends that we know something of the rich culture Islam has brought to the world. Many of us were brought up on stories such as One Thousand and One Nights, wherein Scheherazade tells stories to the vizier, and interrupts them so that he must hear the rest on the next day, instead of killing her. There is an abundant Persian literature. In short, a great literary tradition exists which should be acknowledged and celebrated. The same goes for architecture, painting and music. Health care as well. The ancient history of Islam shows a great concern for the treatment of the sick. Numerous state-of-the-art hospitals were created in the Islamic Empire. Al-Razi (865-925) discovered the effects of bacteria on disease. The most famous surgeon of the Empire was Al-Zahrawi, known in the West as

Albucasis (930-1013). He had great knowledge of
anatomy, and taught how to operate on varicose
veins, to make dental extractions, to reduce skull
fractures, and so on. North Africans introduced
Hindu-Arabic numerals to Europe (the ones we use, 1, 2,
3, etc., as opposed to Roman numerals I, II, III, etc.). We
can also admire their commitment to prayer. Five times
per day is no doubt legalistic, yet how many of us pray
that often? Perhaps the outstanding contribution of Islam
to civilization is in philosophy. During the "Kalam" period
(9th to 12th centuries) wherein scholars such as Mohammad
Ghazali encouraged a revival of religious science, including
jurisprudence and theology. If it were not for Muslims,
particularly Averroes (1126-1198), the West would likely
not known much about Aristotle.

Crucial Issues

Third, then, having said all this, we cannot ignore the
gaping hole in the lives of so many Muslims. Here are a
few of the issues you can discuss with a Muslim friend. To
begin with, God is one, but he is also three, as we have seen
above. Unless carefully explained this idea is shocking to a
Muslim, for he imagines that to have a son, a father must
engage in reproduction, which is profoundly undignified
for God. So you will want to explain that the Father and the
Son are co-eternal. Whatever sonship might mean within
the divine Trinity, it cannot mean anything like physical
procreation. You will also want to explain that God being
three Persons is the basis for all of personality. One God,
who is not three (called monism) cannot be a person. And
so it is that Allah is rather distant and nearly impersonal.
Allah really cannot come down to visit us, as God has done
in Jesus Christ. Allah and the biblical God are radically
different, to the point that we should resist calling Islam
and Christianity monotheistic religions. Islam is monistic,
not monotheistic, that is, the unity of Allah is incapable of
diversity, or true personality.

Another important difference: the Muslim view of sin
is quite weak. According to Islam, mankind was created

fragile, prone to make mistakes. Thus if I become angry with my neighbor or even assault him, that may be wrong, but it is not deeply sinful. The biblical worldview has it quite otherwise. Though originally created upright, man has fallen, and so you and I are profoundly corrupt. Anger and assault are indeed highly culpable. This is the reason that in order to be forgiven, Jesus Christ, God's son had to endure such a hideous death. Nothing else could atone for our sins. Muslims puzzle over our emphasis on the death and resurrection of Christ because they do not have the diagnosis we do.

Yes another difference is between the *Qur'an* and *the Bible*. Again, it is quite confusing to call Islam, Judaism and Christianity "religions of the book." The *Qur'an* was given to Muhammad in numerous episodes, orally. He was illiterate, and so was required to experience a state of ecstasy in order to receive messages from an angel. There were some twenty-nine followers who had heard the Qur'an and committed it to memory. Only later did his followers attempt to put those sayings into some kind of order, and establish an official text. There are 114 Suras, or sections, each with titles derived from themes or events in the history of Islam. The *Qur'an* is meant to clean up and correct elements of Judaism and Christianity that the faithful have got wrong. The Bible is a very different kind of book. It is a covenant constitution, that is, a written charter serving as the foundation for God's people. The various parts of the Bible are revealed over a period of time, in order to give a divine account of the events in the history of redemption. It is complete in itself, and we are forbidden to add or take away from it (Deut. 4:2; Prov. 30:5-6; Rev. 22:18-19).

Perhaps the most important difference is that Muslims are never quite sure God loves them, personally. They may call Allah merciful, but it is a distant concept at best. According to Islamic folklore, two angels will fight over us after we die, the one remembering our good deeds and the other our evil deeds. But you cannot know for sure, today, which one will win. Here is where the gospel of Christ is truly good news. Whoever asks humbly for forgiveness will receive it abundantly. "There is therefore now no condemnation for those who are in Christ Jesus," the Bible tells us (Rom. 8:1). "But if anyone does sin, we have an advocate with the Father, Jesus Christ the righteous" (1 John 2:1).

In my conversations with Muslims this is most often the place where not only our differences appear, but the breakthrough as well. Islam as a religion produces a good deal of fear. One is never quite certain whether Allah is for us or against us. Society must be ordered by a firm rule of law. It is all important for your sons and daughters to marry right. You never know whether the powers that be, whether visible or invisible, will work in your favor or not. In the biblical view, there is a world of difference. God cares deeply about our fears. But he tells us, that in Jesus we can have peace: "In the world you will have tribulation. But take heart, I have overcome the world" (John 16:33). The devil and his co-workers are real, but we are completely well-armed against them. "Resist the devil and he will flee from you," James tells us (4:7). Muslims have no such assurance. That is why they have such an extensive folk religion. Christians should not need to add anything to the finished work of Jesus Christ.

Third, there may be opportunities to spell-out the relationship between the West and the Christian faith. Not always easy to do, since there are very obvious influences from the Jewish and Christian traditions on European and North American civilization, but there are also many points of contradiction. For example, from the beginning Christians favored the practice of medical care and of poverty relief because of their view that human beings were made after God's image.[2] The abolition of the slave trade and of slavery in the British Empire was accomplished largely through Christian reformers, such as William Wilberforce. At the same time, Christian culture was deeply involved in the Crusades, a most sensitive point for Muslims. As we will see in a subsequent chapter, the real story of the Crusades is rather complex, but still, there needs to be wisdom in explaining those wars. Perhaps it should suffice to say that

---

2. See Gary Ferngren, *Medicine and Health Care in Early Christianity*, Baltimore: Johns Hopkins University Press, 2009.

Christian people have not always obeyed their Lord, who specifically forbade the use of violence for the purpose of extending his Kingdom. In more recent times, some Christians showed great courage in protecting the Jews from their Nazi persecutors. But others were silent, or even complicit. Perhaps apologies are needed. Asking forgiveness is not a weakness, but a strength.

The main point, however, is to insist with our Muslim friends that there is not an automatic association between the Christian faith and Western culture. While the Gospel has had a good deal to do with promoting freedom, and to a considerable extent the West has benefitted from that, the kind of license permitted in today's Western culture, including pornography, the downgrading of marriage, the push toward instant gratification, and so forth, has no connection to the biblical worldview whatsoever. One missionary friend of mine has told me there are churches where he could not bring his Muslim friends, because of the way the worship team dresses. While we certainly do not want to start a new fashion code based on modesty, it won't hurt to pay attention to the way we dress.

Political Implications

Finally, the political question will have to be addressed. Perhaps when you are a bit older, some of you may go into politics, either local or national. If you do, you will face the enormous challenge of immigration. Not only Muslims, but many different people are immigrating into the historic countries of the West. How can we receive them with justice, both for them and for those already established there? While this is not the place to go into details, we can suggest a way to think about it. Two approaches should be taken simultaneously. The first is assimilation. When you come to live in another country, it is important to understand its history and values. For example, France defines itself by the three watchwords of the French Revolution: Liberty, Equality, Fraternity. How are these values interpreted by the law? Here is one example. The concept of liberty has been applied by separating religion from the state. Such separation has certain implications for the state schools, as well as for churches and mosques, etc. If you come into France with the hope of living there long term, then you will need to assimilate into that tradition. That does not mean you must give up your religion and become a secular person. Rather, it means churches and individual Christians, just like mosques and Muslims, or atheists, for that matter, must play by the rules.

The second approach is participation. Particularly in a democracy, citizens have the right and the responsibility to join in the ongoing task of shaping towns, counties and nations. The very meaning of a republic (*res-publica*) is "a thing of the public," that is, a public affair. Thus, all people in the particular commonwealth should be represented. That is why we vote for our leaders, and pay taxes so that they may lead. In so doing we hope that the law of the land will truly be just for each and every citizen. True participation is something of a foreign concept for Muslims. They are used to being governed by lawyers who interpret the Sharia system, not by sending representatives to modify the law. Immigrating into a democracy means assimilation into the democratic tradition. But it also means participating in the democratic process. If one is a Muslim then it will mean giving up the hope of theocracy, whereby all of life, including political life, is dictated by religious rule. Yet it does not mean hiding in a ghetto or refusing to participate. Modern democracies are severely tested by the increasing presence of a theocratically minded people. But the Bible gives us sound principles whereby we may promote a just society even when some people may disagree with the biblical worldview.

Discussion

1. Were you surprised to learn about the different places and ethnic backgrounds of Muslims around the world?
2. Can you summarize the basic official beliefs of Muslims? How do they differ from "folk Islam?"
3. How do Muslims view Christians? Can knowing this help with reaching out to Muslims?
4. Why is it not advisable to lump Jews, Muslims and Christians together by such expressions as "religions of the book," and "a common ancestry in Abraham?"
5. Does one issue stand out as being a way to engage with Muslims?
6. What is the best attitude toward Muslim immigrants in your country?

What About the Crusades?

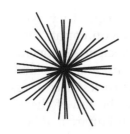

hy does this question come up regularly when discussing the Christian faith with skeptics? First, the Crusades really are a problem for anyone who believes Jesus' way is the way of love, and not force. If it is true that we are meant to "turn the other cheek" rather than compel people into submission, then just what were the Crusades trying to do, and how could they be doing it in the name of Christ?

Second, Muslims remember the Crusades as a terrible way to become victims of European aggression. When President George Bush unwittingly referred to America's "crusade" against terrorism, it drew the ire of a number of Muslims, including Soheib Bensheikh, Grand Mufti of the mosque in Marseille, France, who said the use of the word "was most unfortunate; it recalled the barbarous and unjust military operations against the Muslim world by Christian knights, who launched repeated attempts to capture Jerusalem over the course of several hundred years."

Third, a thoughtful person is concerned about any religion which would try to enforce its practices on a civilization from the top down. Christians, as well as other kinds of believers, are accused today of establishing religious obligations on societies which are meant to be governed by more liberal principles. One of the charges we most often hear is, are you not trying to impose your views on society?

Some History

Each of these concerns deserves a fair answer. What exactly were the Crusades? Basically they were religiously sanctioned military campaigns that occurred between

1095 and 1291 (some would argue they went a bit later). Depending on how you count, there were nine of them. The principal opponents were Roman Catholic Christians and Muslims. The situation in the Middle East ten centuries after Jesus had walked in Palestine was mixed. By the end of the 4th century, a significant part of the Roman Empire had been partitioned off into the Byzantine Empire, which was Christian. Palestine began to be called the Holy Land. There were monuments built above the places where Jesus and the apostles ministered. However, with the rise of Islam in the 7th century, Muhammad's Arab successors began to conquer many parts of the Middle East, including the Holy Land. Jerusalem was particularly targeted because it was believed to be the place Muhammad had ascended into heaven to receive instructions from Allah to take back to earth. The city was captured in 637, after a long siege. Interestingly, Christians and Jews were given freedom to live there and to worship. The occupation lasted about 500 years, although it often changed hands.

In the year 1009 the destruction of the Church of the Holy Sepulcher in Jerusalem was ordered by a powerful Muslim Caliph. The church had been built in the second century, on the ground where it is thought Jesus was crucified. Although the Muslims eventually allowed the Byzantines to rebuild the church (after they had paid an enormous tax!), they nevertheless often persecuted pilgrims who came to it from all over the world. They only relented when they began to understand that much of the wealth they gathered was brought into the city by pilgrims. In 1071 Jerusalem itself was captured by the Seljukian Turks, Muslims by culture and conviction.

Hearing the reports, Europeans were outraged. Well before the actual capture of Jerusalem by Christians Pope Alexander II approved a war by Spaniards against the Muslims, and allowed them to carry the flag of Saint Peter before them into battle. The word "Crusade" literally means, carrying the cross of Christ into combat. The first official Crusade, ordered by Pope Urban II in 1095, was called an "armed pilgrimage." Urban was responding to the urgent request for help against Muslim advances from the Byzantine Emperor Alexius I.

At least nine Crusades followed until the 13th century. After the successful first Crusade, the others were far more of a mixed bag. Thanks to the brilliant Muslim sultan Saladin (1138-1193), Muslims became more united and were able to ward off the Third Crusade. By 1144 Jerusalem was lost again to the Muslims. Major victims included the Jews, who had been living in relative peace in the Holy Lands, but who were often killed off during the Crusades. The end result of all these conflicts is not entirely clear. However, the Muslims basically won by wearing down the European armies.

The Moral Issues

Was anything accomplished during these 200 years of strife? Is there any justification whatsoever for these wars? The common view is that misguided European popes authorized barbarous killing sprees by religious fanatics who thought they were doing God's work in recapturing the high places of the Holy Land. All of this is clear violation of Jesus' teachings about non-resistance. Well, there is a grain of truth to this view. But the Crusades are famous for the misconceptions people have about them. First, in many ways these were defensive wars, not wars of aggression. Muslims had captured these Christian lands and often treated their victims badly. The Emperor therefore sent word to western European Christians to come over and help their friends in the East. And they did. Was this a classic example of a "just war?" that is, when asked by an ally to ward off an aggressor, just war theory allows violence as a last resort. There was Muslim aggression and a cry for help.

Is that all there is to it? No, there is much more. What becomes confusing is that the armies on the popes' side were more than simply combatants carrying out a national cause. A whole culture, a romance, really, of pilgrimages, noble knights, indulgences, and a general ethos of Christian moral traditions, including generosity and honor, gave the Europeans their motivation. These cultural elements gave a legitimacy for the Crusades that went beyond simply a political move or a classic just war. While the Bible authorizes people, Christian or not, to engage in a defensive war against an aggressor, it does not justify Christians in the name of Christ to go to war against unbelievers. What is confusing is that the Crusades had elements of both.

The Crusades thus mixed together a just cause, response to Arab aggression, and a more dubious cause, a culture of Christian honor. The Bible has a good deal to say about honor. It tells us humanity is crowned with glory and honor, simply be being made after God's image (Ps. 8:5). It tells us maintaining honor is a matter of walking uprightly (Ps. 84:11). The righteous man is not afraid of bad news, he gives generously to the poor with no concern for his own security; his honor is intact (Ps. 112:7-9). By contrast, the wicked man is angry and gnashes his teeth (v. 10). God's own honor is maintained not by words but by a heart commitment (Isa. 29:13). The honor of God is kept by serving him with integrity, and praising him as is his due (Rom. 1:21; 1 Tim. 1:17). Jesus Christ is honored because of his suffering and death (Heb. 2:9).

So, honor in itself is fine. War ought certainly to be conducted honorably. But honor alone cannot justify war. So, to our first question, we can answer that going to war is sometimes justified. Jesus' call to "turn the other cheek" is not a blanket statement covering every situation. Such a universal application would be absurd. It would mean we couldn't protect our children against a predator or home owners against a thief. The Book of Romans tells us God has constituted governments for the purpose of protecting its people in the name of justice (Rom. 13:4). So, in part, the Crusades were a defensive war to resist an aggressor. That much we may approve. But then, mixing in all these Christian themes such as the cross of Peter, going to war in the name of Christ and his Church, pilgrimage, honor and the like, these make the Crusades far less commendable. Such a confusion would never have happened had the church and the state been properly separated. But that would not occur until modern times.

The Muslim Perspective

To our second question, about Muslim sensitivity, we may say the following. While the Crusades may not have been the "barbarous and unjust military operations against the Muslim world" claimed by Soheib Bensheikh, it is incumbent upon us today to exercise great caution in the use of terminology that can be unnecessarily offensive. Put yourself in the position of a Muslim. He or she has been brought up to think that the wars of the 11th and 12th centuries were pure acts of aggression by the Roman Catholic church, a sort of holy war against Islam in the Middle East. That view is lopsided at best. But why put vinegar on the wound? Western people owe it to their Muslim friends to be very guarded about such language.

Was President Bush wrong to use the terminology of "crusading" against terrorism? Perhaps not wrong, but certainly unwise. One wonders at the wisdom of calling various political causes or ministries by the name "crusade." Somewhat like playing Tchaikovsky's *1812 Overture* in a French concert hall, at best it shows poor taste. (The program of this composition is Napoleon's defeat at Moscow, ending dramatically with the French national anthem being drowned out by the Russian canons and the Russian hymn "God the Omnipotent.") Language matters, and sometimes we can avoid unnecessary offence by just being careful. Of course we do not need to become absurdly sensitive. I know of people who refuse to sing "Onward Christian Soldiers" because it sounds aggressive. They forget two things, first, the line says "marching as to war," not "marching into war." Second, there is no question that the Bible often speaks of the Christian life using the metaphor of warfare (1 Cor. 14:8; 2 Cor. 10:3; Eph 6:11, 13).

Baptizing Violence?

Finally, the issue of the Crusades raises a larger point. What does the gospel say about the use of force? Does religion lead to violence? Richard Dawkins certainly thinks so. In *The Selfish Gene* he argues that religion causes wars by generating certainty. In this and other writings, Dawkins pushes the envelope. He goes so far as to assert that a religious education is a variety of child abuse! When asked about child abuse by priests, Dawkins of course thinks it terrible. However, he has actually stated that compared to the recent cases of child abuse by Roman Catholic priests, "the damage was arguably less than the long-term psychological damage inflicted by bringing the child up Catholic in the first place."[1] That is quite a statement. And he makes it several times and in several different places, lest we think it's a slip of the tongue. He seems to think religious education prevents one from thinking. An odd assessment indeed.

Of course, there is a surface plausibility to linking religion and violence. Examples are not hard to find. The Crusades seem to be a ripe candidate, although we have tried to show how complex they were. The modern slave trade began with a religious justification for taking Africans into forced labor in the colonies. Islamic Jihad has been used to justify acts of terror. From Turkey to West Africa to Lower Manhattan, the "call for Jihad" has been used to spur leaders on to Islamic conquest. Even within the same basic families of faith, there has been violent conflict. In Northern Ireland, for years "Protestants" and "Catholics" were at war. The unionists and the nationalists were pitted against one another in a bitter and violent conflict over the legitimacy of British rule. Yet religion was at the center. Or was it?

More likely, religious language was used to "baptize" conflicts that stem from a whole variety of motives. From political rivalries to personal revenge, or just plain sinfulness wars are the results of human nature gone wrong, not religion as such (James 4:1-3). Of course, the tendency to war in some religions varies greatly. For example, the conservative branch of Sunni Islam known as Wahhabism defines itself as a religion of holiness, requiring the violent purging not only of non-Muslims but of less-consistent Muslims as well. The classic example of a religion not at all tolerant of violence is the Amish. These folks have more-or-less stopped the clock in the German peasant culture of

1. Richard Dawkins, *The God Delusion*, Houghton Mifflin, 2006, p. 317

the 19th century. Even if provoked they will not retaliate or engage in self-defense. So statements such as Dawkins makes, "religious certainty always leads to violence," should be modified: some religions may be prone to violence, others not.

The Amish are a branch of the Christian faith. They are not the mainstream. In mainstream Christianity some violence is allowable, but only under a very narrow set of circumstances, only what is justifiable capital punishment and the kind of war known as "Just war." This concept only permits duly constituted entities, like the civil magistrate and the armed forces, to repulse aggressors when other options have been exhausted. There have been examples in history of just wars, though no war is totally pure. Most people would acknowledge the struggle of the free world against the Nazis during World War II to count as a just war. The Bible is a realistic book, and asserts that God has appointed governors and magistrates for the good of society. Not only do they reward good behavior but punish evil (Romans 13:1-7).

So, how are we to promote the coming of the kingdom of God ("thy will be done, thy kingdom come, on earth as it is in heaven")? The biblical answer is, primarily by making disciples. Disciple-making begins by the preaching of the gospel. But it is far more. There is a full-orbed program to be imparted. Jesus tells his own disciples to go into the world (the *ethnei!*) and "teach them all that I have commanded them" (Matt. 28:19-20). The New Testament is full of all kinds of teaching. Not only does it address the all-important matter of salvation, but it teaches about every realm of life, from marriage to employment to citizenship... every realm. Each task has its place. Being a husband or wife, being a church member, being a tax-payer, all of these are important. And while each is to be conducted under the Lordship of Christ, there should be no confusion of methods. We don't run the church like a corporation. We don't run the family like a government.

When we have these things straight, we can say what is right and what is wrong about certain wars. While the fundamental basis of the Christian faith is peaceful, the requirements of justice occasionally mean the propriety of civil protection by violence. Jesus indeed taught, "Blessed are the peacemakers, for they shall be called children of God" (Matt. 5:9). Following the Old Testament prophets, Jesus mounted a considerable critique of religion and violence. He was sharply condemning of the established religion of his day, because it was violent. Listen to his language: "Woe to you! For you build the tombs of the prophets whom your fathers killed. So you are witnesses and you consent to the deeds of your fathers, for they killed them, and you built their tombs ..." (Luke 11:47-48)

What about all those wars in the Old Testament, some of them authorized by God himself? This again is a special case from which we may not generalize. Much of the Old Testament brings God's judgments to bear before the end of the world. In that way, while these wars are very real, they also provide a warning, a picture of the end of the world at the last judgment. The Promised Land, won by legitimate conquest, is a picture of heaven. Its civil laws were a picture of the order in heaven. The sacrifice of animals is a picture of the ultimate sacrifice of Christ. Dietary laws forbidding the consumption of certain kinds of meats was a picture of the purity of God's people. And so forth. The wars conducted by men like Joshua and David were real, to be sure, but they announced the larger reality of the judgment to come. They were real justice, wherein evil peoples were eradicated. But those were limited in scope and in time. The fundamental biblical religion is one of peace. David wanted to build a temple to the Lord but was forbidden to do so, because he had gone to war. Even though his wars were approved by God he still could not erect a house for God. That had to wait for his son, Solomon (that name means "peace") to do this (see 1 Kings 5:1-6). The New Testament ushers in the great age of peace, of God's patience, before the world's end. Today, war for the advancement of the kingdom is utterly forbidden.

Perhaps Dawkins' fatal flaw is his rather amazing claim, "I do not believe there is an atheist in the world who would bulldoze Mecca – or Chartres, York Minster, or Notre Dame."[2] Actually the record says the opposite. There has been no more violent régime seeking to destroy churches and monasteries than the Soviet Union, especially under the atheist Stalin. In Romania, under the tyrannical atheist Nicolae Ceaucescu, dissidents like Petre Tutea (1902–1991) suffered unspeakable mental and physical abuse because he was a Christian. His faith actually helped him resist an atheist persecution.

But Richard Dawkins apart, to the larger question posed by our investigation of the Crusades, what does the gospel say about the use of force? We can answer that in the New Testament era, we are not permitted to use force for the promotion of the kingdom of God, except in the case of a legitimate just war, sanctioned by government, and not by individuals. If the Crusades were a mistake, because they confused two different callings, just war and a Christian culture of honor, then what we need to work on is separating those callings, all within the single Lordship of Christ.

Discussion

1. What caused the First Crusade?
2. Were the Crusades in any way justified?
3. How can we best understand the Medieval mentality that led to the Crusades?
4. Do we owe Muslims an explanation or apology?
5. Is it ever justified to use force for the advancement of Christ's Kingdom?

---

2. *The God Delusion*, pp. 303–4.

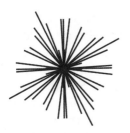

Are there Vampires?

Some may wonder what kind of question this is, and what it is doing in a book on apologetics for young people. Most teenagers know. Here is another worldview, a religion, really, one which is well worth understanding, whether or not you care!

The series of novels, followed by films, by Stephanie Meyer, has become wildly popular among young people. The first story, *Twilight*, climbed up the best-seller list early on, reaching well over one million books and huge box-office sales for the films. These are romance novels about a teenage girl, Bella Swan, whose family moves to Forks, in Washington, where she falls in love with a 104 year old vampire named Edward. At first the relationship is platonic, with no sex. In a following episode the two get married and Bella becomes a vampire in the process.

The story is, as one author describes it, about vampires that are "defanged." Why? Because they bear little resemblance to the older, terrifying vampires who prey on victims to suck their blood.[1] These modern vampires are vegetarians, and the only blood they will have is animal blood. The attraction of the story, especially to teenaged girls, is partly because Edward is very good-looking, but out-of-reach. Not only is he a vampire, and thus potentially dangerous, but he is a bit vulnerable, having fallen in love with Bella, a mortal. Edward worries that he could become violent, which would be according to his nature, but Bella defends him by saying his condition is not his fault.

Furthermore, Bella considers herself to be a typical teen, rather plain and even clumsy, and fears boys will not

---

1. Susannah Clements, *The Vampire Defanged: How the Embodiment of Evil Became a Romantic Hero*, Grand Rapids: Baker/Brazos, 2011.

necessarily be drawn to her. She feels alienated. She asks at one point: "Sometimes I wondered if I was seeing the same things through my eyes that the rest of the world was seeing through theirs. Maybe there's a glitch in my brain."[2] So Edward's attentiveness is welcomed as coming from a fellow outsider. There is a real camaraderie between them. How can they be real equals? Although Edward is in the role of the hero who rescues the girl, he admits at one point that Bella also rescued him. From what? From the terrible fate of being a vampire, condemned to live eternally without the true intimacy of a romantic relationship.

Another reason for the attraction of these stories to teenagers is that they portray romance without sex (at least at first). Many young women long for intimacy, but resent men who want only one thing, their bodies. Bella's relationship to Edward, at least in this regard, seems safe. The love is very idealized. In the first sequel, *New Moon*, Bella tells Edward that her love for him is so committed, he can have her soul. Her love thus trumps any real moral concerns. Every now and then it occurs to Bella that Edward has killed people, but that worry is only fleeting. At one point, she comforts herself with the explanation, "Love is irrational, I reminded myself. The more you loved someone, the less sense anything made"[3]

Vampire stories were never like this in the beginning. Nineteenth-century vampires were scary, blood-sucking creatures who preyed on (mostly) women to make them hideously immortal. Why this shift to kinder, gentler vampires? Why such intense love for a creature who is not quite human? And what does this have to do with apologetics? First, these stories tell us something about where our culture is going. Let's think about the defanging. A fancy word for that is "secularization." We live in a secular world, and vampire stories are a good illustration of that. How did it all happen? Vampire stories are very old, and they are found in many different cultures.

---

2. Stephanie Meyer, *Twilight*, New York: Little, Brown, 2005, p. 12.
3. Stephanie Meyer, *New Moon*, New York: Little, Brown, 2006, p. 340.

Until quite recently vampires represented the embodiment of evil. In Bram Stoker's 1897 classic Victorian novel, *Dracula*, Jonathan Harker wants to visit the Castle where count Dracula resides. Fortunately for him, a local peasant girl gives him a crucifix. Even though he is deeply anti-Catholic, he finally takes it. When he meets the count he finds out how wicked he is. He lives in a coffin. He is awake at night, prowling around with an evil design to suck the blood of human beings in order to turn them into one of his own kind. Eventually, Harker realizes that the cross given to him by the peasant girl can ward off the count. The cross saves him. Unlike many modern movies, where vampires are portrayed more sympathetically, Stoker's Dracula is a horrible, ugly man who crawls about his castle like a serpent. Vampires in these earlier stories are like devils, and are clearly metaphors for sin. Harker is something like a reluctant prophet who discovers that the vampire is a usurper of God's ways. Only by his knowledge of the truth about the vampire can he attain redemption. While one might not call these older stories Christian from beginning to end, they are clearly cautionary tales with a Christian theme.

Not so the more modern stories. Beginning with the tongue-in-cheek *Buffy the Vampire Slayer*, and then Sookie Stackhouse's *Southern Vampire Mysteries*, ones like *Dead and Gone*, we can trace the process of secularization (the loss of a specifically religious interpretation), where vampires become less the symbol of sin and more a romantic hero who is somewhat dangerous. Clearly, the figure of the vampire has changed according to our cultural expectations. Today, religious and theological meaning has been replaced by a more secular or naturalistic worldview in many different realms, so a parallel shift in the vampire genre is not altogether surprising.

The Reality Of The Supernatural

So, vampire culture represents a general cultural drift, namely, secularization. Second, is there anything positive about these stories? Well, maybe. In a day where we often don't stress Christian values, vampires could connect us with the supernatural. Even though they are completely fictitious, they can remind us that there is an invisible world.

According to the biblical worldview, there is a visible portion and an invisible portion to our universe. And there are beings besides God himself who exist in the unseen realm. But not all of them are good. Christians believe we should pay some attention to the reality of the invisible realm, without getting obsessed with it. Although the Bible does not give a great many details here, we know that there are angels, and that they serve God's purposes. Furthermore, there is a real devil and his real minions. It appears there was a fall in the angelic world, and that now demons roam around the earth who wish us evil. These forces are real, and vampire stories remind us of that.

Our response to this reality should not be fear, but sober realism, tempered with hope. The devil is an enemy, but he is a conquered enemy, one who is easily resisted (James 4:7). In this sense the older vampire stories are far closer to the truth than the newer ones. Naturally we cannot ward off demons with crucifixes, but the symbolism is right: through Jesus' death, all principalities and powers have been disarmed at the cross of Christ (Col. 2:11).

True Love

Third, is the observation that the modern vampire stories remind us that we are made for intimacy. Bella's love for Edward is an absurd fiction. But we realize a bit of why so many young women, and a few young men, desire this kind of love. They rightly want a man who will respect them, gently lead them, but not abuse them. True love according to the Bible is not dangerous, of course, it is ultimately quite safe. And yet there is a healthy risk involved in getting close to someone else. Marriage, one of the deepest kinds of love between human beings, has adventure built into it. Young men and young women are right to long for such a journey with a life's partner. The *Twilight* series is hopelessly unrealistic about the nature of the adventure. True love between a man and a woman involves facing life's problems together, with prayer, and with patience and resolve. Of course, one of the main purposes of marriage is to have children. Not every couple can have this gift, but it is central to God's plan for humanity that there be procreation (Gen. 1:28; 4:1; Luke 18:16). While in some of the Vampire stories babies may be born, one does not have any sense that having children is in any way connected to the biblical view of the family.

The traditional wedding vows are neither sentimental nor cynical.[4] "To have and to hold from this day forward, for better for worse, for richer or poorer, in sickness and in health, to love and to cherish, 'til death do us part..." These vows are not in the least sentimental. They are realistic. Things happen even in the best of marriages. Reversals of fortunes, disease, and so forth. Better not be over-romantic about married life. At the same time we don't want to embrace cynicism. The cynic says life is full of problems and the best we can do is be jaded and distrustful. Christian marriage says we can "have" and we can "hold" our dearest friend. A marriage without trust is on its way to disaster. So, Christians will want to be realistic, but full of hope and love.

Good Writing

Fourth, and finally, Christians should be more conversant with literature in general. How is this related to the vampire series? Because they purport to be literature. You see the books in airports and popular bookstores all over. So, how should Christians respond to literature, particularly this kind of genre? Some refuse to read any stories having to do with the supernatural. We may respect that decision. It is a matter of conscience. Yet, this approach is not easy to practice consistently. For example, Christians who refuse to read J. K. Rowling's Harry Potter stories because they portray magic are not averse to reading C. S. Lewis' *Chronicles of Narnia* which also contain magic. They argue that the

---

4. I owe this insight to Dick Keyes, in a wedding sermon.

magic in Harry Potter is not framed properly to portray the standards of good and evil according to Scripture. This is at best a debatable point. A careful look at the Harry Potter tales reveals that while not overtly Christian, there is there a moral structure, and good triumphs over evil in the end. And there is plenty of Christian symbolism throughout. And there is redemption. In *The Deathly Hallows* we have a flashback into the dreadful murder of the Potter family by the evil Voldemort. Just before the flashback, Harry and his friends are visiting the church graveyard on Christmas Eve. They first see the graves of Kendra and Ariana Dumbledore, mother and sister to the late headmaster of the school called Hogwarts (these names are admittedly contrived). On the grave is the inscription, "Where your treasure is, there will your heart be also," from Matthew 6:21. On another tomb one reads "The last enemy that shall be destroyed is death," from 1 Corinthians 15:26. Then the author explains that there is a power greater than the evil of Voldemort, it is the power of a love that is willing to sacrifice life itself for the sake of another. Harry's friends, indeed, stood by him at the risk of their own lives. While these stories are not Christian allegories, they are moral tales and redemption is not far from the surface.

Having said that, the Harry Potter series is not on the level with some of the great classics. Christians have often not been critically aware of the difference between good and bad literature. But, isn't good or bad writing a matter of taste? Taste is important, but it needs to be educated. Just as food and drink can be an acquired taste, so must literature. But how can we know the difference. Consider the following lines from Stephanie Meyer's *Eclipse*:

> 'Bella?'

> Edward's soft voice came from behind me. I turned to see him spring lightly up the porch steps, his hair windblown from running. He pulled me into his arms at once, just like he had in the parking lot, and kissed me again.

> This kiss frightened me. There was too much tension, too strong an edge to the way his lips crushed mine - like he was afraid we had only so much time left to us.

Almost everything about this text is poorly written! Edward is the vampire, the hero of the series. The adjectives used to describe him are so direct, nothing is left to the imagination. His voice is soft. He springs lightly up the porch steps. His hair is windblown from running. Instead of writing more subtly about the tone of his voice, or adding a few similes, this description is stark. Similarly the kiss frightens her because there was "too strong an edge to the way his lips crushed mine." What a statement! Can a kiss have an edge? And what is a too strong edge? The text also contains common mistakes in grammar or usage. One should not write, "just like he did" but "just as he did." Nor is "like he was afraid" quite right. Better to say, "as though he were afraid."

These examples can be found throughout the books. The end result is that the readers are not treated to the riches of metaphor, nor to the colors of a good description.

Compare to these lines from Charles Dickens' Great Expectations:

> Out of my thoughts! You are part of my existence, part of myself. You have been in every line I have ever read, since I first came here, the rough common boy whose poor heart you wounded even then. You have been in every prospect I have ever seen since—on the river, on the sails of the ships, on the marshes, in the clouds, in the light, in the darkness, in the wind, in the woods, in the sea, in the streets. You have been the embodiment of every graceful fancy that my mind has ever become acquainted with. The stones of which the strongest London buildings are made, are not more real, or more impossible to be displaced by your hands, than your presence and influence have been to me, there and everywhere, and will be. Estella, to the last hour of my life, you cannot choose but remain part of my character, part of the little good in me, part of the evil. But, in this separation I associate you only with the good, and I will faithfully hold you to that always, for you must have done me far more good than harm, let me feel now what sharp distress I may. O God bless you, God forgive you!

Here, the hero, Pip, is declaring his undying love to Estella, and compares her presence to the reality of the natural world, even to stones of the buildings in London. He believes in her goodness, and acknowledges her strong influence on him. If you read it out loud, you get a sense of music of these lines. Gentle reader, I would urge you to rediscover such marvelous literature! You can do far better than to fall in love with a defanged vampire!

And by the way, if any of you are called into the arts, this is a noble vocation. Christians in the arts face special challenges and special opportunities. The challenges include the often hostile environment you may face when training with the best. Whether art school, theater training, music conservatory, or film school, you may find that standing up for the Christian faith is hard. This does not mean that to be Christian you must always paint crucifixes or script a happy ending. While there ought to be redemption in your art work it should come through suffering and at the cost of the atonement of Christ. The opportunities include the multiple ways you can enhance our fallen world with beauty, the chance to script something hopeful, or sing songs that are true to our worldview.

Discussion

1. Why is the *Twilight* series so vastly popular among young people?
2. What do "defanged" vampires tell us about our contemporary culture?
3. Is it wrong to long for true love?
4. Are there really invisible creatures? What influence do they have?
5. What is so important about good writing, or good art, or good music?

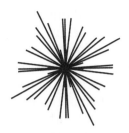

Do We Need God to be Good?

The great Russian novelist Fyodor Dostoyevsky answered this question in his powerful novel, *The Brothers Karamazov*. One of the main characters, Ivan, who is an atheist, made the famous remark: "If there is no immortality then everything is permitted."

What he was saying is that without the absolutes of Christian hope, it is not so much that we will be restricted to a bleak world, but that there will be no restraints. Dostoyevsky was profoundly disturbed by the question of morality without God. His extraordinary novel is the story of an evil father, and of the discussion between his four sons about whether it would be justified to kill him. Zossima Karamazov was a despicable person. He abused almost everyone. He produced a child through the village madwoman. He became rich by ravishing his competitors. Ivan was the philosopher of the group who justified the murder because he believed if there were a God he was unjust. Any God who allows children to suffer is no God at all. In an imaginative chapter, which is famous in all of literature, "The Grand Inquisitor," Jesus returns to a town in Spain controlled by the Inquisition, the arm of the Roman Catholic Church charged with controlling heresy. He preaches compassion and liberty. But the religious authorities capture him and tell him no one can be happy with liberty. Instead, they need "miracle, mystery and authority," that is, the church's control. The catholic church needs to correct God's insufficiencies. For example, Jesus refused to change the stones into bread at Satan's temptation. That was a mistake, because people are hungry.

The novel is disturbing. In the end, one of the brothers, Smerdyakov, does murder their father. He had been persuaded that in a world without God, "everything is permitted." Sadly, the innocent Dmitri was found guilty and condemned to exile.

What is the background for this amazing story? Dostoyevsky was aware of the liberal thinkers of his day who wanted to do away with the cruel Tsars. The idea is very tempting, since these rulers often were arbitrary and evil. But Dostoyevsky in the end cannot endorse their philosophy. The reason is that too much is at stake. The liberals really made no difference between killing the Tsar and killing God himself. As Thomas G. West puts it, "The crude and smirking Smerdyakov, consumed by hate, is the genuine expression of the liberal intelligentsia's revolt against the authority of the biological father, the father Tsar, the fathers of the Church, and God the Father."[1] Dostoyevsky knew that without the ultimate authority of God, even administered through less-than-perfect rulers and fathers, the world would end in chaos. Without knowing it, he predicted the 20th century with its irreligious tyrants, Hitler and Lenin and so many others.

Is it really not possible to be good without God? There are plenty of good people around who do not happen to believe in God. We all know them. And there are plenty of not very good people who nevertheless believe in God. But the real question is not whether there might be individual cases of people who are good or bad with or without God, but whether there is a strong enough fundamental framework for people who actually can practice being good.

Is To Ought

Here is a basic way of stating the issue. David Hume, the skeptical Enlightenment philosopher, once declared that you cannot derive an ought from an is. In his *Treatise of Human Nature* (1739) he expresses "surprise" at how fast one moves from an is statement about, say the nature

---

1. "Sin of the Fathers," a book review of Joseph Frank: *Dostoevsky: The Mantle of the Prophet, 1871-1881*, vol 5 in the series on Fyodor Dostoevsky, Princeton: P U. P., 2002, in *Claremont Review of Books* II/4, Fall, 2002, p. 29.

of God, to an ought statement about behavior, without any real connection. Much later the philosopher G. E. Moore would call this the "naturalistic fallacy," trying to derive ethics from nature.

Plenty of thinkers have developed high ethical systems not apparently connected with nature, or, even less, to God. But can they live successfully within their systems? You may be familiar with Augustine's *Confessions*. It's one of the great spiritual masterpieces. It is a meditation of the 5th century giant, Saint Augustine. It is full of prayer, theological truths, Scripture, and the personal disclosures of a man deeply in need of God, and deeply filled by the loving God without whom we are all restless. In it he tells of his best friend, Alypius.[2] He was a younger man, from the same home town in North Africa. They discussed everything together. Before both were Christians they were professor and student. Alypius had a singular weakness: he "had lost his heart and his head to the games in the amphitheater." You may know about these horrible games, violent, blood-thirsty, where gladiators fought animals and each other to the death, merely for entertainment. At one point, Augustine was used (without knowing it) to prevent him from wasting his talents in: "this thoughtless, impetuous enthusiasm for futile pastimes."

One day Alypius showed up at the lesson and Augustine is illustrating from the arena. His words were used to cure him (at least temporarily) of this habit:

> For after he had heard my words, Alypius hastened to drag himself out of the deep pitfall into which, dazzled by the allure of pleasure, he had plunged of his own accord. By a great effort of self-control he shook himself free of all the dirt of the arena and never went near it again.

But this was not sufficient. Like Augustine, he began to trust in self-control based on a false system of ethics, taught by Manichaeism.

---

2. See *Confessions* VI, 7–9. I have discussed this episode at some length in *Lifting the Veil: The Face of Truth*, Phillipsburg, NJ: P & R Publishing, 2001, pp. 122-6.

He particularly admired the Manichees for their ostensible continence, which he thought quite genuine, though of course it was merely a nonsensical and deceitful method of trapping precious souls which had not learnt to feel the depth of real virtue... (VI.7)

The two men then go to Rome. And here, Alypius had a terrible downfall. He got an "extraordinary craving for gladiatorial shows." And though he tried to resist, his friends enticed him: "you may drag me there bodily... but it will be just as if I were not present, I shall prove myself stronger than you or the games." (VI.8) So he went to a game, but decided he could still resist, by closing his eyes. As Augustine said, though, "if only he had closed his ears as well!" He got right back into the blood and violence of the games. The following description could be a text book account of addiction:

> For an incident in the fight drew a great roar from the crowd, and this thrilled him so deeply that he could not contain his curiosity. Whatever caused the uproar, he was confident that, if he saw it, he would find it repulsive and remain master of himself. So he opened his eyes, and his soul was stabbed with a wound more deadly than any which the gladiator, whom he was so anxious to see, had received in his body. He fell, and fell more pitifully than the man whose fall had drawn that roar of excitement from the crowd. The din had pierced his ears and forced him to open his eyes, laying his soul open to receive the wound which struck it down. He reveled in the wickedness. He watched and cheered and 'grew hot with excitement.' He became a leader in future games.

As Augustine comments,

> This was presumption, not courage. The weakness of his soul was in relying upon itself instead of trusting in you. (VI.8) Yet you stretched out your almighty, ever merciful hand, O God, and rescued him from this madness. You taught him to trust in you, not in himself.

But this was much later. He eventually became a bishop and preached, administered the sacraments and judged.

Why I am telling you this story?[3] For one thing, because it is a great example of pride, spiritual pride. When we think we are strong, danger lurks. When we think we can resist temptation, we are close to falling. The system of ethics taught in ancient Greece was lofty, noble, admirable, but it could not give strength to face the trials of life. Simply put, it had certain high standards. But it lacked the power of goodness. And that is the other thing. We can have a decent ethical system without god, but we cannot have the requisite power to live within it consistently. Only Jesus Christ can provide that kind of power.

Borrowed Capital

So, at one level, of course, you can be good without God. If by "good" you mean "upright," or "generous," or even "honest," we can find many people who have those qualities, while not necessarily depending on God. And these are admirable qualities. God approves them. But he wants something far deeper. He wants for us to find our meaning, our purpose, our hope in him through the gospel. The Christian faith is not first and foremost about moral improvement. That comes in the bargain, no doubt. But it is first and foremost about friendship with God. It is first and foremost about a relationship.

Indeed, being good in the biblical sense is to have received the free gift of God's righteousness so that we may be buried with Jesus into his death and raised up with him into his life (Rom. 3:22-26, 6:1-4). God wants us to know him, a knowledge that is life (John 17:3)! Jesus has prayed that we may be one with him, with the same oneness as the Father has with the Son (John 17: 11). This is friendship at the deepest, most spiritual level. Our usual sense of goodness is far, far too petty, compared with this lofty one.

The great danger is that in trying to be good without God we might have those good surface virtues, but not

---

3. I have told it elsewhere in a slightly different light. See *the face of Truth: Lifting the Veil*, Phillipsburg, NJ: P & R Publishing, 2001, pp. 121-5.

the knowledge that leads to life and friendship. One reason the Pharisees come in for a strong drubbing, is because they not only fancied themselves good, which in a certain sense they were, but because they thought that is all God wanted of them. And the truth is, they weren't as good as they imagined. Their hearts were not clean at all. "Woe to you, scribes and Pharisees," Jesus declared, "for you clean the outside of the cup and the plate, but inside they are full of greed and self-indulgence" (Matt 23:25). They had surface goodness. And some of them were better than others. But they lived on borrowed capital, not on the heart of the gospel.

Only if you are a true Christian can you begin to have any kind of significant moral life, that is, the goodness that is based on the knowledge and friendship with God himself. Then we really can experience being dead to sin and alive to the new life in Christ. Now, that's true goodness.

Discussion

1. Are there good people in the world who do not need God?
2. How does Dostoyevsky explain that without God you cannot be truly good?
3. How does Alypius reveal the impossibility of finding moral power without grace?
4. What is the fundamental nature of goodness, according to the Bible?

These books are representative, rather than exhaustive. They vary in their level of difficulty, so young people should not be discouraged if not all of them are equally accessible. There is something here for everyone.

General Principles for Doing Apologetics

Jerram Barrs, *The Heart of Evangelism*. Wheaton: Crossway, 2001

G. K. Chesterton, *Orthodoxy*. Garden City: Doubleday, 1959

Charles Colson, *Loving God*. Grand Rapids: Zondervan, 1983

G. K. Chesterton: *The Everlasting Man*. Fort Collins: Ignatius Press, 1999

William Edgar, *Reasons of the Heart*. Grand Rapids: Baker/Hourglass, 1996

William Edgar, *The Face of Truth: Lifting the Veil*. Phillipsburg: P & R, 2001

Jean Bethke Elshtain, *Who Are We?* Grand Rapids: Eerdmans, 2000

John M. Frame, *Apologetics to the Glory of God*. Phillipsburg: P & R Publishers, 1994

Michael Green & Gordon Carkner, *Ten Myths about Christianity*. Batavia: Lion, 1988

Os Guinness, *The Journey*. Colorado Springs: NavPress, 2001

Timothy Keller, *Counterfeit Gods*. New York: Dutton, 2009
_____ *The Prodigal God*. Dutton/Adult, 2008 (see also the DVD & discussion guide)
_____ *The Reason for God*. Dutton/Penguin, 2008

C. S. Lewis, *Mere Christianity*. New York: Macmillan, 1960

David Lyon, *Jesus in Disneyland: Religion in Postmodern Times*. Cambridge: Polity Press, 2000

K. Scott Oliphint, *The Battle Belongs to the Lord: The Power of Scripture for Defending Our Faith*. Phillipsburg: P & R Publishing, 2003

James I. Packer, *Knowing Man*. Westchester: Cornerstone, 1979

Francis A. Schaeffer, *The God Who Is There*. Downers Grove: InterVarsity Press, 1968

R. C. Sproul, *Reason to Believe: A Response to Common Objections to Christianity*. Grand Rapids: Zondervan, 1978

Cornelius Van Til, *Why I Believe in God*. Philadelphia: Great Commission Publications, n.d.

Worldview and Our World

David Aikman, *Great Souls*. Dallas: Word, 1998

Harry Blamires, *The Christian Mind*. London: SPCK, 1963

David J. Bosch, *Believing in the Future: Toward a Missiology of Western Culture*. Harrisburg: Trinity Press, 1995

Michael W. Goheen & Craig Bartholomew, *Living at the Crossroads: An Introduction to Christian Worldview*. Grand Rapids: Baker, 2008

Mark R. Gornik: *To Live in Peace: Biblical Faith and the Changing Inner City*. Grand Rapids: Eerdmans, 2002

Os Guinness: *The Call: Finding and Fulfilling the Central Purpose of Your Life*. Dallas: Word, 1998
_____ *The Last Christian on Earth*. Regal, 2010

David Bruce Hegeman: *Plowing in Hope: Toward a Biblical Theology of Culture*. Moscow: Canon Press, 1999

Dick Keyes, *Seeing through Cynicism*. Downers Grove: Inter-Varsity Press, 2006

Abraham Kuyper, *Lectures on Calvinism: The Stone Foundation Lectures*. Grand Rapids: Eerdmans, 1931

Paul Lakeland, *Postmodernity: Christian Identity in a Fragmented Age*. Fortress, 1997

Kelley Monroe, *Finding God at Harvard*. ed. Grand Rapids: Zondervan, 1995

Richard J. Mouw, *Distorted Truth: What Every Christian Needs to Know about the Battle for the Mind*. San Francisco: Harper & Row, 1989
_____ *When the Kings Come Marching In*. Grand Rapids: Eerdmans, 1984

Lesslie Newbigin, *Foolishness to the Greeks: The Gospel and Western Culture*. Grand Rapids: Eerdmans, 1979

Mark Noll, *Turning Points: Decisive Moments in the History of Christianity*. Grand Rapids: Baker, 1997

James I. Packer, *Knowing Man*. Westchester: Cornerstone, 1979

Francis A. Schaeffer, *How Shall We Then Live?* Old Tappan: Fleming Revell, 1976

James K. A. Smith, *Desiring the Kingdom: Worship, Worldview and Cultural Formation*. Grand Rapids: Baker, 2009

John R. W. Stott, *Your Mind Matters*. Downers Grove: InterVarsity Press, 1973

Steve Turner, *Imagine: A Vision for Christians in the Arts*. Downers Grove: Inter-Varsity Press, 2001

Albert M. Wolters, *Creation Regained: Biblical Basics for a Reformational Worldview*. Grand Rapids: Eerdmans, 1985

N. T. Wright, Simply Christian. San Francisco: HarperOne, 2010

Specific Applications

J. N. D. Anderson: *Christianity and World Religions*. Downers Grove: InterVarsity Press, 1984

Jerram Barrs & Ranald Macaulay, *Being Human: The Nature of Spiritual Experience*. Downers Grove: InterVarsity Academic, 2005

D. A. Carson, *How Long, O Lord? Reflections on Suffering and Evil* Grand Rapids: Baker, 2006

Douglas R. Groothuis, *Unmasking the New Age*. Downers Grove: Inter-Varsity Press, 1986

Os Guinness, *Time for Truth*. Grand Rapids: Baker Books, 2000

S. Mark Heim, *Is Christ the Only Way?* Valley Forge: Judson Press, 1985

R. Hooykaas, *Religion and the Rise of Modern Science*. Grand Rapids: Eerdmans, 1972

Charles Hummel, *The Galileo Connection*. Downers Grove: InterVarsity Press, 1988

Craig Keener & Glenn Usry, *Defending Black Faith: Answers to Tough Questions about African-American Christianity*. Downers Grove: Inter-Varsity Press, 1991

I. Howard Marshall, *I Believe in the Historical Jesus*. Grand Rapids: Eerdmans, 1977

Dan McCartney, *Why Does It Have to Hurt? The Meaning of Christian Suffering*. Phillipsburg: P & R Publishing, 1998

Alister E. McGrath, *The Foundations of Dialogue in Science and Religion*. Oxford: Blackwell, 1999

Richard L. Pratt: *Every Thought Captive: A Study Manual for the Defense of Christian Truth*. Phillipsburg: Presbyterian & Reformed, 1979

Vern S. Poythress, *Redeeming Science: A God-Centered Approach*. Wheaton: Crossway, 2006

Hans Rookmaaker, *The Creative Gift: Essays on Art and Christian Life*. Westchester: Cornerstone, 1981

R. C. Sproul, *Surprised by Suffering*. Wheaton: Tyndale, 1988

John R. W. Stott, *Our Social and Sexual Revolution: Major Issues for a New Century*, 3rd ed. Grand Rapids: Baker, 1999

Theodore Turnau, *Pop-ologetics: Popular Culture in Christian Perspective*. Phillipsburg, P&R Publishers, 2012

Steve Turner, *Hungry for Heaven: Rock 'n' Roll and the Search for Redemption*. Downers Grove: InterVarsity, 1995

Other titles that may interest you from Christian Focus...

THE DAWKINS LETTERS
CHALLENGING ATHEIST MYTHS **DAVID ROBERTSON**

The Dawkins Letters

David Robertson

When Richard Dawkins published *The God Delusion*,
David Robertson wanted there to be an intelligent Christian
response. So he wrote an open letter to Richard Dawkins
on his church website. This found its way into Richard
Dawkins' website, where it generated the largest response
of any posting up to that time.

The ferocity of the responses and the shallowness of
the thinking that it exhibited, spurred David to write this
book. Christians need to know where Dawkins is weak and
we need to explain things better! It draws upon David's
experience as a debater, letter writer, pastor and author.

This is a very honest book. It agrees with Dawkins
where appropriate but also does not hesitate to point out
where some of his thinking does not hold together—It is
written in a gentle spirit of enquiry.

ISBN: 978-1-84550-597-4

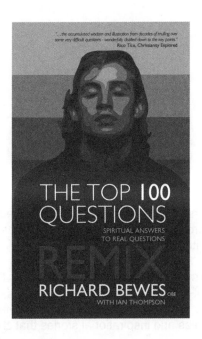

> "...the accumulated wisdom and illustration from decades of mulling over
> some very difficult questions - wonderfully distilled down to the key points."
> Rico Tice, Christianity Explored

THE TOP 100
QUESTIONS
SPIRITUAL ANSWERS
TO REAL QUESTIONS
REMIX

RICHARD BEWES OBE
WITH IAN THOMPSON

Top 100 Questions Remix

RICHARD BEWES

As a popular media broadcaster and conference speaker, Richard Bewes often faces tricky questions about the Christian faith. This book collects answers to the top 100 asked by people from all opinions and religious beliefs—remixed for young people.

These are not 'pat' answers to make you feel smug and the questioner seem stupid—they are the sort of thing you could use in a conversation—if only you had thought it out in time!

When you socialise with friends or course mates, living out the Christian faith in the 21st century naturally attracts questions. Here is some instant experience to stop you slapping your head and saying 'if only I'd said that!'.

Top 100 Questions: Remix—it's a great way to answer your mates' questions and help you explain why you are a Christian.

ISBN: 978-1-84550-191-4

CHRISTIAN FOCUS PUBLICATIONS

Christian Christian CF4K Mentor
Focus Heritage

Christian Focus Publications publishes books for adults and children under its four main imprints: Christian Focus, CF4K, Mentor and Christian Heritage. Our books reflect our conviction that God's Word is reliable and Jesus is the way to know him, and live for ever with him.

Our children's publication list includes a Sunday School curriculum that covers pre-school to early teens, and puzzle and activity books. We also publish personal and family devotional titles, biographies and inspirational stories that children will love.

If you are looking for quality Bible teaching for children then we have an excellent range of Bible stories and age-specific theological books.

From pre-school board books to teenage apologetics, we have it covered!

Find us at our web page:
www.christianfocus.com

CF4 •K
Because you're never
too young to know Jesus